LTD
ED COVER

The Headquarters of The Scottish Football League.

THE SCOTTISH

FOOTBALL LEAGUE

THE FIRST 100 YEARS

written by **Bob Crampsey**

© Copyright of The Scottish Football League
188 West Regent Street, Glasgow, G2 4RY.
ISBN 0 9516433 1 2

The contents contained in this publication will not be reproduced in whole or part, stored in a retrieval system, or transmitted in any form, or by any means, electronic, mechanical, photocopying, recording or otherwise without the prior permission of the publishers, The Scottish Football League.

Produced on behalf of The Scottish Football League by
M & A Thomson Litho Limited, 10/16 Colvilles Place,
Kelvin Industrial Estate, East Kilbride, Scotland.
Tel: East Kilbride 33081/2/3/4.

Published by The Scottish Football League and
Printed by M & A Thomson Litho Limited.

FOREWORD

It is indeed both a privilege and a great honour to represent The Scottish Football League in my role as President during the course of its Centenary celebrations.

It is a time to celebrate, for let us all not forget that The Scottish Football League, rightly, has much to be proud of and has been in the forefront of the development and expansion of the game on a worldwide scale over the years. I am sure, however, that the small group of men that met in Holton's Hotel, Glasgow on 20th March, 1890, to form The Scottish Football League, never quite imagined the manner in which this organisation would develop and expand in the years that lay ahead.

The evolution of the game and the continuing advancement in technology has ensured that Association Football will never remain the same from one generation to another and over succeeding decades, The Scottish Football League has never been slow to recognise this and indeed has on many occasions led the way in change. One of the comments that is regularly heard in the grandstands, terracings and enclosures of League grounds is that "it is not the same as it used to be," although I have no doubt that this can be said about every aspect of life. Each era of League football in Scotland has produced considerable change, which on many occasions have provoked much comment and disagreement. One only has to look at the criticism that was directed at this embryo organisation on its formation 100 years ago together with the legalisation of professionalism three years later.

It has been mentioned on many occasions that League football is very much the "bread and butter" side of the game and undoubtedly, this is very true. It provides the player with the opportunity of displaying his soccer skills on a week to week basis to a discerning but nevertheless, appreciative audience and also affords players with the chance to play at the highest level. At the same time, the League was set up to guarantee clubs matches on a regular and organised basis and ultimately reward the most successful clubs. In turn this now provides both the player and the club with the opportunity to play at an even higher level through the European club competitions and the International arena. I think that these reasons alone are most significant when trying to quantify the importance of The Scottish Football League.

The League Management Committee was delighted when Bob Crampsey agreed to undertake the daunting task of writing the official history of The Scottish Football League. As a respected historian of the Scottish game, he has vividly and candidly set-out to document the history of this organisation and its member clubs from its conception, the acceptance of the paid player, the expansion of League football throughout the country, the popularity and prominence of Inter-League matches for the first seventy years or so, the introduction of automatic promotion and relegation, the disruption of football because of two World Wars, the innovative League Cup Competition, the expansion of the game at world level and its effects on Scottish football, right up to the present day, with Freedom of Movement for players and high profile sponsorship by multi-national businesses together with the effects that television and more especially satellite broadcasting will have on our game in Scotland in the future.

However, in an age of rapid expansion and advancement in technology, we must never forget that League football has and always will be about the player and the spectator. Without the player, there is no game and without the spectator, there is no atmosphere. The combination of the two, with skilful, exciting and entertaining football being played in front of a packed and enthralled audience creates a spectacle and an atmosphere that cannot be matched by any other sport.

I have no doubt that all football fans have a wealth of stories about the Scottish game. Some accurate, many embellished and a few that have adopted numerous versions through the passage of time. I hope that "The First 100 Years" recreates these memories and offers you an unrivalled insight into the history and development of The Scottish Football League.

The Scottish Football League is steeped in tradition and proud of its achievements. However, it realises that time will not stand still for anyone and that it cannot live on its past glories. The Scottish Football League has over the years been fortunate in the quality of leadership at legislative and administrative level, and I am delighted that this factor is very much in evidence today. I am confident that The Scottish Football League will continue to play an important role in the development of football in the years ahead.

Here's to the next 100 years of The Scottish Football League.

JACK STEEDMAN, *President*
The Scottish Football League

ACKNOWLEDGEMENTS

I have to thank many people who greatly lightened my task. Both League Secretaries during the time of research, Jim Farry and Peter Donald, were unfailingly supportive and Jim Farry made time to be interviewed during a particularly busy spell in his career.

The office staff of The Scottish Football League never failed to find me a corner, often a fairly luxurious corner, in which to pursue my researches and they invariably found a cup of coffee as well. Any query addressed to them was resolved promptly and cheerfully and they have my gratitude. On frequent visits to the League office, the President, Mr. Jack Steedman of Clydebank was encouraging and helpful.

In the early days of preparation I had the considerable benefit of advice from two noted historians of the Scottish game, Mike Watson, M.P., and Pat Woods. Their help was much appreciated.

In response to an appeal from the League many followers in Scotland sent in football memorabilia. I thank them all and in particular Allan Geekie, Blair James, Bob Laird, John McLennan, Andy Mitchell, Jack Murray, Mrs. Eileen O'Donnell for permission to use her father's wartime scrap book and Jimmy Inglis, ex-Falkirk, for a similar permission.

Inevitably, one relied heavily on sources such as the Mitchell Library, Glasgow, and the Glasgow Herald library and nothing was too much bother for the respective staffs. For permission to use photographs from the past forty years, thanks to the *Daily Record*, *the Scotsman* and the *Glasgow Herald/Evening Times*. Senga Murray played a crucial role in the production of the book with her quite excellent portraits of various celebrated Scottish players over the years.

The staff of Thomson Litho, East Kilbride, in particular John Mackay, Bert MacMorris and Jim Thomson, who displayed their customary humorous imperturbability in the face of approaching deadlines and were always willing to consider the wishes of the author.

Beyond all others I am indebted to David C. Thomson of The Scottish Football League. Immersed in the game, a percipient and unforgiving taskmaster, he was both a joy to work with and a conveyor-belt of good ideas and suggestions for the shape of the book. Many of his ideas were accepted, all were valued and his cheerful thoroughness was very much enjoyed.

One of the great bonuses for the author in writing the book was to have his love of the game re-kindled by the constant evidence of the affection for the game and deep knowledge of it which so many Scottish fans possess. No one can understand industrial Scotland fully who does not appreciate the enormous attraction which association football has had for the working man. If this book succeeds in conveying anything of that fascination then those named above have legitimate cause for pride. And, lastly, amid the helpers let me mention an opponent, the splendidly gloomy editor of *Scottish Sport* who predicted a century ago that the whole enterprise was doomed to inglorious failure!

CONTENTS

Chapter		Page
1	IN THE BEGINNING	1
2	BASE AND TEMPTING GOLD	17
3	THE AGE OF EXPANSION	35
4	LEAGUE FOOTBALL IN SCOTLAND IN THE FIRST WORLD WAR	57
5	1920–39 THE YEARS BETWEEN	71
6	SCOTTISH LEAGUE FOOTBALL IN THE SECOND WORLD WAR	105
7	THE POST-WAR YEARS	129
8	THINKING ABOUT CHANGE	167
9	THE PREMIER DIVISION IN THE 1970s	197
10	THE SCOTTISH FOOTBALL LEAGUE IN THE 1980s	211
11	THE LEAGUE CUP — A TOURNAMENT REDISCOVERED	233
12	THE LEAGUE ON THE FIELD — INTER-LEAGUE MATCHES	243
13	THE RUNNING OF THE LEAGUE	257
14	THE LEAGUE REACHES ITS CENTURY — TRIUMPHS AND CHALLENGES	263

Chapter One

IN THE BEGINNING

A HUNDRED YEARS OF
THE SCOTTISH FOOTBALL LEAGUE 1890–1990

In the whole of sport there is no greater paradox than that which made an upper-class game, the rules of which were an amalgam of those of half a dozen English public schools, into the fervent and abiding passion of Scotland in general and the West of Scotland, which was the very model of a smoky, industrial, working-class society, in particular.

The affection of the Scots for association football was immediate and permanent. It offered a platform for the display not only of courage and stamina but of those individual skills which could not easily be demonstrated in the more traditional artistic fields. The game was not over-demanding in the amount and cost of equipment required, nor did its pitches require the same amount of expensive cosseting as did cricket grounds and tennis courts.

Although association football developed almost simultaneously in Scotland and England, there was a difference in ethos and approach almost from the outset. In England soccer was originally neither more or less than one of those vigorous, manly ball-games which so delighted late Victorians and which served the very useful purpose of allowing pupils who had left home for their schooling to work off surplus energy without resorting to crime, hooliganism or dangerous liaisons. It was not originally envisaged in England that this rough, turbulent game would provide a livelihood for anyone and for many years the officials of the Football Association were drawn almost exclusively from members of the middle class for whom the playing of professional sport would have meant social death. It was otherwise in Scotland where from the very earliest days there was a realisation that this new game might not simply afford an enjoyable pastime but could well provide an escape route from the drudgery of heavy industry for those fortunate enough to be gifted footballers.

There was football in Scotland before the creation of The Scottish Football League in 1890, more, there was organised football in

Scotland before then. Scotland's premier club, Queen's Park, had been constituted as far back as 1867 and although in the next five years its fixtures were few and haphazard, Queen's Park not only preserved an unbroken existence but attracted imitators. It was not surprising that England, whence the initial impetus had come, continued to lead the way in the organisation of the game and this was evidenced in the foundation of the Football Association in 1863. In the formation of a national association and a football league, in the creation of a cup competition and, perhaps oddly, in the adoption of professionalism, England would lead and Scotland follow shortly behind in each case.

Queen's Park as the most renowned Scottish club were invited to take part in the F.A. Cup in 1872 and were promised exemption to the semi-final if they agreed to enter. This was the very first year of that competition and the Glasgow club was drawn against the famous Public Schools side, Wanderers. There was a delightful informality about proceedings. Wanderers, as their name implied, were nomadic and Queen's Park accepted the invitation on the strength of a membership of 60 and a bank balance of less than four pounds. The trip to London was financed by personal subscriptions and the abandonment of a projected tour to the Tweed Valley where the game was to be introduced to the Borderers. The fact that the tour was never made allowed the rival game of Rugby Union to be introduced to the area from the North of England and has meant that South-East Scotland is the one region of the northern kingdom where association football cannot claim to be the pre-eminent game.

The Football Association was extremely accommodating towards Queen's Park. Considerately, the other semi-final, Royal Engineers v Crystal Palace, had been played off beforehand so that if Queen's Park were to triumph against Wanderers, a remote contingency in the view of most, they could stay over and play the final on the day after, thus avoiding any necessity for a second trip south. In the event, the Wanderers match resulted in a goalless draw and this was the equivalent of a defeat, since the Scots were unable to afford an extended stay and perforce had to scratch.

Nevertheless, they had created a most favourable impression and when the first official International match with England was played in Glasgow in November 1872 and attracted an unlooked-for crowd of over 4000 spectators, the popularity of the game was assured. Rivalry with England was to be the oxygen which kept the fire of Scottish football burning. Here was an area where Scotland could compete with remarkable success against its much bigger and wealthier neighbour, here was a theatre in which the Scots sense of nationhood and difference could assert itself. A country lacking in political and artistic self-expression turned to its footballers as other small European countries were turning to their composers, their artists and their writers as visible proofs of national identity and uniqueness.

The partial successes of Queen's Park and Scotland against the Englishmen had a climactic effect. Almost overnight football became a booming sport in Scotland with an overpowering necessity for the creation of some form of organisation to control it. The obvious solution was the formation of a Scottish Football Association on the lines of the Football Association and this came about in 1873, eight clubs, Queen's Park, Third Lanark, Vale of Leven, Clydesdale, Eastern, Dumbreck, Granville and Rovers agreeing to sponsor a cup competition and also to form The Scottish Football Association "for the promotion of football according to Association rules." Of these founder members only the first named, Queen's Park, survives to the present day. In the early days of The Scottish Football Association some of the leading Scottish clubs retained membership of the Football Association as well but eventually the Scottish body put a stop to this duality.

The Associations in both countries were the creation of the original legislators, the Leagues were that of the second generation. The Associations were the aristocrats of the football world, the Leagues distinctly more workaday. We have to consider the reasons which led to the emergence of league football and the needs which it was designed to meet. The early functions of the Associations were to act as legislative bodies, to run the Challenge Cup competitions and to select representative sides to play in international matches. Beyond that, they had little or nothing to do with club fixtures. At a subordinate level there were county associations which ran cup competitions, second only in importance to those of the F.A. Cup and Scottish Cup in early days, and various charity competitions of which the Glasgow Charity Cup was by far the most prestigious. These cup competitions provided perhaps half a dozen fixtures per year and the club fixture list was mainly composed of friendly matches, or "ordinaries" as they were called, which by the early and mid 1880's included several against leading English clubs in the case of the more powerful Scottish combinations.

This was a haphazard arrangement which worked well enough in the days when football clubs were loosely organised along the lines of their tennis, cricket and golf counterparts but the one thing that association football could do and the three other sports could not—at least in Scotland—was to attract people to watch in large

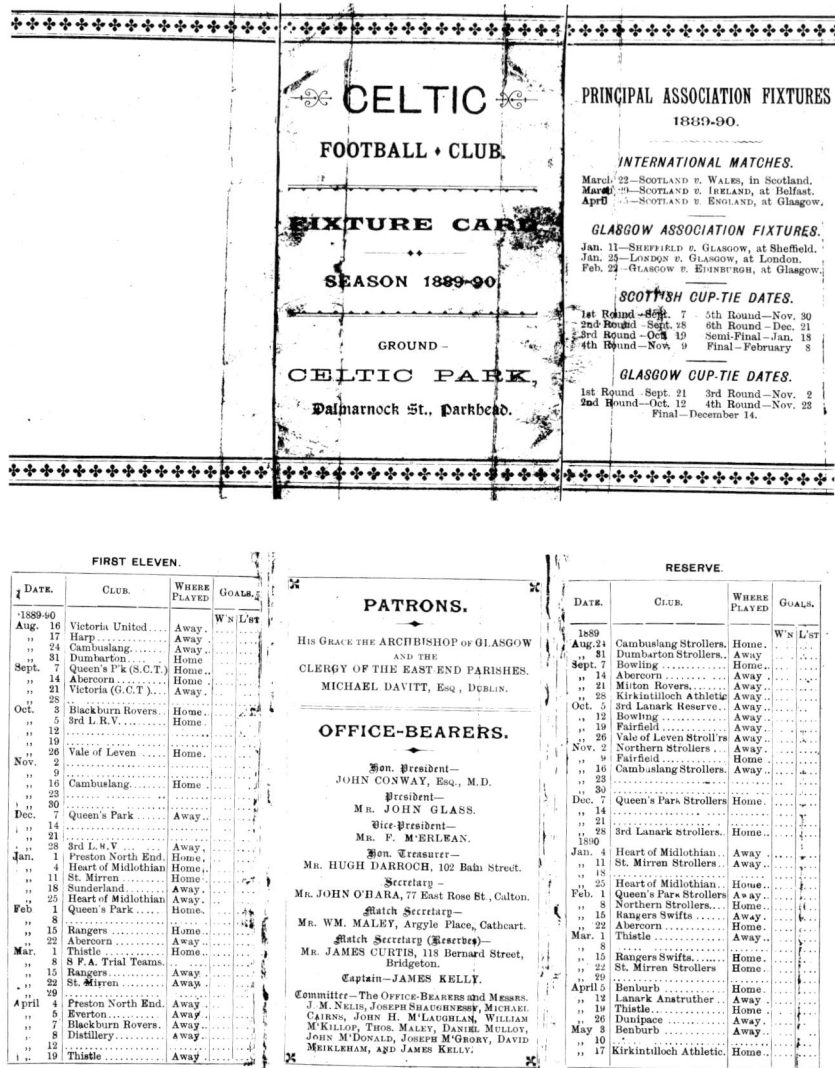

Celtic's very first Membership Card, that of 1889–90 shows the curious mix of famous English sides and village teams. Note the number of blank dates and note too that either Celtic or Queen's Park would have been out of the Scottish Cup as early as September 7th.

numbers and pay for the privilege of so doing. By the middle of the 1880s Queen's Park and Vale of Leven could draw 10,000 spectators to witness a challenge match, i.e. a friendly match, and as clubs became aware of the existence of gate revenue, and in-

IN THE BEGINNING

evitably grew dependent upon it, the match card could no longer be left to chance. The twenty years between 1880 and 1900 would see the game in Britain change from pastime to well-run amateur sport to a business, a weird and bizarre business it is true, but one in which the balance sheet was crucial. There was a need for more direction within the game and the feeling that the Associations were not the ideal bodies to provide it; some other form of government was required.

It was provided in England by a Scot. There, professionalism pre-dated the beginning of league football, whereas in Scotland it was to follow it very shortly. On March 2 1888, William McGregor, an official of Aston Villa, proposed in a letter to certain kindred spirits that "ten or twelve of the most prominent clubs in England combine to arrange home and away fixtures each season." The response was extremely positive and by the end of the month a provisional set of rules had been drawn up and approved of which Rule 3, enjoining each club to play its strongest available side in all matches, has proved to be the most durable. The Football League began operations in the late summer of 1888 with the following clubs in membership, Accrington Stanley, Aston Villa, Blackburn Rovers, Bolton Wanderers, Burnley, Derby County, Everton, Notts County, Preston North End, Stoke City, West Bromwich Albion and Wolverhampton Wanderers.

The choice of title, The Football League, has earned William McGregor some undeserved hostility from some of his fellow-Scots who have seen that choice as élitist and exclusive. In this they did and do him an injustice on two counts. McGregor as a committed Scot was scarcely likely to slight his fellow-countrymen, rather his hope was that in the future Scottish clubs could be admitted to membership, hence the careful choice of name. In any event "English League" would have been misleading, as another glance at the founding members will reveal that there was not one side included from south of Birmingham and indeed it would be another thirty years before The Football League made any impact whatever in the South of England.

As has been said, the game at top level in England was now professional, it had been so since 1885, and already some of the leading clubs were formed on the lines of limited liability companies. Their directors had a wage bill to meet every week and this could only be done if supporters were provided with a steady diet of top-class opposition. There was no room now for the informal coming together of secretaries to arrange fixtures. That system had never worked particularly well anyhow and many were the instances of a small town eagerly awaiting the arrival of the stars of a leading club only to find that the latter had received a late but better offer and would not be appearing, having "chucked", in the vigorous if inelegant phrase of the time.

Players were being paid in England and many of those who were receiving money were Scotsmen. Their skill and straitened working circumstances made them prime targets for the great northern English clubs and the "Scotch professors" as they were known, became the sporting equivalent of the seventeenth-century Scottish mercenary soldier. In the earliest days some decent pretence was made of finding normal employment for these imports and one Wilson, goalkeeper of the Vale of Leven and a dyer to trade, was offered a job in Blackburn for £1 per week. In addition, Blackburn Rovers, who had fixed him with this post, would pay him £3-10-0d per week for playing football which was clearly to be the more important of Wilson's two occupations.

English football exercised the same lure for Scots players as the West End did for English provincial theatre. With a small population, heavily concentrated in the Forth-Clyde Valley, it appeared that Scottish football could only survive if a league were organised on similar lines to that of England and if professionalism were to be adopted. Both proposals would eventually triumph but not before they had overcome some formidable opposition.

Unlike the English pattern the establishment of a league would precede the adoption of professionalism in Scotland. The first steps were taken in March 1890 when Peter Fairly, Secretary of Renton Football Club, sent the following letter to several kindred spirits:—

Renton Football Club
Renton, 13th March 1890

To the committee . . . . Football Club.

Gentlemen,

You are requested to send two representatives to attend a meeting to be held in Holton's Commercial hotel, 28 Glassford Street, Glasgow, on Thursday 20th inst. at 7.30 p.m.

Yours truly
(Signed) Peter Fairly, secy.

BUSINESS:—To consider the question of organising League matches in Scotland.

Fourteen clubs were invited but only twelve, Abercorn, Cambuslang, Celtic, Cowlairs, Dumbarton, Heart of Midlothian, Rangers, Renton, St. Bernard, St. Mirren, Third Lanark and Vale of Leven attended. The two absentee clubs were Clyde and Queen's Park. The former would very soon join the league ranks but Queen's Park would hold aloof for a considerable time and as they would be in the vanguard of the opposition to the league it is worth while setting out their reservations in some detail.

Ostensibly the reason for the non-attendance of their Secretary at that preliminary meeting was that the gentleman in question, Mr. J. McTavish, claimed that the letter had not informed him of the purpose of the meeting nor the agenda to be followed but this response seems less than candid. Scotland's oldest club was implacably opposed to the pursuance of league football and its reasons were by no means totally selfish. It was self-evident that any league must eventually entail professionalism, something that a club devoted to the amateur principle could scarcely welcome, but Queen's Park also saw that a league would eliminate many of the weaker and smaller clubs and the famous Hampden side had always preferred fostering to euthanasia. Indeed if anything Queen's Park under-estimated the rationalisation that the league would bring, for six of the founder members, Abercorn, Cambuslang, Cowlairs, Dumbarton, Renton and Vale of Leven would be out of top-class football before ten years had passed and their signature of adherence to the league was the signature of their own death warrant.

All this is to run before our horse to market. Of all the Scottish League minute books only that covering the first season is totally gone, but reporters in those early days were admitted to meetings and the popular sporting paper of the time, *Scottish Sport*, was able to supply its readers of March 22 1890 with a typically orotund Victorian view of proceedings. It made no pretence at impartiality as can be seen from the heading of the piece.

WITH THE LEAGUE AGITATORS
[By "Number One."]

"Tis Thursday night. The modest little 'alarm' on the far off corner of the sanctum has claimed the hour of seven; *Sport* has just gone to press, and the P.D. has left me alone, leaving behind a hideous caricature of old 'scissors and paste.' A bundle of unopened editorial communications lie on the desk usually occupied by 'Ye Journiemanne,' while everything around is a chaos of confusion and darkness. I was about to depart when the word 'League,' written in bold characters on the margin of a rejected pile of manuscript, arrested my attention. Look at the word again, write it slowly, ponder over its significance, and mayhap similar feelings of curiosity and excitement will pervade you as they did me. Suddenly I recollected that the epistle heretofore mentioned referred to a meeting to be held in the short space of half-an-hour, for the purpose of discussing and, if possible, establishing a football League in Scotland. Here was a chance not to be lost, and in the language of the melancholy member of our staff, I wended my way to Holton's Hotel 'with mingled feelings of pleasure and regret'—pleasure at the probable privilege of listening to proposals, fraught with the most momentous issues, with just the possibility of a direct revolt to usurp the power of the institution which has so long, so honourably, and so faithfully guided the destinies of Scotch football; regret at the not too inviting prospect of undergoing the humiliating process of being 'chucked out.' My perturbed state of mind was somewhat relieved when I discovered I was the first arrival. Something new in my experience this, so take a note of it. Here, in a rather plain and cheerless apartment at the far end of the lobby, free from the intrusion of the usual 'commercial' intruder, was the trysting place. A small wooden table, with five wooden chairs to keep it company, were arranged almost in the centre of the room, and immediately behind the chairs three wooden school forms, with no resting place on which to lean a wearied back, were arranged. The materials for a fire were in the fire-place, but there was no light. I was beginning to despair of visitors, when in pops the burly, if not commanding proportions, of Mr. P. Campbell, of Renton, along with several inferior (in bulk, of course) co-workers. At the suggestion of one of these a light was applied to the fire, and the aspect of affairs changed completely.

With the exception of the Queen's Park and Clyde, all the clubs circulated sent two representatives, and quite an air of importance and influence attached to the gathering, as the following list will show, viz.:—Third Lanark, Celtic, Rangers, Cowlairs, St. Mirren, Abercorn, Renton, Dumbarton, Vale of Leven, Cambuslang, St. Bernards, and Heart of Midlothian.

Mr. Lawrance (Dumbarton) was asked to preside, and, in doing so, stated he yielded to the desires of the meeting in this line fo conduct. So far as his club was concerned, he was not present in an official capacity, prepared to vote on whatever proposal might be adopted. He administered a mild exhortation to his audience to be reasonable, dispassionate, and not too easily awayed by the arguments which would be adduced in favour of the proposal. The Dumbarton were prepared to support it on the lines he indicated at a later stage of the proceedings.

IN THE BEGINNING

At the request of the Chairman, Mr. Graham (Renton), as taking the iniative, rose and prounded his views. These may be briefly summed up as a protest against the existing cup tie arrangement, the derangement of the fixture card, and the frequent class of matches they were compelled to play. He further declaimed the impression which had gone abroad that the Renton were agitating for the introduction of professionalism in any shape or form. This was to be distinctly understood, and he was conscious those present would give Renton every credit for their loyalty to the very spirit of amateurism. The invitation to participate in the proceedings was extended to all, and Mr. J. H. McLaughlin, in his eloquent and deliberate style, stated the only parallel they had to go upon was the Football League in England, an institution which had created a greater interest than formerly existed in the game across the border. The League has the advantages of a first-class and attractive array of fixtures, without the spirit of acrimony or rough play, which was conspicuous in cup-tie engagements. Mr. John Thomson (Third Lanark) was also in sympathy with the movement, as being beneficial all round.

Mr. Reynard (Cambuslang), whose face throughout the evening was wreathed in smiles, now rose, and with inspiration derived from the exhilarating effects of a cigarette, stated his club had discussed the matter in committee, and he was there by invitation to hear and report all that passed. The Cambuslang were quite prepared to support a qualifying competition. He considered it a very great hardship that clubs of such status as Queen's Park and Celtic should be drawn together in the first round. Once out of the ties the club was insufficiently supported, and the sooner something was done to maintain the interest the better.

A look of the tenderest sympathy with the object under discussion overspread the facial development of the representative of the Vale of Leven, as the chairman politely requested his opinion. The eloquence of previous speakers, however, seemed to have overawed him completely, for a modest assent of approval with what was going on was all that could be eliminated from the delegate of the famous club on the banks of the Leven. Things certainly were looking up, and everybody seemed delightfully contented as one after another orated on the eventualities of the future. When Mr. J. Mellish (Rangers) got to his legs, the interest heightened, and anxious anticipations were depicted on the faces around. One whose knowledge and splendid powers of organisation would be invaluable to the movement under weight, would surely carry conviction. I thought, and eagerly I hung—so to speak—on the utterances of the representative of the S.F.A. Without lacking the firmness, regularity of speech, and air of conscious ability which usually characterises his appearances, the speaker began. I was disappointed with his short speech, probably because I had expected a longer one, and probably because he had nothing in the way of originality to enrapt the attention. My feelings must have been akin to the hot-headed politician, whose favourite hero had only bowed from the railway carriage, after he had tramped 20 miles to applaud his harangue. Mr. Mellish's words, as I have said, were few, but were those of a diplomatist. In conjunction with Mr. Wilton, he had come there to listen and report. Provided the League was got up in a proper way, and for the benefit and furtherance of Scottish football, he could see no harm in the departure, but it *must* be *strictly* amateur [emphasis, Mr. Comp., on the words in italics], and recognise the S.F.A. as the governing body. He had no instructions to act definitely.

The next speaker—Mr. George Henderson, whose long connection with the Cowlairs instinctively made me grasp my pencil and hurriedly turn the leaves of my note-book, in case I should omit some sentence of infinite moment and purport—began, 'well, Mr. Chairman and gentlemen, we have had this matter before our committee and fully discussed it, and our recommendation is in favour of a League.' This all in one breath, and with a flow which conveyed to me the impression that he was afraid his tongue might drop out ere he completed his peroration. "They had got up such a thing in England, and it would be to the advantage of clubs in Scotland to follow suit. The question of gates would require to be settled when the League was formed. We are quite prepared to settle definitely any proposal that might be adopted, provided it was organised in proper form, and looking to the interests of the Association. We hope the Association would grant a qualifying competition and it would be a very good thing, indeed.' (Cheers.) With wonted timidity, and leaning hard on the handle of a stout umbrella, Mr. Smith (Heart of Midlothian) 'modestly addressed himself to speech.' The Hearts never did seriously discuss this matter, or consider its details, but they were just in this position—ready to go with the times.

Somebody whispered Mr. Lamb (St. Bernards) had just come in, and though the Queen's Prizeman said, looking in the direction of the door, 'Mr. Lamb,' that individual answered ne'er a word, but kept fondly gazing at the ring on his little finger, in the hope evidently of gleaning something bright.

One volunteer is worth three pressed men any day. So thought Mr. Towns (St. Mirren), who quickly mentioned the fact that the St. Mirren had talked *it* over—(fancy only talked it over)—and that they thought it a very good thing, too. Loyal to the Scottish Association in the meantime, and also that it be amateur, was his parting salute. Thinking, no doubt, it would never do for St. Mirren alone to embody Paisley's opinion, the Abercorn delegate, Mr. Hastie, gaining confidence as he proceeded, mentioned that his club had the subject discussed on Tuesday night, but they were not prepared to submit anything definite. You will observe, gentle reader, the similarity of the speakers' sentiments. Mr. Hastie proceeded to say he was not prepared to say anything officially. It was his opinion the League, if amateur, would be a welcome change, and a great aid to the match secretary. League matches would draw better, and they would have increased gates, which was much needed in these days of increased expenditure and improved grounds.

Mr. Lamb had by this time got his sea legs. He is better, Mr. Editor, at waving the umpire's flag than making a speech in the Council Chamber. He had nothing new to say beyond informing the meeting Mr. Walker and himself were commissioned to attend and report result. It was certainly the St. Bernard's desire to support the League movement, if it did not go in opposition to the existing Association, and [in a lower tone, as if he was afraid of the sound of his vocal organ] that it be strictly amateur.

The discussion was all on the same lines, and the Cambuslang representative again took relief in a cigarette, at which his colleague, Mr. R. Livingstone, seemed dreadfully tickled. Don't confound this latter gentlemen with the genial one of our staff, who would as soon be found blowing the big trumpet in a Salvation Army band as sitting discussing a project which had in any wise a contrary policy to the powers that be. The tobacco was contagious, and Mr. Henderson lit his pipe.

Mr. Lawrance again aired his views to the enlightenment of those around. The mild and discriminating nature of his remarks met with my approval. Generally speaking, he said there was a decided feeling against the proposed League taking any form of cognisance of professionalism or clashing with the S.F.A. The Dumbarton were strongly opposed to professionalism, which must not be encouraged in the slightest degree. If at all possible, he urged the League should be worked with the S.F.A. as a head centre. Then its matches would clash as little as possible with Scottish Cup ties. If the League would interfere with the progress of the smaller clubs it would be a hardship, and, he considered, if this were so, they would not be justified in doing anything like that. It would be beneficial were the Association to exempt certain clubs and work at the same time, the League matches. Some arrangement could be made for this purpose. He thought the best idea would be to approach the clubs at the general meeting in May. The proposal was not a new one, for five or six years ago the representative of their club had advocated unsuccessfully before the S.F.A. that a proportionate number of clubs be excluded from the cup competitions for a certain length of time. Now he found the present agitation was only the germination of that scheme on a much wider basis.

The remarks from the chair led to a considerable discussion on the details involved by the adoption of the scheme, and the avoidance of friction with the S.F.A. The representatives all expressed themselves, however, favourable to the formation of a League, and for a time lost sight of a motion, by Mr. M'Laughlin, to press its adoption, in their anxiety to discuss issues. The chairman said the sentiments of some of the speakers were not his own, and urged that no alternative be put to the Association in the event of their failing to grant any proposal that might be decided at this meeting. The feeling, however, was decidedly in favour of a constituted League apart from the Association, and yet paying all due respect to its laws. Mr. Mellish pointed out that, before taking any definite steps, the representatives would require to have their various committees' instructions. A small committee should be appointed to draft out the Constitution and Rules of the proposed League, and submit it to the clubs.

The Chairman again pressed that they should run parallel with the S.F.A. The Celtic representative asked the meeting if they imagined the Association would bear evidence, and adjudicate protests on their behalf. Were they to run the League on the lines of County Jurisdiction? Mr. Lawrance thought the S.F.A., if reasonably met, would provide some arrangement for a satisfactory method of working the League. Messrs. Henderson, Smith, and M'Laughlin, sustained the discussion, which now veered round to another tact. Mr. Montgomery (Third Lanark) considered the term 'League' obnoxious, which brought out the retort from the Cowlairs man, amid laughter, that 'they were not leagued together for evil purposes.' Mr. Montgomery thought the preferable name would be 'The Football Union.' Mr. Smith increased the hilarity by stating it ought to be 'The Football Benefit Society.' The meeting was most harmonious, and eventually the following motion by Mr. J. H. M'Laughlin, seconded by Mr. Richardson (Heart of Midlothian), was approved of unanimously:—'That a committee be appointed from this meeting to draft the rules and constitution of the proposed League, and submit them to the various clubs determined upon; and that these clubs be requested to send representatives with full powers to a meeting to be afterwards convened.'

The following were appointed a sub-committee to draft rules and constitution:—Messrs. Henderson (Cowlairs), Lawrance (Dumbarton), Graham (Renton), Towns (St. Mirren), Thomson (Third Lanark), M'Laughlin (Celtic), and Wilton (Rangers). In so far as taking a minute of the proceedings was concerned, Mr. Lawrence allowed his name to stand as secretary *pro. tem.* Mr. Mellish was proposed for convener, but declined to go on the committee. Mr. M'Laughlin agreed to take the duties, after some pressure. The initial resolutions to the S.F.A. for a qualifying competition were, by request of the meeting, to be moved in the name of the Renton, in virtue of the prominent part that club had taken in connection with the whole affair. The clubs present pledged their united support.

The curtain falls on the first part of a drama which marks a distinct epoch in the history of Association football in Scotland. Is it the beginning of the end?

The league, inaugurated on April 30 1890, would therefore in the absence of Queen's Park and Clyde proceed with the distinctly unprofessional and unbusinesslike number of eleven clubs in its first season—St. Bernard's[1] were not elected—although a combination of circumstances would almost immediately reduce this to a more workable ten. Mr. J. H. McLaughlin of Celtic was appointed as League Secretary, a man of outstanding organisational and literary ability and one who carried on the tradition of the English founders of the game in that he himself had attended an English public school, Stonyhurst in Lancashire.

The brave new title The Scottish Football League was misleading, however unintentionally so, and the fledgling body could just as well have been called the Forth-Clyde League since it contained no members north of the Forth and no clubs south of the Clyde. The game itself was as yet scarcely national and with the singular exception of Queen's Park all the great Scottish footballing powers were contained therein. J. H. McLaughlin persuaded his committee that the League would only work if it adopted the

---

[1] The Edinburgh club were in their earliest days often referred to as St. Bernard. The more common name will normally be used.

procedures of a closed shop. Not only must League games take precedence over all other matches, excepting Scottish Cup ties and county cup ties, but members were forbidden to play friendly matches against non-League clubs in towns where a League match had been arranged for that day. It could well prove to be an expensive business to be outside the ranks of the League clubs.

Almost the first warning shot came from a very unlikely source, the *Lancashire Evening Post* of June 28 1890, which had this to say: "To all appearances the Queen's Park Football Club will, during the ensuing season, be left out in the cold so far as the principal clubs in Scotland are concerned. The members of the newly-formed League have all replied to the Queen's invitations for games to the effect that they cannot oblige, so that the leading club of the country will have plenty of time to go in for propagandist work."

This was true enough, Mr. McTavish the Queen's Park Secretary had been rebuffed by Third Lanark, Vale of Leven, Rangers and Dumbarton. These were indeed grievous blows since each of these clubs was a considerable attraction. Clubs kept their home gates (although the League would partially share gates from the outset) and moreover, Queen's Park had built a large ground and were well placed to profit from this arrangement in the normal run of things. Now the big Scottish clubs would not be calling, nor would the leading lights in England, unavailable for the same reason.

The Scottish sporting press, especially the highly-influential *Scottish Sport*, was not well-disposed towards the Scottish League initially, indeed *Scottish Sport* was prepared to die in the ditch for amateurism. It replied thus to the gloomy forecasts of the *Lancashire Evening Post*:

> "If the Queen's Park have acted stupidly in the matter of the League, let us be content to have that demonstrated by results, not by prophecies and threats."

Just before the start of the first-ever season of League football in Scotland, a contributor to *Scottish Sport*, using the name *Pertinax*, had this to say in the issue of August 5 1890:

> "Where the incongruity of the League appears is in the fact that it desires to be fostered under amateur laws which at the very foundation it is opposed to. One thing the League has done and which will meet but with scant commendation is that it has brought on the beginning of the season much earlier than usual. Very few of the clubs in the League will have had more than two months rest."

IN THE BEGINNING

Scottish Sport had a nice line in invective and did not believe in wrapping its opinions in honeyed words where the League were concerned. In another issue of the time it thundered:

> "Our first and last objection to them (the League) is that they exist. The entire rules stink of finance, money-making and money-grabbing."

From the outset of the League the game would certainly become less sociable and even such sympathetic witness as John McCartney, later manager of Hearts and Portsmouth, regretted the disappearance of the after-match teas. Clyde had run cricket and tennis clubs in conjunction with their football team when amateur, and indeed had in addition Dramatic, Musical and Literary Sections but none of the outcrops would survive the change to the professional game.

Not that the game was as yet professional in law or organisation. Clubs were happy to let committee men act as referees in League matches, and the first programme of League football, carried through on August 16 1890, produced one extremely gratifying result and one legal *cause célèbre*. Four matches were played and as they were the very first it is worthwhile to give the results in full.

Celtic	1 v 4	Renton
Cambuslang	8 v 2	Vale of Leven
Dumbarton	1 v 1	Cowlairs
Rangers	5 v 2	Heart of Midlothian

The good result referred to was not a win, loss or draw but the size of crowd at Ibrox Park for the match between Rangers and Heart of Midlothian. Even *Scottish Sport* was compelled to concede that "the crowd was a good one. Between 3000 and 4000 assisted which is marvellous for an Edinburgh side, they being proverbially bad drawers in Glasgow."

The crowd at the Celtic-Renton match, 10,000 was much larger, but the opening day of League football could scarcely have been more disastrous for Celtic. Not only were they thrashed 4-1 but they had recently landed in further severe trouble for taking part in a benefit match for a Renton player, James McCall. Worse was to follow, for in their next two league matches they played an unregistered player, Bell of Hurlford, in goal and although they won both matches, two points per game were deducted under rule. Cowlairs, guilty of a similar infringement in the same two matches, found themselves even worse off as their win and draw translated to minus one point.

On May 31 1890 Celtic and Old Renton (a transparent attempt

to disguise identity) had played a benefit match for James McCall at Celtic Park. Celtic, realising that they were on thin ice, since benefit matches were not permitted unless a player was retiring from the game through illness or injury and there was no indication that James McCall was doing either, hastily prepared their defence. It was their contention that the match was simply a half-gate fixture and that it was no concern of theirs that Renton should have given their own money to the McCall Testimonial Fund. Celtic themselves had given their share of the gate (£217 had been drawn) to four specified charities. The Scottish Football Association was not impressed and McCall and Kelly of Renton—also deemed responsible as captain—were "held suspended" without any limit of time set.

The Scottish League had got off to a messy start. The officials were determined to impress on member clubs that such matters as registration had to be taken seriously. The game was still remarkably informal for another club, Cowlairs, did not even have a ground of their own when the League got under way.

Scottish Sport lost few chances of criticising the new organisation and in September 1890 it published a long article lamenting that, because of the greediness of the League clubs, the Dundee sides were finding it increasingly difficult to get fixtures of any importance and there was therefore the fear that the game might die out in the Jute City. This story, interesting enough as it was, would soon be replaced in the public interest by the allegations of professionalism which would ensure that the initial League career of Renton would be of the briefest.

Chapter Two

BASE AND TEMPTING GOLD

For the first three years of its life, perhaps even longer, The Scottish League led a placid, Limbo-like existence. It had been brought into being to provide order but the early conduct of the competition was not particularly business-like. Seldom, if ever, did all ten clubs play off matches on the same day, with the inevitable result that certain clubs had long completed their programmes whilst other member clubs still had several matches outstanding. There was therefore, equally inevitably, a diminution of interest in the competition.

All ten clubs, yet the League had started with eleven. The casualty, the first in the history of Scottish League football, was Renton and the circumstances were these.

In September 1890 a club named Adventurers protested against St. Bernard after they had lost a cup-tie, on the grounds that the Edinburgh side were professional, having lured a player named Ross to Edinburgh from Dunfermline Athletic and paid him a weekly wage for playing football, although there was also the bait of a job in a biscuit factory. This job would pay him less than he had earned in Dunfermline but there would be an additional payment of ten shillings per match. It was widely felt that in making this protest Adventurers were merely the mouthpiece of Dunfermline Athletic who had harboured a grievance against St. Bernard ever since the transfer of Ross.

On September 25 1890 St. Bernard were found guilty of concealed professionalism and suspended by The Scottish Football Association. Nothing daunted, the members met in the clubhouse the same evening and formed another club called Edinburgh Saints with much the same membership and playing personnel. They arranged to play Renton in a friendly on the following Saturday and the latter club sought clearance from the S.F.A. They were refused it and warned in the clearest possible terms not to carry out the match but Renton decided to go ahead. The Association saw this as a deliberate challenge to its authority, a viewpoint trenchantly propounded by *Scottish Sport* on October 3.

> "Renton seem set on ruling the Association. First of all the Renton are a disappointed club. The Association and its cup ties are of little account in its purview now that the club has been ousted from the ties. The jurisdiction of the Association extends beyond the cup-ties however. The parent body exercises a paternal supervision over all matches played by its clubs."

Scottish Sport had put its finger on a great weakness of Scottish football's early years, to wit, the organisation of the Scottish Cup. This tournament began early in the season and with no form of seeding within the various geographical zones the strongest clubs could be, and often were, drawn against one another and for a prestigious club like Renton to be free of Scottish Cup ambitions as early in the year as September was indeed a heavy financial blow. *Scottish Sport* now proceeded to turn its batteries upon St. Bernard.

> "The managers of the St. Bernard (the definite article was obligatory in Victorian description of teams) must have been very short-sighted indeed if they imagined that the mere change of name was sufficient to clear the club of the consequences of their peregrinations in the paths of professionalism ... The sentence is a severe one,—the expulsion from the Association of the two clubs, the suspension of the players involved until the end of the season, and the social annihilation of the officials concerned."

In that last phrase is revealed the strong streak of snobbery that coloured attitudes to sport. The same publication could say, a few years later in December 1894 that "Bailie Primrose, the honorary president of Rangers, is not ashamed to confess publicly that he numbers some of the Rangers' professionals among his personal friends" condescension dripping from every syllable.

The St. Bernard scandal called forth one last attempt by the authorities to maintain the amateur status of the game. The Professional Committee of the Association required 45 clubs to submit their books to them for investigation. This was a ploughing of the waters for it was an open secret that most clubs kept two sets of books, one for just this kind of emergency and the other which showed the actual state of affairs. There was the strong presumption that the S.F.A. was not too enthusiastic to discover details of wrong-doing, since it had no clear idea of what it would do in the light of such a revelation.

Certainly clubs had been acquitted in highly suspicious circumstances. In 1887 Hibernian won the Scottish Cup, defeating Dumbarton in the final. Dumbarton's near neighbours Vale of Leven, acting as their agents as Adventurers had done for Dunfermline Athletic, hired a private detective named Morton who established that one of the Hibernian players William Groves, had been paid up to four times his wages as an apprentice stonemason as "broken time", to enable him to turn out for the club. Moreover, in the "whitewash" set of books presented by Hibernian, it was observed that although the club had certainly had three distinct secretary-treasurers in the last five years, nevertheless all the entries for that period were made in the same hand. Despite this overwhelming evidence, Dumbarton's eventual protest was rejected and Hibernian remained in possession of the Scottish Cup. Justice of a sort followed for some weeks later, the Hibernian treasurer, Mr. McFadden, was reported as having absconded to Canada with club funds and money belonging to the Archdiocese of Edinburgh!

This investigation of 1890 did bring the occasional touch of panic. Celtic's submission was more than a week late, explained by the fact that there was fever in the Secretary's house and that the books could not be delivered on account of the danger of infection. They had to go to the Sanitary Authorities for disinfecting, after which they were handed over, but they passed muster as indeed did those of all clubs excepting only the unfortunate Cowlairs.

For the moment Renton were out of the League, indeed out of football altogether, and the League reduced to ten clubs. There was a suggestion that the Renton fixtures might be assumed by Queen's Park but nothing came of it. The League operated with ten clubs and then in October the unthinkable happened. Renton took the S.F.A. to law, to the undisguised scorn of *Scottish Sport*:

> "For my part I don't see that they have a leg to stand on. There is nothing for it but to turn professional and work the oracle as best they may, or allow their best players to be bought up by English clubs".

Renton had the courage to think they knew better and they did bring an action, claiming £5000 from the Scottish Football Association on the grounds of loss by their engagements being cancelled, the vested interest in their fame as a club—they had after all been unofficially and self-styled "champions of the world" after their defeat of the F.A. Cup holders West Bromwich Albion—their expenditure on ground and pavilion and injury to their patrimonial rights in the Association itself and in its funds. By December 1890 *Scottish Sport* had changed its tune rather and was coming round to the view that the Association "could be in trouble over the Renton business for not having given them a hearing".

Indeed it was. In an action raised on behalf of Renton in the Court of Session by lawyers Messrs. Angus Campbell and McKenzie judgement was given for the football club with costs. Renton had their day in court, triumphed and were restored to the ranks of The Scottish Football Association and later on to The Scottish League, although their first-ever League season had ended after only five matches. Meanwhile, not without fits and starts, the League proceeded with the completion of its initial competition.

It had established priority of matches except where cup ties and representative games were concerned. These last did not simply consist of internationals but matches between various Scottish and English county associations, Glasgow v Sheffield being a typical case. Intercity matches were extremely important occasions in those early days and under the rules of the Edinburgh Association, clubs such as Heart of Midlothian and Hibernian were obliged to furnish at least three players if selected. As in 1890 intercity dates had been fixed before the League was even formed, it was necessary for Hearts to seek agreement with Celtic for a postponement which was granted. More cavalier was the attitude of the Paisley club Abercorn who in December lost heavily to Cambuslang because neither of their full backs bothered to turn up and as none of the second eleven was available, they had to scratch around to raise a team.

Tentatively, the first League campaign came to a close, producing the only case in the entire century of its existence of a shared championship. Dumbarton and Rangers, each finishing with 29 points, drew 2–2 in a play-off and no further method had been devised of separating them. It had been a cautious beginning, not that one would have thought so from the report of the Secretary J. H. McLaughlin at the first Annual General Meeting of 1891. He was not prepared to give the Doubting Thomases an easy passage.

> "I have very much pleasure in presenting to this body its first annual report. I say, advisedly, much pleasure, because so many were the prophecies of an early death for the bantam League when it first saw light, and coming as they did from men 'of light and leading'—at least in their own estimation—the wonder is that the tender infant, if I may call it so, did not die right off through sheer terror.
>
> But, gentlemen, in spite of these malignant prophecies, the infant has waxed fat and strong beyond belief; its crowing is heard over the land and the kick of its infantile foot strikes terror into the

BASE AND TEMPTING GOLD 21

The early Scottish Football League matches were rough and ready affairs. In this 1894 match between Clyde and St. Mirren at Old Barrowfield Park there are no goal nets although their use had been sanctioned in 1891.

hearts of its venerable brethren when they are unfortunate enough to come into contact with it. I think that we, the tender guardians of the League, may well be pardoned if we feel proud of our nursling. When we consider the chorus of calumnious misrepresentation that greeted our advent, the almost universal condemnation that was visited upon us by press and public alike, the apparently insuperable difficulties and dangers that beset our career during the eventful season just past, the opposition, hidden and open, that encountered our every step, and last, but most galling of all, the vicious misinterpretation that greeted our every action—when we consider all these and look at our position now, I say again, gentlemen, we are justly entitled to feel proud of the successful issue of our labours."

Given that in addition the League had made a profit of £62-7-0d on its first season's working. J. H. McLaughlin's enthusiasm was understandable if a touch overblown. He would have an enlarged League on which to report the following season, for although the landless Cowlairs withdrew from the roll of original entrants Renton rejoined and the numbers were made up to twelve by the addition of Clyde, who had clearly reconsidered their early decision to hold aloof, and Leith Athletic, whose inclusion was testimony that the game was beginning to take hold in the East of Scotland.

Membership in the League's three years of existence before the adoption of professionalism went from 10 to 12 then back to

10 again. At the end of the second season, a season in which Dumbarton won the League title outright, Cambuslang and Vale of Leven withdrew. In the new, more highly-organised version of the game there would be no room for what were in reality village clubs and not even the fact that the geographical area from which Vale of Leven took their name was in a very real sense the cradle of the Scottish game could save them at top level. At the outset of the Scottish League that area had provided three members, Renton, Vale of Leven and Dumbarton, but the pull of the cities and England and the collapse of the textile industry within the Vale itself would make it impossible for the local teams to compete at the highest grade.

The onset of professionalism could no longer be delayed, for the current situation had become a public scandal, strongly analogous to that of athletics 100 years later. Everyone knew that players were being paid for it passed belief that young working men could frequently take time off to play away matches against English clubs without in some shape or form being recompensed. Yet the opposition was able to fight a skilful delaying action, their spokesman being Mr. A. Lawrance[1] of Dumbarton who marshalled his forces to resist the attack of those who favoured open professionalism, J. H. McLaughlin in the van.

Scottish Sport displayed its usual ability to disregard the way things were going. The adoption of professionalism in England in 1885 had made it impossible for Scottish clubs to hope to retain their best players. The top English sides recruited them mercilessly through the means of "agents" whom they employed in Scotland. These agents were hated, feared and not infrequently assaulted as in one celebrated case in Kilmarnock station where the locals got wind of an attempt to seduce the famous "Bummer" Campbell, but they existed and were on the whole successful.

In vain did the sporting press launch tirades against the poaching of players from Scotland by agents of English clubs. Taking the highest-possible moral ground *Scottish Sport* had thundered in December 1888:

> "What Scot worthy of the name would be so base as to deliver a fellow-countryman into abject relations of humiliation and subserviency?"

The answer of course was that quite a few Scots would. Those who went south to play shut their ears to the departing censures of

---

[1] There is a variant of this spelling, Lawrence but I have used the earliest and less common form.

the papers. The dyer, Wilson, who had gone to play certainly for Blackburn Rovers and dye possibly, was urged in the same newspaper to "weigh against tempting gold the moral and physical shipwreck inseparable from the life of a professional football player." No future career was envisaged for the ex-professional other than the ownership of a 'dramshop', indeed it was pointed out acidly in the very last years of amateurism that several prominent members of the Celtic Football Club, notably James Kelly, (father of Sir Robert Kelly, later President of the S.F.A. and of The Scottish League) had mysteriously and suddenly become possessed of the means to set themselves up as keepers of taverns.

The amateurs, the 'Simon Pures' in the phrase of the day, died hard. On April 1 1892 a Special General Meeting of the S.F.A. rejected the notion of the paid player but by the comparatively narrow margin of 71–54. Those who wished to legalise professionalism had high hopes of their motion succeeding at the A.G.M. of the following month but again it went down 104–78, largely because of the opposition of the "backwoods" clubs for whom the paid player was not remotely an option. But professionalism was an idea whose time was at hand and as so often in those early days, J. H. McLaughlin found the phrase to articulate the viewpoint declaring, "You might as well attempt to stop the flow of Niagara with a kitchen chair as to stem the tide of professionalism."

After a long and sometimes heated debate professionalism was adopted in Scotland at the Annual General Meeting of the S.F.A. in May 1893.

The meeting was chaired by Mr. J. Sliman of Heart of Midlothain and there could be no other standard-carrier for the advocates of change than J. H. McLaughlin. The following report of his speech contains the gist of his argument.

He began by saying that professionalism did exist, they knew it existed and anyone who said that it did not at once showed that his views were of very little account. Recognising this, what were they to do about it? They could not kill it. Five years ago the S.F.A. had tried to kill it, with the result that it flourished more and more every year. In every sport where money could be made professionalism must creep in and so they had professional golfers, cricketers, billiard players and Volunteers. (This last was a dig at Mr. Lawrance of Dumbarton who was a noted exponent of rifle shooting at Volunteer meetings and was suspected of having accepted prize money.)

They could not continue the organised hypocrisy of last year— they must take it in hand, legalise it, keep away all possible evils but derive all possible benefits. Whether they approved of it or not they ought to control it. Football in Scotland was on the wane and the cause was simply the importation of their players into England. He thought legislation would stop this poaching but they would at any rate be in no worse position than now. If England would not enter into a protective treaty—and he thought that she would—they would have this advantage, that they could go to England and bring back their players. Dealing with the argument that the country clubs would suffer he pointed out that under professionalism they would at least be certain of a team for a season which they were not at present. Just now, with veiled professionalism, players were masters of the clubs and could go and debauch themselves without being called to account; but under the new system clubs would be masters of the players and the standard would rise accordingly.

The motion was carried by a large majority but there were the predictable prophets of doom. A correspondent from Ayrshire wrote:

> "Legalisation of professional football simply means sounding the death knell to first-class football so far as Ayrshire is concerned. There is not a single club in the country that could afford to keep a team of paid players even at the most nominal sum per week."

Within ten years there would be three Ayrshire clubs in membership of The Scottish League, not for the first time the gift of prophecy had been denied.

Scottish Sport sought comfort where it could. On May 3 1893 it said its last words on the subject with the weary grace of Lee surrendering his sword at Appomattox.

> "The League has all along been put down as a professional body; in fact its unpopularity in certain quarters at the time of its inception was largely due to the foreboding that it would one day assume the role of promoter of the system of openly paying players in this country. The ruling body has now approved of the change. Yet amateurism is not dead; players, if they choose, can still stand aloof from all mercenary inducements, can still wear the white flower of amateurism, the badge of sport for sport's sake.
>
> "Our professionalism will not be so professional as to permit our players making football their only living, doing nothing else but train and play. They will go on very much as they have been going, working as well as playing, only more amenable to the control of their committee, which will in itself be a great gain."

The Song of the Good Old Queen's Park F.C.

Tune—"Scots Wha Hae."

Scots wha hae wi' "Spiders" played,
The good old "Black and White" Brigade,
Never shall your glory fade,
Who made the old Q.P.
Sillars, Arnott, Gillespie (goal),
Campbell, Berry, swell the roll,
Smellie, Lambie, Bob McColl,
All Stars of Old Q.P.

We've still good "Spiders" on the ball
In Craigie, Clark and Harold Paul,
And Ramsay, trickiest of all,
A Nipper for Q.P.
Anderson clean heels can show,
Drummond makes the rest look slow,
While "Hector" lays usurpers low,
Who dare to face Q.P.

As sportmen they have made a name,
As Amateurs they're still the same,
They always try to play the game
Just like the old Q.P.
Here's to the good old Premier Team
Whose history reads like a dream,
May Good Luck always brightly beam
Upon the old Q.P.

R. F. Morrison

No. 2240—*Copyright.*

Most Clubs had semi-official songs, those of the weaker clubs being the more vainglorious. This one from the first decade of the 20th century extols the merits of internationalists R. S. McColl and Harold Paul among others.

There had been strong hints from the advocates of professional football that clubs would impose a stricter control on their players and this indeed proved to be the case. By the early 1890s Celtic had issued their players with a list of training regulations and dietary advice. Nor was conduct omitted in Willie Maley's somewhat ominous phrase: "the player who cannot conduct himself on and off the park has no peg for his suit at Celtic Park."

The practice grew up of insulating players from the temptations of everyday life before important matches. In April 1895 the St. Bernard football team went to Burntisland for a week to prepare for the Cup Final. Cup ties were still seen as the really big events at this time. The following March Heart of Midlothian called in their players to stay in an Edinburgh hotel for a few days before another important cup match. The players trained at the ground as usual but were not allowed home to their wives, something more often associated with today's Italian football. They passed this monastic spell in visiting Cooke's Circus, the Lyceum Theatre in Edinburgh and an excursion to Gullane.

It was becoming more difficult with every year that passed to combine top-class football with a heavy manual job. In September 1895 Allan Martin of Celtic fainted after a Glasgow Cup tie against Linthouse. Subsequent enquiries established that he had worked a double shift as a furnace-man in an iron works immediately prior to playing. He had been forced to do this in order to get time off to play. With the increasing rigour went an element of paternalism. Players still received wedding presents from their club, Sandy McMahon of Celtic received a very handsome gift to the value of £20 in May 1896. Nor was it all unremitting grimness. In February 1897 a King's Park player was so disgusted by his colleagues' performance against Dundee that he left the field before the end of the match.

In general then there was more stringent supervision. It was in the interests of the clubs to do this and it had the added advantage of silencing some of the critics of full-time football who were not slow to use the "idle hands" argument when players fell foul of the law.

The decision to pay the hands had no adverse effect on the number of applicants who wished to join the League, quite the reverse. In the summer of 1893 Hibernian, St. Bernard (back with the old name) Cowlairs and Dundee were all forward to join the one-division League.

They were unsuccessful but managed to gain election to the newly formed Second Division, also of ten clubs, which was largely formed from the already existing Scottish Alliance. The new division was made up of the following clubs—Dundee, Hibernian, Morton, Motherwell, Northern, Partick Thistle, Port Glasgow Athletic, St. Bernard, Thistle and Cowlairs.

A word needs to be said about the creation of this division. Clearly, St. Bernard and Cowlairs had purged their contempt and there were interesting extensions of the boundaries of League football to Tayside and industrial Lanarkshire, to say nothing of Lower Renfrewshire. There were four Glasgow clubs, which was certainly too many, but a real wrong had been righted with the admission of Hibernian. That club had been amongst the earliest pioneers of the Scottish game but mismanagement, plundering and prejudice had joined to force them briefly out of football. For the mismanagement they had themselves—and chiefly Mr. McFadden—to blame but they had been deprived of six of their best players when Celtic set up in business in 1888 and they suffered considerably from the fact that they were closely identified with Ireland and Home Rule in the volatile political climate of the 1880s. So closely indeed were they identified with the Home Rule movement that, in London for a friendly match, the team spent their free time at the trial of Piggott, who stood accused of forging and uttering letters over the signature of Charles Stewart Parnell, the celebrated Irish politician.

For several years Hibernian were refused admission to the S.F.A. on the grounds that "the Association was founded for Scotchmen" and they were not admitted until 1876. The League was scarcely more welcoming. In their first season of membership Hibernian won the Second Division comfortably but were not admitted to the First Division, although it has to be said that promotion would not become automatic until season 1921–22. Cowlairs, who finished behind them, were not promoted either, that distinction falling undeservedly to Clyde. When Hibernian again won the Second Division in 1894–95 they were rather grudgingly admitted to "uppah succles" as Victorian sports writers loved to describe the First Division, Dundee, who had finished second, receiving 14 votes to 11 for Hibernian. Still, in the First Division they were and Edinburgh was now strongly represented there with three League clubs and a fourth (Leith Athletic) just along the road.

The Hibernian situation reflected a demographic situation which was very different in Scotland from that of England. In the wake of the Great Famine of 1846, tens of thousands of Irishmen had come to Scotland with their families. Distrusted, feared, despised, they tended to remain within their own ethnic group even when forming clubs for the playing of sport. If Hibernian were perhaps the most politically-conscious example of this, they were by no means the only one, for Celtic in Glasgow, Harp in Dundee and smaller organisations such as Broxburn Shamrock all looked back tenaciously across the Irish Sea to their origins. This would strongly affect the ethos and intensity of football in Scotland.

But, for the moment professionalism had come and was adopted with undiscriminating enthusiasm, indeed without a thought as to its long term viability. Each division of the League was to manage its own affairs, with the home club retaining two-thirds of the gate receipts, something which would heavily favour the city clubs whose grounds were larger and population base stronger. There was a guarantee of £5 to visiting clubs, oddly enough the same sum pertained in both divisions, but there was a recognition of rank in the subscriptions to the League, First Division clubs paying £3 while Second Division clubs were required to find only £2-10-0d.

By 1894 almost 800 players had been registered as professionals by 83 clubs. Inequalities persisted from the start with a Kilmarnock player getting ten shillings per week plus half a crown per point whereas Celtic and Rangers players were earning three pounds a week before the turn of the century, almost double the wage that a skilled tradesman, such as a cobbler or a fitter and turner could hope to make.

The game would henceforth be more honest. In John McCartney's phrase, written in his book *Story of The Scottish Football League* "legalised professionalism meant, to use a colloquialism, the end of the man with the muck-rake." There was now no place in the game for the seedy men on the fringes who scavenged a living by reporting infractions of rules by players, infractions real or imagined. The game however would henceforth be played in a rather less amicable spirit, undoubtedly some of the conviviality had gone for good as McCartney also trenchantly observed:—

"However keen the battle raged and whatever spasm of temper or chagrin crossed the struggling players, the tea and social after the match wiped the slate. Where, oh where, have these happy functions gone?"

They were gone for good, since the new regime had no place for those little civilities of life which had seen J. H. McLaughlin of Celtic act for several years as pianist/accompanist to the Rangers Glee Club. This was the price paid for improved facilities and indeed these could have stood improvement. McCartney again:—

"It is instructive to contemplate the little wooden shanties holding to suffocation 22 players with an unlimited number of 'Kommittee' men, plus several frenzied 'rabids' hollering in at the door and window (in some cases there were two) 'what had to be done' and 'who had to be watched.' The rear of these cabins generally had a construction, disclosing the hall-mark of ancient architecture, for the display of a few tin basins containing rancid or stagnant water. With only one piece of soap and perhaps a couple of towels, players were expected to purify themselves. A shower bath could be obtained simply by tipping overhead a basin (if you were fortunate enough to secure one), of equal parts mud and water."

The League was thriving if unsociable. It was becoming an extremely powerful organisation which bade fair to achieve parity of influence with the S.F.A. This was especially so after the development of a Second Division, since the League now included the most powerful and influential clubs in the country with the singular exception of Queen's Park. J. H. McLaughlin saw this expansion as a great step achieved. In his annual report to the League in 1893 he had stated:

> "I refer to the proposed extension of this body to include a Second Division. The time seems right for this step. It will add to the weight and importance of the League as a body and will, I believe—and this is of course, the more important consideration—increase the prosperity and consequent usefulness of the clubs included in that supplementary division."

McLaughlin would be in spirited mood because in the third and fourth seasons of League competition his club, Celtic, had won the championship outright. In the summer of 1894 Airdrieonians, Morton and Dundee Wanderers were elected to the Second Division. The last-named, an all-amateur team, had a very brief and stormy career which lasted but the one season and was the starting-point for the debate, which continues today, as to whether the city of Dundee is capable of sustaining more than one top-level side.

Relationships with the Football League and with individual English clubs were still being worked out. Celtic were put on the boycott list of the Football League for having signed a player, Lee, formerly with Lincoln City. The Scottish Football League Secretary was instructed to enquire of his Football League counterpart if Scottish clubs were not perfectly at liberty to engage players, formerly with English clubs but now free, without the consent of the said English clubs. If they were permitted to do this, then he was to ascertain the grounds on which Celtic were being boycotted.

Complaints still abounded that League fixtures were not carried out sufficiently briskly or punctiliously. Ammunition was not lacking for such critics. Thus in the Second Division in 1894-95, Renton, who did seem to have a collective death-wish, did not appear at Dundee for their return fixture with Wanderers and forfeited the points. In the same season Leith and St. Bernard protested that they had been ordered to play their match by the referee when in their opinion the rain was too heavy. Their attempts to have the match treated as a friendly were thrown out by the League Management Committee to the glee of *Scottish Sport* which had been bending a threatening eye on such proceedings.

"Last Saturday (December 29 1894) three League matches were cancelled. In addition, the superlative daintiness of the referees at Ibrox and Barrowfield (the home of Clyde) metamorphosed these two matches into harmless friendlies. In each case a match WAS played, and although conditions were not of the best, they were good enough for a cup-tie, which is more important than a League match any day of the week. If miry ground, even ankle deep, is to be sufficient excuse for cancelling a League match and substituting a friendly, then it would be better for the League to consider whether they should not refrain from playing their competition in winter at all."

The report went on to note that to date there had only been 60 League matches played by the end of December, a decrease of four from the previous year. This situation had been exacerbated, not only by severe weather but by the fact that such holidays as the Glasgow September Monday and New Year's Day were traditionally kept for attractive friendlies with English sides. Thus on the first day of 1895 Third Lanark had played London Casuals, Dundee had met Sheffield United and Celtic had encountered Everton.

Even at this early stage the smaller clubs were caught in an economic vice. Port Glasgow Athletic survived in the Second Division because, alone among the League clubs, they had remained amateur. In Dunbartonshire the game was in a desperate position. *Scottish Sport* again:

"The Vale of Leven club have gradually dropped out of sight, we believe almost out of existence. We feel pretty safe in saying that it is questionable whether Dumbarton will attempt to run a professional team next season. The opinion of most of those at the head of football affairs in Dunbartonshire is that Scotland can only support about half a dozen professional teams of high standing and that country clubs cannot hope to keep in the running with them."

The early winter of 1895 was marked by very severe weather and the inevitable hold-up in the fulfilment of the fixture list led to a slackening of public interest. The League Management committee did its best to keep things going, refusing to approve the decision of Referee J. Richardson to declare the match between Celtic and St. Mirren a friendly game AFTER it had been played. Oddly enough, this move was approved by the waspish *Scottish Sport* although it was unable to resist its by now customary dig:

"If a ground is good enough for a friendly it is also good enough for a League match which is practically a friendly with a special significance."

One club was in increasing danger of being frozen out both literally and metaphorically. On January 15 1895 a little paragraph in the *Glasgow Evening News* carried the information that Queen's Park were unfortunately without a definite fixture for Saturday first. The lagging League fixture list was thrown even further into disarray by the fact that twice in the initial stages of the campaign in September, referees had failed to appear, causing those matches (between Celtic and Clyde and between Dundee and Hearts) to be played as friendlies and requiring that new dates should be found for them.

Unfavourable comparisons were being drawn with England, where there was very little playing fast and loose with league fixtures. A correspondent writing to *Scottish Sport* made the point firmly that League fixtures should be sacrosanct. "Only firm management in the immediate future will prevent the League competition becoming a dragging, upsetting nuisance as the season closes."

Country clubs suffered especially as the icy weeks dragged on. The solution to Renton's problems, caused by the impossibility of generating adequate home gates in what was a Dunbartonshire village, was seen as removal to Glasgow, where there was plenty of room for them and a suitable ground could easily be obtained.

In the midst of all difficulties, *Scottish Sport* could be relied upon to campaign for high moral standards from players both male and female. These last, the depraved members of the newly-formed Ladies' Football Association, came in for some fundamentalist denunciation. "The members of the new Ladies' Football Association, of which we have lately heard so much, do not play in fashion's dresses, but in knickers and blouses. They actually allow the calves of their legs to be seen and wear caps and football boots. The more shame to them, is our retort."

This brought forth a vigorous if ambiguous letter from a lady contributor who volleyed: "Hands down, all ye crusaders against knicker-attired females!" The newspaper certainly saw itself as the guardian of probity on the field and addressed a problem which remains unresolved almost a hundred years later: "Is it not about time that the referee should interfere and stop the aggravating caddism that deliberately kicks away a ball which is placed for a free kick?"

There were still areas in which priorities would have to be resolved between the Scottish Football Association and the younger League. Already League clubs were showing a great attachment to Saturday fixtures and the S.F.A. were unpopular with League clubs when they intimated their intention of holding international trial matches on a Saturday but the senior organisation prevailed on this occasion and the trials went ahead.

By the end of March 1895 Heart of Midlothian had taken the championship by the comfortable margin of five points and Dumbarton had not only finished bottom of the First Division but had required to revert to amateur status since there was simply no money available to pay their players. The original aristocrats of the game, Vale of Leven, Renton and Dumbarton had indeed fallen upon hard times. Dumbarton were going to the well too often and would not be voted back again when they did the same the following season.

Various beverages came from that well in the 1890s. In April 1895 Dundee were rather disconcerted when having provided the usual "hard stuff" and refreshments for the visitors' dressing-room in the course of a friendly match with Sunderland, they were informed by the trainer of the English club that half a gallon of tea would be preferable for his charges. The old, easy ways were going. Queen's Park signified their customary willingness to play Charity Cup ties on the last Saturday in April and the first two in May but the League clubs could not see their way to sacrifice so many Saturdays to charity. The paybills of the League clubs were too great an item to tackle with no income.

As April moved into May in 1895 there was more than the usual lobbying for changes in the composition of the two Divisions of the League. Dundee were most anxious that the number of First Division clubs should be increased to 12, seeing themselves as the most likely beneficiaries, but there was never any real chance of that since it was difficult enough to get the fixtures played off to time in a 10 club League. There were local league fixtures to fit in, i.e. those of the Glasgow and Edinburgh Leagues, as well as local cup competitions which in those days had a high degree of priority. Nor was Dundee's case helped by the ricketty existence of their amateur fellow-townsmen Dundee Wanderers who finished ninth of ten in the Second Division and who might not even have done that had they not been awarded two points for a match in which Renton failed to appear, having chosen to play a friendly match against Queen's Park instead. (One cannot but marvel at the patience shown by the Management Committee towards the Dunbartonshire club). The Divisions stayed at ten and ten but Dundee Wanderers did not stay with them. They were voted out along with the terminally-ill Cowlairs whose financial and legal problems had become insuperable. In their room came Kilmarnock and a club from the south side of Glasgow, Linthouse.

The year 1894–95 had been by a comfortable or uncomfortable

margin the most difficult that the infant League had yet experienced. It appeared to be faltering and *Scottish Sport*, never slow to put the boot into a fallen opponent, quoted approvingly from the letter of a reader:—

> "That this year's competition has been a greater failure than last year's is admitted, and the conclusion is almost forced upon us that, unlike England, we have not the number of populous centres nor the money to successfully carry through a competition of this kind."

The first tentative looks at rationalisation were being taken. Could Paisley sustain two First Division clubs? Some did not appear to think so. It was alleged that St. Mirren's antipathy towards Abercorn was so great that they were trying to drive the other Paisley club out of existence, a charge which St. Mirren officials strongly refuted. But if Paisley could sustain two First Division clubs, surely Edinburgh could support three and this made the grudging admission of Hibernian to the First Division at the A.G.M. of 1895 all the harder to understand. Their gate-drawing powers had been amply proved but perhaps their overtly sectarian origins, or rather those of the previous Hibernian club, had counted against them.

At the Annual General Meeting of 1895 J. H. McLaughlin of Celtic resigned as League Secretary. He had done an admirable job in launching the organisation and his quick mind and eloquent tongue had done much to minimise the considerable opposition that the very notion of a League had originally aroused. He was succeeded, most fortunately for the League, by another man who, differing in character, was every bit as able, William Wilton of Rangers who would later manage the Ibrox club. Wilton moved to the Secretaryship from the post of League Treasurer and his last act in that position was to pass to his successor, Mr. Montgomery of Third Lanark, a credit balance of £300. The Press could snipe as it liked, the League was doing well and was soundly based.

Now that play-offs have become an accepted feature of the Football League set-up in the 1980s it is interesting to note that they were being suggested by the Second Division clubs in Scotland in 1895. The procedure then used for movement between the two divisions was that three sides were selected from the bottom three First Division clubs and the top three Second Division clubs by the remaining seven First Division clubs. There were obvious dangers in this method. A club could win the Second Division on merit, might even win it two years running on merit and yet fail to gain admission to the top Division because it lacked friends at court. What the Second Division clubs proposed was that the top club in their Division should automatically be admitted to Division One and that "test matches" be held to decide the remaining two places. The leading clubs were not averse to the notion that the top club should come up from the Second Division but they certainly wished to retain voting rights on the other two places. It would be another quarter of a century before automatic promotion and relegation came to Scotland and it would come not from motives of genuine conviction, but from the threat of concerted external action.

The vexed question of player registration received some attention. At that time a player available for transfer could not play in League matches for his new club if he had turned out in a League fixture even once for his previous club. With League fixtures becoming ever more important this clearly would not do, and this restriction was removed. Renton—who else?—were not at the A.G.M. to assist in its removal. They were marked absent and subsequently claimed not to have received official notification of it. They were living dangerously.

Chapter Three

THE AGE OF EXPANSION

There was now no doubt that the long-term future of the Scottish League was assured. There was the best possible evidence of this in the large number of clubs which annually tried to secure admission to its ranks. Failure to gain admission to the charmed circle or a refusal to apply for such admission was increasingly damaging. Celtic withdrew from a fixture with Queen's Park at Hampden which would certainly have been one of the great money-spinners of the season for the amateur club on learning that the match would have been played in opposition to a Third Lanark home League match just down the road.

Occasionally, League clubs overdid their bid for protection. When Clyde complained about the action of Celtic in running a "strong reserve team" to compete with their own home League games they were told firmly that there was nothing that The Scottish Football League could do in such cases. In this particular instance Celtic do seem to have been at fault in that the posters advertising the match did not make it clear that they would be fielding a reserve eleven.

Gradually the notion was spreading that the use of club members, committee men most often, as referees was increasingly becoming inappropriate and that neutral officials should be employed who would be paid for their services. A tariff was drawn up whereby referees received half a guinea (ten shillings and sixpence) for officiating at a match within 30 miles of their home, fifteen shillings where the distance was 50 miles and a guinea for longer journeys. The function of the referee was still rather like that of a cricket umpire, for interestingly at this time (1895) a penalty kick could only be awarded if a claim was made by the players, rather like an appeal at cricket.

Gradually too the demarcation lines between League and Association were being drawn. It was established that Scottish Cup-ties would take precedence over even Inter-League matches and Rangers and Hibernian both had to withdraw players who had been selected for such a fixture. This, one may say, was greatly to the relief of the clubs concerned. The new League Treasurer, Mr.

D. R. Montgomery of Third Lanark announced that as the campaign against liability for Income Tax had been unsuccessful, the imposition would have to be met. The Secretary was instructed to insert a note in the Minutes that such a payment was not to form a precedent for subsequent years although, given that the amount involved was only eightpence, the League did seem to be erring on the side of excessive caution.

At the end of the 1895–96 season Celtic were champions, for the third time in six seasons. In the course of his report the new Secretary, Mr. William Wilton, was able to note:

"I record the fact that in the whole course of ninety games played not a solitary player was brought under the punishment of the League." This was one in the eye for those Jeremiahs who had been emphatic that the creation of a professional league would be the occasion for unbridled thuggery on and off the pitch.

Dumbarton, having finished in bottom place for the second consecutive year were denied First Division status which necessarily led to the resignation of their representative, Mr. A. Lawrance from the presidency of the League. He was succeeded in that office by the senior Vice-President, the pawky J. H. McLaughlin of Celtic. Motherwell, Morton and Linthouse were all voted back to the Second Division and in an oddly contradictory phrase it was decided that "a player was not cup-tied in League matches (*sic*) unless he had played four for his previous club in Division 1 or five in Division 2 and even then dispensation could be sought in the latter case".

Protests, often frivolous, were the bane of the late Victorian football legislator's existence and in an effort to cut down their number, J. H. McLaughlin suggested neutral linesmen in the more important League matches. He was slightly ahead of his time and the move failed but only temporarily. Questions of precedence remained to be decided and the League scored over the S.F.A. in deciding that even Glasgow League matches were more important than the Qualifying Cup Final, and that the Saturday in dispute could not be left free.

The Scottish Football League was by now measuring its playing strength against other such organisations, a facet of the League's activities noted at much greater length elsewhere in this book. Some of the early briefings survive. Thus for the match against the Irish League in Belfast in 1897 the purchase of playing kit (uniforms, in the terminology of the day) was to be left in the hands of Mr. Towns of St. Mirren with full powers. The Friday before the match would be spent in Bangor with lunch at Mrs. O'Hara's Hotel. The players were each to receive a guinea plus travelling expenses and the League clubs were encouraged to release their star players by the assurance that the League would pay the wages of any player injured and unable to appear for his club side the following week.

The Irish League was defeated as was, for the first time, the Football League, to commemorate which latter victory President McLaughlin was given a special gold badge. The League was in fairly affluent circumstances and felt able to make the quite substantial donation of £50 to the Indian Famine Relief Fund. On the field power shifted temporarily at least to the East with Hearts and Hibs in the first two places and St. Bernard occupying a relatively respectable seventh spot. For the second year running, no player had been reported to the League Committee.

Abercorn, finishing at the foot of the First Division, found few prepared to keep them there and they were replaced by Partick Thistle. More surprisingly Falkirk, applying for membership of Division Two and coming from an area which by Scottish standards was densely-populated, did not muster a seconder! Even worse was the fate which awaited Dumbarton. The famous old club had finished in last place in the Second Division despite having reached the Scottish Cup final. They now suffered the mortification of being voted out of the League altogether and that a mere five years after they had been outright champions.

More important than any of these happenings, at least in the long term was the instruction given to the Secretary that he should write to his English counterpart expressing the willingness of The Scottish Football League to sign an agreement recognising each other's registration of players.

The area which caused most difficulty in the negotiations concerned those Scots players who had returned from England. Clearly the Scottish League could be no party to such players breaking a contract but equally it could not countenance a system in which such players were held for ever to their English club on tenuous evidence. Agreement was finally reached on the following terms:

> "All Scotch players registered with the Football League who have never played for the English club for which they are registered shall have their registrations cancelled by the Football League, but players who have played in England and are now engaged with Scotch clubs may be still held by the League club for which they are registered in England, in addition to their present Scotch club, but for no other English club without the consent of the Scotch club."

This agreement was a great gain to both associations but as the tide always flowed strongly south the Scots might reasonably be said to have got the better of the bargain.

The season of 1897–98 saw the county of Dumbarton incur another prominent casualty. Renton's association with the League, which had always been stormy and uneasy, came to an end. After four matches they found themselves unable to meet their obligations in the way of gate guarantees and were allowed to resign "without penalty". It was a melancholy departure but the truth was that there was no place in League football for the village side with its spartan ground, Tontine Park, and regular crowd of a few hundred. Their departure led to one of the most confusing episodes in Scottish football history. Hamilton Academical[1] were brought into the Second Division and given the remaining fourteen Renton fixtures but many League tables show Hamilton as having played all 18 matches whereas there is no doubt that Renton themselves discharged the first four. Hamilton Academical showed an opportunistic relish in ditching the Scottish Combination to which they had previously been attached and they were rewarded with confirmed Second Division status at the A.G.M. of 1898, Ayr having previously replaced Dumbarton. Now that agreement had been reached between the Leagues on registration of players, the next logical step was the formation of an International League Board to deal with matters of common concern. At an early meeting in December 1897 it was decided that, with immediate effect, no amateur would be allowed to play in League games unless first registered with the Secretary of the appropriate League.

The need for neutral linesmen, previously highlighted by J. H. McLaughlin, emerged again in the course of a Management Committee debate on whether linesmen were allowed to go on to the pitch and coach in the course of a game. To the general relief it was decided that they were not. There were turbulent players too. Three of them, Kelso, Blessington and King struck before the Inter-League match with the Irish League in February 1898 at Dundee. Their grievance was that the League had decided to give players only medals and expenses. In an early demonstration of player power, the three demanded to know if they would be paid for playing and the inference was that if they were not they would not. They were eventually given the usual terms of one guinea, not an over-generous provision since the gate drawings amounted to £229-10-8d.

---

[1] This is the official name of the club although in everyday usage they are invariably referred to in the plural.

THE AGE OF EXPANSION

There were foreshadowings of a much later Premier Division debate when J. H. McLaughlin suggested that three down from ten, or three possibly down from ten, remembering that relegation was not automatic, was far too many and that the number should henceforth be reduced to two. This proposal was adopted at the A.G.M. at the end of the season by which time Celtic had won the championship once more.

Despite the rumblings at Dundee it had been a highly successful year once more as League Secretary William Wilton was not slow to observe.

"The mutual recognition of registrations means the practical amalgamation of two Leagues, involving 56 clubs and almost 2700 players. We have met and defeated both the other Leagues. In conclusion I can only comment on the success of our competition. During the season it has drawn crowds second only to the great International itself. The day has gone when professional clubs can afford to be outwith the League and, that being so, it is in the interests of us all to do all in our power not only to maintain interest in the games but to see to it that the rivalry is of the healthiest nature possible. Thus will we continue a power in the land and the benefactor of the many toilers in our towns and cities who need so much the exhilaration which our competition provides."

After such an inspiring address it was only to be expected that the last three clubs in Division One, St. Bernard, Clyde and Partick Thistle would be voted back and that a similar fate would be accorded the three Lanarkshire Second Division basement-dwellers, Motherwell, Airdrie and Hamilton. Clyde had applied for re-election to the First Division for three years in a row and the hollow, ghostly laugh heard in the council chambers no doubt came from Dumbarton direction.

There was a growing recognition that, for their own protection, referees had to be distanced from the clubs if possible. An instance of this was the decision that referees should now be paid a standard match fee of one guinea plus a Third Class return railway ticket and that this payment should be made by the League Treasurer rather than by club officials, a practice which in the past had led to several highly embarrassing scenes. The need for this change was all the more evident in that various League committee members, including the President himself, were still acting as referees.

Just before Christmas 1898 there was a nasty shudder when it seemed that Dundee would go to the wall. They failed to appear for a match against Celtic and the report spread that the club was going into liquidation. It was vital that the game should survive in what was then such an important outpost and to achieve this the League offered to guarantee Dundee their wages and travelling expenses for the remaining four League matches by making good any deficit that might not be covered by gate receipts. They did set a prudent upper limit of £25. The League's intervention had the desired effect and Dundee, under new management, survived the season comfortably enough.

That particular season 1898–99 was distinguished by the astonishing performance of Rangers in winning the League title with maximum points, 18 matches played 18 matches won, so that they took the title from Hearts in second place by the relatively huge margin of ten points. In his valedictory as Secretary, he was about to be succeeded by Willie McAndrew, William Wilton permitted himself a quiet chortle at the success of his team.

"Modesty, born of my close connection with the champions, hampers my eulogising them to the extent that their great performance warrants. A world's record, however, especially when it is an unbeatable record, is an achievement that will speak for itself as the years go by." It was indeed a remarkable performance and although Celtic have gone through an entire League campaign undefeated, no club has come particularly near the exclusively winning performance of Rangers.

The Annual General Meeting of 1899 saw Ayrshire gain First Division representation for the first time when Kilmarnock were promoted. Dundee, despite their financial upsets were retained in the First Division—it was important to have a top-flight presence north of the Forth-Clyde Valley if at all possible—while Linthouse and Abercorn found their Second Division colleagues in lenient mood and both clubs were voted back.

In the autumn of 1899 coming events cast their shadows in a bizarre way. Third Lanark complained to the League about the condition of the ball used in two of their matches. It was then ordained that all League matches must be started with a new ball. In the last three years of Third Lanark's existence, i.e. 1965–67, failure to provide just such a new ball would be one of the charges levelled at the Cathkin club. The League was now less inclined to make excuses. Hearts,[2] fined for a late start in a match at Kilmarnock, were disposed to blame the late arrival of their train. They were told to pay the fine of £10 and recover it from the Glasgow and South-Western Railway Company.

---

[2] The style, Heart of Midlothian, is used in League tables, Inter-League sides etc. In narrative Hearts will often be used.

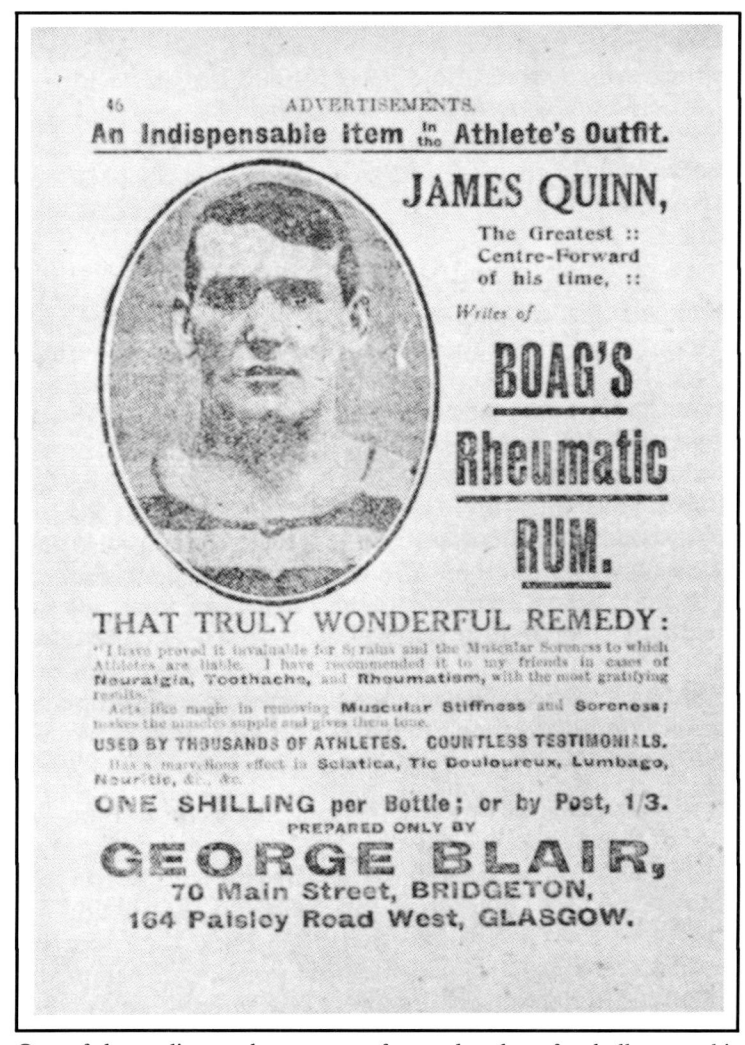

One of the earliest endorsements of a product by a footballer was this one by Jimmy Quinn of the marvellous properties of Boag's Rheumatic Rum.

The country was by this time at war in South Africa but the Boer War was largely fought by professional soldiers and the effect on the population at home was not great. Nevertheless the Second Division (the divisions were still run separately in some aspects) voted an unspecified sum to the Fund for the relief of wives and children and other dependents of soldiers and sailors who had been impoverished by the death of their bread-winners, and also of the families of reservists and militia not otherwise adequately provided for.

The League had now been going for almost ten years and to mark this Mr. J. H. McLaughlin was presented with a diamond ring for services to that body since its inception. Mr. McLaughlin having "feelingly replied, the remainder of the evening was spent in a harmonious manner".

The tardy train used by Heart of Midlothian had its consequences. A new bye-law was formulated which read as follows:—

"All games must be started at the agreed or advertised times. In the event of any game being unfinished on account of insufficiency of light or otherwise, both secretaries of the competing clubs shall report the matter to the Committee who shall have power to fine the offending club or clubs."

No rule could be found to cover the mysterious case of Referee A. A. Jackson who had claimed to be sick for the match between Linthouse and Motherwell but who had, several Motherwell officials averred, subsequently been seen on the ground. No confirmation could be had of this and Mr. Jackson's pleas of illness were accepted. Mr. Jackson would not be at Govandale Park, the ground of Linthouse, in sickness or in health the following season nor would any other referee as the little Govan club decided not to offer itself for re-election. Rangers had that particular district of Glasgow much too firmly sewn up. The place of Linthouse was taken by East Stirlingshire, a surprising choice given that Falkirk already looked the stronger of the two clubs in the town of that name.

The First Division saw an even greater case of injustice. Clyde had yet again finished bottom of the division with a miserable four points, eight points behind St. Bernard in ninth place. Yet the Edinburgh club were voted out of the First Division on the first ballot while Clyde, despite a prolonged and proven record of non-success tied with Partick Thistle for the remaining top flight place. Unusually indecisive, perhaps because two Glasgow clubs were involved, J. H. McLaughlin drew lots to decide rather than use his casting vote and justice was partially done when the name of Partick Thistle came out of the hat. Such unlovely lobbying made the case for automatic promotion and relegation much harder to resist.

There was a certain application of double standards here. Glasgow's appetite for football was held to be insatiable, not without reason, whereas there may well have been the thought that for Edinburgh, where rugby had much more of a hold, top grade clubs should be limited to two. That said, it is difficult to avoid the conclusion that St. Bernard had been shabbily treated. They were replaced by Greenock Morton.

THE AGE OF EXPANSION

The summer of 1900 saw two interesting developments in League politics. A motion came before the Annual General Meeting that the rules of the League should be altered so that each division of the League would manage its own internal affairs. The Management Committee would take charge of all Inter-League matches and all business affecting the League as a whole. The motion was lost but by the narrow margin of 19–15.

At the same time the great prodigal came in from the cold. Queen's Park were elected to membership of the First Division which thus for a year stood at the nonsensical number of eleven clubs. They had acquired League status not a moment too soon. In

Back Row: W. McClelland *(Trainer)*, J. Lynch, J. Jackson, T. MacArthur *(President)*, [*Photo by Turnbull & Sons, Glasgow*]
A. Gordon *(Linesman)*, J. Miller, J. Munro, J. A. MacDonald, J. MacKenzie *(Ass. Trainer)*.
Front Row: G. Hamilton, P. Hagan, J. Montgomery, I. Findlay, R. Martin, R. Findlay.

Magazines often gave coloured photographs of teams as supplements. Port Glasgow Athletic were a First Division side from 1902–1910 but so struggling financially that they were an amateur Club.

---

fact, their great days were already behind them and special arrangements had to be made to save them from the pains of relegation. Without these they would certainly have made themselves acquainted with Division Two as their playing record up to the outbreak of war in 1914 was, to put it charitably, undistinguished. Shortly after their admission to the League, autonomy was granted to each Division with the promise that the eleven-club First Division would last for a season only. Gates were to continue to be split two-thirds one-third in favour of home teams and the guarantee for First Division matches, indeed for a time Second Division matches also, was to be £10.

There was an inevitable gulf between life at the top and life as experienced by struggling Second Division clubs. In October 1900 Port Glasgow Athletic uttered a heartfelt complaint that the visitors' dressing-room at Airdrie was not watertight and that their players' clothes had got very wet. Airdrie were ordered to bring the visitors' dressing-room up to the same standard as the one used by their own players. There was too a certain lack of confidence in the product. Arthurlie, elected to the League at the A.G.M. of 1901 soon afterwards requested that one of their home matches should be switched to Airdrie because the date for it clashed with the local Co-operative procession in Barrhead.

The season just ended in May 1901 had seen Rangers champions again with Queen's Park creeping into eighth position on goal difference. The Management Committee had been gratified to note that there had not been a single protest all season and transfer traffic with England was in a remarkable state of equipoise, 29 players having gone to England and 23 having returned.

The League was acquiring a political sense. The clubs which comprised its membership were increasingly aware that they represented the most important and most successful element in Scottish football and buoyed up by a record 6-2 victory over the Football League, decided that there should be a slate in the coming elections for President and Vice-President of the S.F.A. and that certain agreed candidates should be supported.

The fact that financially the League was doing well was not the signal for its embarking on a spendthrift course of profligacy. When a referee, one Mr. Nisbet, claimed expenses for a postponed match between Queen's Park and Kilmarnock these were allowed, with the exception of the one shilling and sixpence which he had claimed for his tea. The Committee pointed out sternly that he could easily have returned home for this meal. Their judgment of character appears to have been fairly accurate as shortly afterwards the same referee was struck off the list for having made a monumental mess of an Old Firm match in which his impartiality came under some well-merited scrutiny.

The Annual General Meeting of 1902 saw much more sensible choices made in regard to League composition. Dundee and Morton were re-elected to the First Division and with Port Glasgow Athletic also going up Renfrewshire now had three First Division clubs. Partick Thistle also benefited from the decision to expand the First Division to twelve clubs and this made room for the long overdue admission of Falkirk to the Second Division. With the entry of Raith Rovers another very important area of population in Scotland, Fife, was now exposed to League football.

Lines on the IBROX DISASTER

Brightly dawned that April morning,
  Blue skies bade us haste away
Where the flower of Scottish football
  Meant to show their might that day.
East and west, from every quarter
  Happy hearts come trooping in.
Till the gates of sunny Ibrox
  Close on the great crowd within.

Ne'er a thought of pending danger,
  All are eager for the fray;
Quip and jest and friendly jostle
  While the waiting time away.
Hark! is that a sound of creaking?
  Timid ones grow pale with fear;
But the thought is soon forgotten,
  The contending teams appear.

Free and fast the game is raging,
  Scotland's sons are pressing sore;
On the tiptoe of excitement,
  All expect them soon to score.
Then is heard a mighty uproar,
  "God have mercy!" someone cried;
Panic-stricken, there's a stampede
  Which all human power defies.

High above the seething tumult
  What an awful sight is seen,
Only a great gap remaining
  Where the cheerful crowd had been.
Down below are dead and dying,
  Mangled forms lie all around,
Broken—limbed, and bruised, and bleeding;
  Like a shambles is the ground.

Willing hands, their hearts nigh failing,
  Go to work with tender care,
Till the long, long list of injured
  of their help receive a share.
Brightly dawned that April morning,
  Blackest night has been the close;
Our sympathy is with the suffering,
  Rest the dead in steet repose.

The collapse of part of the terracing during the International of 1902 between Scotland and England was commemorated in these unattributed verses.

The next few years would see a steady growth in size of the top division. With only ten clubs in 1901 it would have exactly doubled in size by the time war in 1914 came along. In between times there were the usual spats and feuds which demonstrated that association football was a physical contact sport, and that not solely where the players were concerned. Thus in September 1902 one McAvoy of St. Mirren was accused of kicking the Hearts linesman, neutral linesmen having once more been abolished in the interests of economy rather than impartiality. The said linesman refused to turn the other cheek and used abusive language and his flag against McEvoy. Both men were dismissed with a stern rebuke but the day of the coaching, stick-brandishing linesman was surely limited.

An interesting development at this time was the use of Inspectors at matches. In a way these were the forerunners of the modern Referee Supervisors although their function was not so much to report on the performance of those officials as to report offending players to the League Management Committee. There were obviously great dangers of a conflict of jurisdiction between Referee and Inspector and after one or two instances in which Inspectors attempted to enter dressing rooms to remonstrate with erring players the procedure was abandoned.

The A.G.M. of 1903 saw the First Division increased to 14 clubs with two new names joining the Second Division in Albion Rovers from Coatbridge and Ayr Parkhouse. There was an attempt to gain immediate First Division status for Aberdeen but this foundered, possibly because the newly created Aberdeen had only emerged from a combination of clubs in that city and it was not until the following year that the northern side appeared in the Second Division in place of Ayr Parkhouse. One year in the lower grade was enough to convince their *confrères* that Aberdeen should be promoted to glory, despite having

There was always a touch of the dandy about this Kilmarnock and Celtic winger. He was renowned for his mass dribbling and fearless nature, once entering a cage and putting his head in a lion's mouth.

THE AGE OF EXPANSION

finished a modest seventh, 11 points behind Clyde who won the Division in a canter but failed to gain election to the First Division. They could scarcely complain however, having been previous beneficiaries of the inequitable system.

In passing it should be noted that Ayr Parkhouse led an eventful life at this time. They were back two years later, then after a further four years of mediocrity merged with the Ayr club to become Ayr United. This is the only one instance of an amalgamation of two league clubs in the one Scottish town working smoothly, or indeed, even being attempted. In the clash of business rationalisation and sentiment which is forever at the heart of Scottish football, familial and tribal loyalties have effectively stopped such mergers. Even today the most likely result of a blending of the Dundee clubs would the disappearance of large numbers of supporters of both sides who would be unable to muster much interest in any new-developed hybrid.

First of the Tynecastle stars, Bobby Walker was one of the outstanding players in Scottish football in the first years of this century.

The Ayr situation was resolved successfully because at the time of an expanding First Division, the town had much more chance of gaining one of the extra places available if it could field one strong side rather than two indifferent ones. Ayr United first took the field in 1910 and by 1913 they had become members of the First Division.

It had been a condition of the admission of the new club, Ayr United, that the former clubs Ayr Parkhouse and Ayr, would each liquidate their own responsibilities by September 30 of the following season, 1910–1911. The new club would be run by three neutrals and four committee members from each of the two previous clubs. Ayr United should actually have been promoted in 1912 when they topped the Second Division but the First Division clubs decided to defer the automatic relegation of St. Mirren who had incurred a heavy wage bill for the new season and while this was not a consideration for the second worst club, Queen's Park, a special

THE THIRD LANARK CHAMPIONSHIP SIDE OF 1903–04
Back row (l to r): *Graham, Raeside, Sloan, Campbell, Neilson, Cross.*
Front row: *Barr, McIntosh, McKenzie, J. B. Livingstone, Wilson, Johnstone, Wardrope (Chairman).*

Between 1904–48 only Motherwell in 1931–32 prevented a total domination of championships by Celtic and Rangers.

THE AGE OF EXPANSION

tenderness, as on other occasions, was extended to the Amateurs.

The season of 1910–11 also saw the last creation at senior level of a side based partly at least on ethnic origins when Dundee Hibernian were admitted to the Second Division, although they were not anything like so overtly sectarian as their predecessors Harp had been. The new creation showed a refreshing confidence in their ability to stay the course since they took over the disused Clepington Park just across the street from Dens Park, the home of the senior club, Dundee, and re-named it Tannadice Park.

The geographical composition of the League was tilting eastwards and northwards as the First Division grew. When it reached 16 clubs in 1905, Cowdenbeath had come in to make up the Second Division. In 1911 when 18 clubs could claim First Division status, St. Johnstone were admitted, giving Perth a League side surprisingly late in the day. In 1912 the admission of Dunfermline gave Fife a third club which made economic sense, more than could be said about the decision to replace Port Glasgow Athletic, a failed team from a small Renfrewshire town, with Johnstone, another exact such.

In the summer immediately before the outbreak of World War 1 the great shipbuilding centre of Clydebank and the Fife coal town of Lochgelly each saw the local team achieve League status.

One of the weaknesses of Scottish football had by this time become starkly apparent. Third Lanark had won the League Championship in 1904, but it would be their sole success, and for the next 28 years only Celtic and Rangers would experience triumph. Each of these powerful clubs chalked up multiple wins, Celtic setting a new record with six successive wins after the lone Third Lanark triumph. Rangers then took three League flags in a row before power returned to Parkhead during the First World War with four Celtic championships one after the other. All too often the League title would be decided by New Year's Day and even the clubs from the larger cities, such as Hibernian, Heart of Midlothian, Aberdeen and Dundee could offer no serious challenge.

Whenever the winter weather was unusually severe there would always be pressure on dates and potential friction between the League and the S.F.A. In February 1910 the League International with England was fixed for a Saturday, as was indeed customary. That date, however had already been allocated for Scottish cup-ties which had been postponed and an approach was made to the S.F.A. to consider further postponements of the ties. Before the S.F.A. could adjudicate on this, Hearts had anticipated a negative decision and withdrawn their international forward Bobby Walker

Back Row: W. Chambers *(Assist. Trainer)*, G. McTurk, H. McL. Thomson, A. S. Maley *(Sec. re Manager)*, A. Watson, J. Wylie, G. Robertson, Major R. L. Stevenson *(Director)*. R. Greer, P. Travers, T. McAteer, W. Mossman *(Chairman)*, W. Struth *(Trainer)*.
Front Row: J. Kerr *(Director)*, J. Gilligan, W. McCartney, J. Chalmers, W. Walker *(Captain)*, J. Blair, J. Stirling, T. Booth, T. M. Colquhoun *(Director)*.
[Photo by Agnew & Son, Glasgow]

CLYDE F.C. SEASON 1909–10

The back row is of special interest. On the extreme right is William Struth who would later manage Rangers, fourth from the right is Paddy Travers who managed the Clyde Scottish Cup winning side of 1939 and fourth from left the then manager, Alec Maley, brother of Willie Maley of Celtic.

---

from the Inter-League side so that he could represent his club in the Scottish Cup. Hearts were fined £20 for acting against the interests of the League while Dundee and Hibernian suffered half the penalty for opposing the League's suggestion that the cup-ties should be put off on the day of the Inter-League game.

More constructively, agreement was reached with the Southern League, in which the overwhelming majority of South of England professional clubs played, on the question of mutual recognition of registrations. That was comparatively easy for the Management Committee who were asked at this time to adjudicate on some tricky cases. Was a request by Hamilton Academical for a switch of venue for their home game against St. Mirren justified because the Lanarkshire Junior League were playing the Irish Junior League at Motherwell? Answer, it was not. Port Glasgow Athletic had gone to the wall, owing money to several clubs, Clyde and Airdrieonians in particular. How could these two clubs be recompensed? Answer, the League would compensate them and recoup the money from transfer fees received from the sale of the former Port Glasgow players whose registrations would now revert to the League. Queen's Park complained against Clyde who had made an approach to one of their players, Willie McAndrew, in the course of the season and they asked for some protection for amateur

JIMMY BROWNLIE
One of Scotland's greatest over goalkeepers and a noted servant of Third Lanark. In later life he managed Dundee United.

players. Answer, Queen's Park were given the right to retain their players until April 30 each year.

The League Secretary and Management Committee had to be aware that clubs and for that matter players might constantly be endeavouring to twist the rules to their own advantage. In May 1911 the League had made an award of £30 to Celtic to commemorate their unprecedented feat of winning the League six times in succession. Two months later the club was on the mat when their own player, James Hay, complained that Celtic had retained him without making him an offer. At first sight it looked like faithful employee hardly dealt with by unfeeling employer. The club refuted Hay's version of events and was able to produce a minute book in which their offer was recorded. Not particularly magnanimous in victory, Celtic decided that as a mark of their displeasure they would not at the moment place Hay on the transfer list. Finally John "Sailor" Hunter of Motherwell asked for a free transfer from Clyde to Motherwell as he was now an amateur. As

52 THE FIRST 100 YEARS

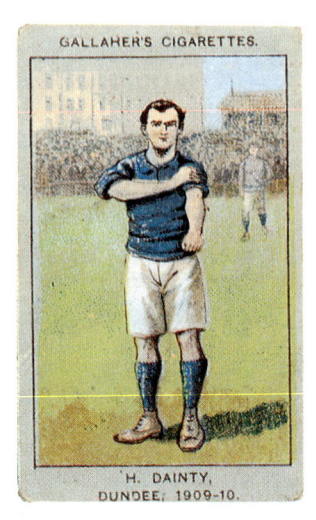

THE AGE OF EXPANSION 53

**COLLAGE OF
SCOTTISH PLAYERS
OF 1910**

he was also now Secretary of Motherwell Football Club his application was given short shrift.

Sometimes it did seem that the League brought some of its troubles on itself. Thus in July 1912 when the fixtures for the season to come had been published, Mr. Danskin of Rangers made the eminently reasonable request that his club might be given at least one home game during the month of October. The allocation of fixtures seemed still a little on the primitive side.

It was an age of slow, strong and skilful football. Many of the players still worked in heavy industries and were not finely-trained as players in the modern sense would understand it. Yet the period produced the surpassing craftmanship of Patsy Gallagher and Jimmy Gordon of Celtic and Rangers respectively, and of Bobby Walker of Hearts. It saw the strength and manly endeavour of Jimmy Quinn of Celtic, and Willie Reid of Rangers at centre-forward, the bravery—and goalkeepers needed to be brave—of Celtic's Charlie Shaw and Rangers' Herbert Lock. Keepers were not only courageous—they had to withstand the intensive charging of opposing forwards—but now more instantly recognisable since the rule of 1910 that compelled them to wear distinctive-coloured jerseys. Till then they had been distinguished only by their flat caps or 'hooker doons" which frequently got dislodged in goalmouth scuffles. In the thinking positions of wing-half and inside-forward Alec Raisbeck of Partick Thistle and Jimmy McMenemy of Celtic demonstrated weekly that speed of thought was more important than speed of foot.

Players being young, untutored men for the most part, their sense of responsibility was not always of the strongest. Around this time Motherwell signed Willie Loney from Dundee Hibernian but it proved an injudicious speculation and Mr. Loney haunted the office of his manager, that very "Sailor" Hunter who had sought a free transfer from Clyde on discovering the joys of being an amateur again. In November 1913 Loney missed training for an entire week and when taxed with this said that he was so upset by the big beating which the side had sustained the previous week that he was very foolish and the worse for liquor over three days. He asked for another chance which he got but failed to avail himself of and he was dimissed the following April for intemperance and breach of training regulations. The case was reported to the S.F.A. and the player placed on the Open to Transfer list.

In January 1912 The Scottish League was notified that players in Scotland had decided to join the Association Football Players Union. This brought a wary response from the League as did the players' request that the top club from the Second Division

THE AGE OF EXPANSION

should automatically be promoted. The Union was recognised while the Management Committee at the same time fired this warning shot:—

> "This Committee strongly disapproves of the system of players forecasting the probable results of games in newspapers and also of betting on results of games by coupons or otherwise and that the same will be considered offences liable to be dealt with."

The League was also asking clubs to make up their minds as to where their commitment lay. At that time the Scottish Consolation Cup was still in being, a competition designed, as its name would suggest, for those clubs knocked out in an early stage of the national trophy. The League looked upon it with disfavour as it required Saturday dates which interfered with their own fixtures and Albion Rovers, Arthurlie, Johnstone, Leith Athletic and Vale of Leven were warned against participation in this competition.

In March 1913 the League, through the medium of the International League Board, took up the cudgels with Mr. F. J. Wall, the Secretary of the Football Association who had written to the Secretary of The Scottish League requesting that the word "international" should not be used for games between The Scottish League and the Football League. The Board wrote to Mr. Wall as follows:—

> "While acknowledging the right and jurisdiction of the Football Association in regard to the match when it is played in England, the Board are unanimously of the opinion that the advertisement of the match in Scotland is a matter solely for Scottish jurisdiction and discretion and regrets that any attempt should be made to interfere with the authority of The Scottish League."

Officialdom, as has been mentioned, was strongly and rightly against the practice of betting on the outcome of individual matches, deeming such a practice to be an unnecessary temptation for the very occasional crooked player. On most grounds programmes were sold through the National Football Programme Company and it was a condition of sale that such programmes contained no advertisements for betting. In addition, players would be forbidden after the end of the 1912–13 season from contributing articles on football over their own signature to newspapers or magazines.

Promptitude in carrying out League fixtures was still the major League concern. Willie Maley of Celtic moved successfully in

April 1913 that "First Division clubs which may be drawn against each other in the Scottish Cup must play off any drawn tie on a week day." This was a step forward and the next stage was a demand to the S.F.A., resisted successfully for the moment, that the full International matches against Wales and Ireland should be played in mid-week. Showing that the League had a heart as well as a head there was agreement that sides should be provided to play benefit matches for Alec Bennett of Rangers and Alec Raisbeck of Partick Thistle. About this time too, the League acquired new offices of its own at 179 West George Street, Glasgow. The increasing power and scope of the League had shortly before brought yet another motion from Willie Maley of Celtic successfully moving "That the party holding the office of Secretary of this League in future devote his whole time to the business of the League and not be allowed to take part in any other business." The time had gone when the League's affairs could be run in the intervals of the life of a busy accountant or solicitor.

So, with a First Division of 20 clubs and a Second of 14, Clydebank and Lochgelly being the new enlistments, the League drifted placidly towards the First World War. It was just short of its silver jubilee and coincidentally its golden jubilee would likewise be shorn of formal celebration because of conditions of war.

Chapter Four

LEAGUE FOOTBALL IN SCOTLAND DURING THE FIRST WORLD WAR

In August 1914 Britain went to war in a frenzy of enthusiasm and ignorance. Very few thought the war would last as long as a year and the obsession with "doing one's bit" meant that for almost four years the armed services were manned without recourse to conscription. Whether a man joined up or not depended on his own response to the situation or very often upon how much moral pressure was exerted upon him. The result was that even in the small world of football, response to the colours was uneven. Some clubs, notably Queen's Park and Hearts, saw their first teams enlist almost *en bloc*, others, especially Celtic and Rangers, were much more cautious in their response to the trumpets of war.

The Government was prepared to allow association football to continue on a modified scale, but eventually provided that no one should make his entire living from playing the game. They also saw the football grounds as excellent theatres of recruitment. Regular soldiers visited them on match days and made strenuous and successful efforts to persuade spectators to "take the shilling." The first official pronouncement came on September 3 1914 from League President Mr. Thomas Hart of St. Mirren. He referred to the war cloud hanging over the nation at present and enjoined every club to do its utmost for the recruiting of members for the army which was presently being raised by Lord Kitchener. The League also put its hand where its pocket was and subscribed £300 to the National Relief Fund inaugurated by H.R.H. the Prince of Wales.

The outbreak of war had occurred within ten days of the start of the new season and the easiest thing to do appeared to be to continue as normal. This caused some adverse public comment about players chasing a ball while their brothers and cousins died in France, but more immediately damaging were the gaps on the terracings which the absence of those same brothers and cousins

ST. MIRREN. — W. O'HAGAN, O.H.M.S.
THIRD LANARK. — J. BROWNLIE, O.H.M.S.
QUEEN'S PARK. — E. S. GARVIE, DIED OF WOUNDS.

WORLD WAR INJURIES

Cigarette cards continued to be issued during the First World War, even of players killed in action.

caused. Attendances dwindled, compounded by the fact that increasingly other men were working Saturday shifts in munitions factories. By the first Christmas of the war a meeting was held to discuss the general financial position and it was unanimously agreed, with a view to enabling all clubs to complete their fixtures, to recommend all Second Division clubs to reduce their players' wages by not less than fifty per cent. This had the effect of flushing out not a few players into heavy industry. As a cost-cutting measure it was further decided that the services of neutral linesmen would be dispensed with for the duration of the war. Less logically, given the decision to continue League football, it was felt that the running of the Scottish Cup competition would be inappropriate and although one or two suggestions were made for the running of a substitute tournament they came to nothing.

The maximum wage for First Division players was reduced to £4.10.0d per week and close-season wages became a thing of the past. Players would not now be paid between May 1 and the resumption of training in late July. Even this reduction proved wildly unrealistic and when it was decided to carry on the First Division the following season it was claimed to be impossible to pay more than £1 per match. In the unlikely event of a club making a profit however, it could retrospectively make additional payments to its players provided such payments did not amount to more than an additional £1 per week with effect from July 26 of the previous season.

The decision to carry on in some shape or form had been taken after a meeting of the four Leagues (Football, Scottish, Irish and Southern) at Blackpool in July 1915 after which the following statement was issued:

> "This Conference, having carefully considered all the arguments in favour of and against the continuance of the game, are satisfied that the best interests of the nation and those engaged in the war and preparing munitions of war, as well as the considerable number of people who are by various reasons unavailable for the purpose of the war will be best served by the continuance of the game.
>
> Having regard to the varying conditions experienced by the Leagues here represented, the Conference is of opinion that each League should be left to carry out such programme as may be thought most advisable in such way as shall best recommend itself to the League concerned.
>
> We suggest that each League consider the advisability of approaching the national governing association to discontinue the registration of professional players during the coming season and that for such period all players should be made amateurs as in the case of professionals who have joined the army and navy and in such cases automatically become amateurs."

This was a bold idea but might have failed signally to attract too many players willing to play for no financial reward. At all events, it came too late for the Scottish Second Division clubs. They had been losing money hand over fist and could not possibly contemplate another such season. The First Division had already indicated that it would function in 1915–16. The lower Division now asked for the creation of two Scottish sectional leagues, East and West, thus anticipating interestingly enough the Southern and North-Eastern Leagues set-up of 1941. The First Division clubs refused to accede to this suggestion and the Second Division ceased to exist for the duration of the war. Indeed, as we shall see, it ceased to exist for some little time after the signing of the Armistice and in that cessation lay much trouble.

The second season of wartime football, with Scotland, unlike England, keeping its official League going, brought enormous problems. Although conscription was still well over the hill, Partick Thistle's old stalwart, Alec Raisbeck, now managing Hamilton Academical, was driven to ask permission to play for his new club in an emergency. The permission was forthcoming. In November 1915 Rangers were asked to explain why they fielded only nine players in a match against Falkirk. They explained that illness, injury, Government work and fog had deprived them of eight of the 17 players they had available, and there were other clubs with far more players in the Forces.

As the third season of the war started in 1916, in the wake of the bloody battle of the Somme, there was no lack of hostile outside sources scrutinising football clubs for infringements of Government regulations or even rules of decent conduct. Until conscription came in the last year of the war neither Rangers nor Celtic had any great record of player representation in the forces, despite the fact that a Celtic reserve won the Victoria Cross and a royal investiture was held at Ibrox by King George V in the course of which hundreds of Servicemen were decorated.

This did not go unremarked. In August 1916 the *Daily Record* reported that a First Division club had sent its players to Seamill Hydropathic for special training, a practice frowned on if not prohibited under wartime conditions of football. The club involved, Celtic, emphatically denied the charge. Five of their players had indeed been at Seamill, they conceded, but with a view to having their recovery from specific injuries expedited. This had also facilitated the players' returns to their everyday occupations and receipts were produced to refute the charge that the players had been there for special training.

There was some evidence that even at the height of the war not all players took their civilian occupation too seriously. The prodigiously gifted inside-forward Patsy Gallacher of Celtic was convicted by a Munitions Tribunal of bad time-keeping and attendance at the engineering factory in Dalmuir where he was employed during the week. As it was a condition of being allowed to play football that all players should have another major occupation, Gallacher was suspended for five weeks and Celtic fined £25 for playing him after his conviction came to their knowledge.

Celtic, with much the same side as immediately pre-war, won the first four wartime League championships, championships which unlike those of the second global conflict were official. When conscription came in 1918 eight of their side were called up and they lost the championship that year to Rangers who could still call on the majority of familiar faces.

Other clubs were less fortunate, or less far-sighted. In April 1916 Heart of Midlothian scratched from a League fixture because they could not raise a side worthy of the club. Somehow clubs managed to fulfil their League commitments and to spare players for matches for wartime charities. Thus a series of games in September 1916 raised over £1100 for War Funds and the money was allocated

THE SCOTTISH FOOTBALL LEAGUE.

Army and Navy Fund.

Application by Dependant of Sailor or Soldier.

1. Name of Soldier.......... Peter Johnstone
2. Regiment and number...... 14th A & S Highrs. No 285250
3. Date of joining.......... 25 May 1916
4. Club connected with...... Celtic Football Club
5. Married or single........ Married
6. Occupation............... Collier
7. Earnings before joining.. £5 per week
8. When killed.............. 12/16 May 1917
9. Name of Applicant........ Isa Johnstone, Widow.
10. Relationship to Sailor or Soldier............ Widow
11. If not Widow, how much did Soldier contribute to household before joining..............
12. Particulars of any other income...... £2 per week from Newspaper shop
13. Amount of pension................... 50/-
14. Particulars of any other Dependants:-

Names.	Ages.	Earnings.
Nelly	8	
Peter	4	

Isa Johnstone
20 Rose St
Kirkcaldy

PENSION FUND FORM

For many years after the First World War the Scottish Football League administered the Army, Navy Fund for dependents of professional footballers who had been killed or wounded. This is a typical Application Form.

to the Lord Provosts of Edinburgh and Glasgow and the Provosts of Motherwell and Greenock for the relief of families of men serving with the Forces.

Playing manpower became an increasing problem, though microscopic compared with the military shortage. It was seriously proposed in December 1916—and the fact that the proposal went down by only one vote indicates the volume of support for it—that the duration of League matches should be cut by ten minutes in December and January because of the difficulties experienced by players in getting to grounds from their work. It became clear too that there would have to be some modification in the composition of the 20 club League. In January 1917 Ayr United complained that because of the poor wartime train service they could not get to Aberdeen and back on the same day. This was the beginning of a campaign to have the northern club dropped from the League.

Rules became increasingly elastic where registration was concerned. Players could now turn out for a club other than their own without being formally transferred providing that the club playing the player had the consent in writing of the club with whom the player was registered. There were even blatant infringements of accepted rules. On January 20 1917 in a match against Rangers, Partick Thistle had been allowed to introduce a substitute player in a League match. The Partick Thistle manager, Mr. Easton explained that the player had been hurt after only three minutes and with a view to maintaining interest in the game he had sent out a replacement player, Rangers having generously agreed to this. War or no war, the Management Committee looked unkindly on this arrangement and warned sternly against any repetition of it.

By April 1917 the fabric of the League was under considerable strain. Clubs who had dropped out of wartime football were expected to continue to pay their subscriptions but no fewer than eight of them, Abercorn, Arthurlie, Clydebank, Dundee Hibernian, East Stirlingshire, Johnstone, Leith Athletic and Vale of Leven were seriously in arrears. They were given until April 30 to pay their dues. In order to complete the fixture lists clubs were having to play twice on the same day. Celtic recorded dual victories against Raith Rovers and Motherwell while Clyde played twice on April 4 against Motherwell and Third Lanark.

It was clear that matters could not continue as before and in June 1917 Aberdeen, Dundee and Raith Rovers were asked to retire from the League in the coming season because of travel difficulties. Their oncost charges would be met and to achieve this there would be a deduction of 5% from the gate drawings of those clubs continuing in active membership. The three retiring clubs would retain full rights as First Division members including the right to be represented at meetings of the League. To avoid the odd number that the withdrawal of the three clubs would leave, one new side would have to be admitted. Albion Rovers, Stevenston United and, a name from the past, Vale of Leven all made application for the vacant spot but the choice fell upon Clydebank. The last-named side had enjoyed one season of Second Division membership in 1914–15 and their inclusion in the First Division now was probably due to the war-time boom in the town among shipyard and munition workers.

Still the strict application of peace-time rules was relaxed. Clubs could now play four untransferred players in away games and two in home matches provided the permission of the club holding the player's registration was obtained in writing beforehand. The Scottish League wagged a prudent finger in the direction of the three dormant clubs, reminding them that they must set any sum obtained for the use of their players or any other non-football revenue against their oncosts.

The game, truncated and enfeebled as it was, could still generate primitive passions. Referee G. H. MacKenzie reported ordering H. Higginbotham of St. Mirren from the field against Hearts for jumping over the fence of the enclosure and chasing a spectator along the front of the stands. The League took the sensible pragmatic view on another occasion involving Hearts when owing to the late arrival of their train in Glasgow, only 40 minutes each way could be played against Clydebank. It was decided that the result of the abridged match should stand.

It was however, determined to carry out to the letter the provisions regarding players working. A second player, Neil Harris of Partick Thistle, was accused of bad industrial time-keeping. His club were aware of the situation and suspended him pending investigation of the circumstances. Harris was able to satisfy the football authorities that his absence had been caused by the illness of his wife and child and that he had furnished Ministry of Munitions officials with the appropriate certificates. The meeting of January 1918 which deliberated on this case also noted with pleasure the conferral of the honour of C.B.E. on Provost David Martyn of Airdrieonians, a future Scottish League President.

In the final season of the war, 1918–1919 conscription was biting savagely. Yet another player, Felix Gunn of Dumbarton, was arrested for failing to return the certificate exempting him from military service because he was a miner when he had been unemployed as such for a number of months. In their defence Dumbarton said that they had no knowledge of this and were surprised as "Gunn's appearance was always clean and tidy", a somewhat disingenuous explanation as at least sometimes Gunn would have had to come to the park straight from work.

The emergency provisions regarding unregistered players were being cheerfully abused on all sides and in an attempt to regularise the situation it was decreed that no club could play the same player under emergency provision more than twice in any one month and thereafter a clear month had to elapse before the said player was eligible to play again.

The League had found itself in something of a dilemma in the summer of 1918. It was beginning to look as if the war might finish quite soon, but not before the season was due to start in August. War conditions still prevailed, players were short and transport difficult. This lay behind the proposal, which was approved in July 1918, that Ayr United and Falkirk should be dropped from the League for the coming season. This brought about furious protests from the two clubs concerned. A mass meeting in Ayr attracted 800 as an audience and, in a calculated side-swipe at the Old Firm, it was maintained that it was ridiculous to drop Ayr United from the League, a club whose contribution to the Forces in manpower was exceeded only by that of Hearts and Queen's Park. Very properly, the League thought again and allowed the two clubs to continue in active membership. Certainly if the decision was taken for reasons of transport difficulties there were no grounds in logic for allowing Glasgow clubs to pass a shuttered Brockville Park, Falkirk, while en route by train to play matches in Edinburgh, 20 miles further to the east.

The signing of the Armistice meant that the rest of the season was played out in a peculiar half-world. Peace in France did not necessarily mean goodwill at home as Referee James S. Sinclair who had been in charge of a match at Airdrie could testify:

Kelso Buildings
Thornliebank
November 3 1918

Dear Sir,

I must take exception and report Manager Chapman of Airdrieonians for using language to me (before the Balcony Seat holders) when I was entering my dressing room. He seemed to feel against a decision which was not awarded (sic). He made the remark "Ah, you twister! Was it going to burst your coupon if Airdrie won?" Immediately the spectators from the Balcony heard his remarks they too had language to use which I am sure could and should have been left unsaid. I may add that instead of some of the Officials being there as a protection against such conduct, I am sorry to say they started a scene which I trust I will not figure in again.

Yours truly,
Jas. S. Sinclair

Under examination the Airdrie manager, Mr. Chapman, admitted using these words but claimed that he had done so in a jocular manner. The Management Committee, unconvinced, jocularly fined him four guineas.

In December the Scottish League announced that to mark the Allied victory, home and away matches would be played with the Football League for the first time since 1915. It was too late to institute a Scottish Cup competition and in any case the S.F.A. were constrained by the fact that so many of their member clubs had been absent from competitive football during the war. As a substitute it was decided that the 18 League clubs and 8 Western League clubs—the Western League was an organisation which had given refuge to some pre-war Second Division clubs—should take part in a Victory Cup. If a Western League club were drawn at home in one of the ties it was empowered to surrender ground advantage for a payment of £50 if it so wished.

The war was over, the first Servicemen were returning and the players were no longer prepared to operate under wartime conditions. They wrote to the Scottish League Secretary.

William McAndrew Esq.
Secretary   Glasgow
Scottish Football League   December 14 1918

Dear Sir,

A meeting, at which all the First League clubs were represented by their respective captains or their deputies was held in Glasgow on Saturday December 14 1918 to consider the players' position regarding the wage question.

After having fully discussed this question from various points of view it was agreed that the time had now come for the restrictions on wages, which have been in force for the last four years of war, to be raised and that the Scottish League Committee be asked to sanction the return to pre-war conditions of wages.

Further, the representatives would ask the First League clubs to grant free transfers to all players who have been on the books of their club for two years, provided the clubs do not offer these players, on or before the 30th April, remuneration at the rate of £156 per annum. The ban on mid-week games has been raised and the arrangement of Cup-ties and International matches permitted, and now the players ask your Committee to give their case for wages their full and prompt consideration.

The meeting decided to recommend January 1 1919 as the starting point for the new conditions. Any bonus money or extra money due to the players before that date would, of course, be paid to them in full.

When it is considered how loyally the players have stood by their clubs during the last four years in order to keep the game prominently before the public, and how well they have succeeded in doing so despite adverse conditions and low wages, it is felt that their demands cannot be termed extortionate.

Signed (among others) by Charles Shaw, Celtic; James Bowie, Rangers; Jackie Wright, Morton; William Bulloch, Partick Thistle.

The League answered promptly with a four point reply:—
1. They felt that January 1 1919 was too soon to revert to pre-war conditions.
2. The present wage of £1 per week should continue, but clubs in profit could apply such to pay an extra pound up to 31 December 1918 and £3 per week thereafter.
3. Such deferred pay should not be given until the season's end.
4. There could be no action on the question of transfers until after a conference with the Football League.

The Scottish League did however agree to meet the players but there was little joy for the latter from the meeting.

It was therefore with a sullen and discontented labour force that League football moved into 1919, with the knowledge that the following season would be the first post-war one but with considerable uncertainty as to what form Scottish football should take. There had been in some quarters the unspoken hope that the stresses of war would deal the final blow to some of the smaller clubs who were basically unwanted as members of The Scottish Football League. This had not happened, and of the clubs who had made reputations in Scottish football only Abercorn were beyond thinking of a resumption of League status. The others had managed to keep going quite happily in the Eastern and Western Leagues.

There was still a period of a few months in which to work out what form the League should take in 1919–20. In the meantime there was a difference of opinion with the Football League over the

IBROX PARK

A view of a match taken about 1920. Note the almost total absence of vehicular traffic and the curious double-barrelled roof on the enclousure.

venue for the Inter-League Victory match in England. The Football League had nominated Birmingham as its location and the Scottish League, unhappy with this suggestion, countered with Liverpool, Manchester or Sheffield and, when these found no favour with the hosts, Newcastle. The Football League was immoveable and maintained that the venue was the sole concern of the home league. The match was duly played in Birmingham, the Scots going down 3–1 but it contained one curiosity. There was a substitution in the Scots side, P. Nellies of Hearts going off before half-time and being replaced by J. Richardson of Ayr United, again presumably with the concurrence of the opposing side. Matters became satisfactorily even-handed when The Scottish Football League won the return match at Ibrox Park 3–2.

By the summer 1919 the decision had been taken not to operate a Second Division of the Scottish League although the First Division was expanded to 22 clubs. Aberdeen, Dundee and Raith Rovers, who for geographical reasons had been dropped for the last two seasons of wartime football, came back and the fourth club added was Albion Rovers from Coatbridge who were moving into a new ground at Cliftonhill.

The news that there would only be one Division operating led to what was potentially a most damaging situation in Scottish football.

Some of the spurned clubs sought refuge in the Central League, a body whose main strength lay in the counties of Stirling, Fife, and

West Lothian. At first sight it did not look particularly enticing, the clubs in membership being Bo'ness, Dunfermline Athletic, East Fife, Hearts "A", Alloa, Armadale, St. Bernard, Bathgate, Broxburn United, Stenhousemuir, Falkirk "A", East Stirlingshire, King's Park and Clackmannan, but this initial impression was misleading. For a short time after the end of World War 1 the coalmines of Fife and the shale oil industry of West Lothian did comparatively well and workers had money to spare for football matches. In particular Dunfermline Athletic were a sound and financially strong club as were, in the very short term, East Fife and Bo'ness while the reserve sides of Falkirk and Hearts attracted reasonable crowds.

In addition, the Central League possessed the considerable advantage of not being affiliated to the Inter-League Board and therefore was under no obligation to recognise that body's registration system. The Central League therefore proceeded to recruit where it willed and several very prominent players were soon found in its ranks, including such Scottish international stars as Andy Wilson of Chelsea, Jimmy Gordon, formerly of Rangers and the former Hearts international centre-half Bob Mercer. In theory no Scottish League club could be certain that it would not lose a top player to a Central League side without any financial recompense or indeed warning.

The Scottish League was divided on what should be done. The hardliners on the Management Committee argued that this was a temporary blip and that the Central League would not long be able to afford the inflated wages that the players just named were receiving. When two years passed and there was no sign of the Central League collapsing the waverers began to become more influential. They argued that if The Scottish Football League were to survive, it must revert to a two Division system and the Central League clubs must be admitted.

It was clear that the latter would only agree to this if part of the arrangement was the introduction of automatic promotion and relegation, since clearly there would be little incentive for Dunfermline Athletic to leave the flourishing Central League for a spot in a Second Division from which only influence, rather than ability, could rescue them. As a *quid pro quo*, the star players who had been successfully wooed by the Central League would have to return to their own clubs.

The expected ferocious debate on these proposals which had been expected at Scottish League Management Committee level did not eventuate. In a splendid article on the subject, W. G. Gallagher, who was better known as "Waverley" of the *Daily*

Record maintained that the hardliners of the Scottish League suddenly saw the enormous possibilities of this suggestion. This is how he described it.

> "The places left vacant by the departed stars (of the Central League) were, perforce, filled with mediocrities, and the fans refused to hand over their cash to look at small-timers where once they enjoyed the skill and artistry of the top-of-the-bill fraternity. Gates crashed and within a couple of years or so insolvency stalked the townships where there had once been football prosperity. Clackmannan, Lochgelly United, Armadale, Broxburn United, Bathgate, fell by the wayside to be followed by others who either put up the shutters or sought sanctuary in a lower grade of football. The same was happening to those brave hearts of the Western League, most of whom had their being in the mining towns of Ayrshire. On their death-bed they cursed the day on which they had fallen for the wiles of the Scottish League intelligentsia. These gentlemen knew what they were doing. They well realised that the country clubs could not stand the pace of automatic promotion and relegation and that the cold hand of extinction would close on them."

There is one word in the above passage, "township", which is the nub of the matter. Places with populations little in excess of 3000, e.g. Clackmannan and Broxburn, were now indulging in the totally unrealistic pipedream of being able to sustain a League club. England, with a population of some 45 million people was content with 88 League clubs. Scotland with fewer than five million inhabitants would attempt the experiment in season 1921–22 of running 42 clubs, or in other words almost half the number that England could sustain with nine times the Scots population. The Central League clubs had applied to join *en bloc* but this was seen as something too much savouring of capitulation by The Scottish Football League. They were therefore accepted on an individual basis. Of the pre-war Second Division clubs only Abercorn, Arthurlie and Leith Athletic were missing, although the last two had still a vigorous-enough existence. On the opening day of the 1921–22 season eleven clubs could boast Scottish League membership for the first time, Alloa Athletic, Arbroath, Armadale, Bathgate, Bo'ness, Broxburn, Clackmannan, East Fife, Forfar Athletic, King's Park, and Stenhousemuir.

A First Division of 22 clubs was over-large and it was ordained that in that first season of automatic promotion and relegation three clubs would go down and only one come up from the Second

Division. Alloa came up at their very first attempt and were passed on the way down by Dumbarton, Queen's Park and Clydebank. It was a harder world now and there could no longer be any question of special treatment or exemptions for the amateurs of Hampden.

The introduction of automatic promotion and relegation to Scottish football created an intractable problem. If Manchester City lost First Division status in England they could expect gates to decline from 30,000 to 20,000 in their home fixtures. In Scotland relegation for a club such as Dundee meant the difference between 15,000 at Tynecastle and, with luck, 1500 at Stenhousemuir. The penalties for failure in Scotland were and would remain for very many years savage in the extreme. Yet, equally, there had to be the guarantee of promotion for an ambitious club and at the end of the day in a competitive sport, playing ability had to be taken very seriously and indeed accorded priority. Automatic promotion and relegation might be and on occasion was highly inconvenient, but there was a manifest injustice in exempting any side from its provisions, even when that side had as distinguished a past history as Queen's Park. The new system might be draconian but would be accepted if all were vulnerable.

Chapter Five

1920–39 THE YEARS BETWEEN

A case can be made that the opening of 1922 saw the real return to a pre-war structure. The next 18 years would see the renewed revelation of the paradox at the heart of Scottish football, an abundant supply of skilled individual players but an almost total lack of real and sustained competition. Between the wars the League championship was to all intents and purposes a Rangers monopoly, the Ibrox club being triumphant on all but five occasions. Motherwell had one successful challenge and a few brave tries, Airdrie in the middle Twenties might well have succeeded but for the financial stringency which compelled them to transfer their leading forwards of the day such as the great centre-forward Hughie Gallacher to Newcastle United and, even more damagingly, the powerful inside forward Bob McPhail to their arch-competitor, Rangers. Elsewhere Hearts would in the 1930s have a side full of attractive players such as Alec Massie, Dave McCulloch, Andy Black and Tommy Walker, Aberdeen had genuine stars in Willie Mills, Matt Armstrong and Billy Strauss, but none of it added up to a realistic bid for the championship.

Football was now more accessible than it had been pre-war with the development of both rail and road transport, especially the latter. Few if any supporters travelled by horse waggonette after the First World War in the way that the old Brake Clubs had done before 1914 but the old title stuck, now almost always used in a pejorative way. In September 1920 Kilmarnock had submitted a letter to the Management Committee directing its attention "to the menace which the brake club fraternity are to the game" and requesting the Committee to take some action conjointly with the S.F.A. to protect clubs from the undisciplined multitudes. Kilmarnock added that as a precautionary measure they themselves intended to prohibit anyone from entering their ground in future if carrying either a ricketty or a flagstaff.

Few if any of the publications totally devoted to games and pastimes such as *Scottish Sport*, had survived the Kaiser's War but

DUNDEE.
A. TROUP.

ST. MIRREN.
D. C. WALKER.

AYR UNITED.
J. J. QUINN.

ALBION ROVERS.
W. REID.

ALLOA ATHLETIC.
R. ORROCK.

1920–39 THE YEARS BETWEEN 73

F. & J. SMITH'S CIGARETTES

CELTIC.
A. MCNAIR.

F. & J. SMITH'S CIGARETTES

DUMBARTON.
D. COLMAN.

COLLAGE OF SCOTTISH PLAYERS OF 1920

F. & J. SMITH'S CIGARETTES

CLYDE.
T. SHINGLETON.

F. & J. SMITH'S CIGARETTES

ABERDEEN.
J. MILLER.

F. & J. SMITH'S CIGARETTES

AIRDRIEONIANS.
J. REID.

there was still tremendous interest shown by the press in the reporting of football. Coverage was comprehensive and not always, the newspapers felt, did the game take account of their own pressures and difficulties. In the autumn of 1920 the Scottish Daily Newspaper Society asked that the time of kick-off should be moved back to 3 p.m. from the customary 3.30 p.m. to assist them in meeting their deadlines, particularly important in the case of the evening papers. It took some time for this to happen but by 1939 the earlier kick-off was almost universal.

At the same time the League took the decision that henceforth it would itself be the direct paymaster of all those players selected to play for it in representative matches. Hitherto badges had been given to the players and the match fees sent to their clubs but now all players and reserves would be given £5. There was just a hint in the new procedure that not all the money previously earmarked for players had necessarily reached them.

The proliferation of benefit matches was becoming a serious problem. The League was often asked to supply a side to take part in such games and the public purse was not bottomless, especially once the post-war boom petered out. There was a serious danger of such matches being overdone so that Celtic's application for a side to be provided to play them in a match for the benefit of Alec McNair in January 1921 received an understandably grudging approval.

> "The Committee, while deprecating applications of this nature, in view of the long and honoured service of A. McNair to the game resolved to grant the request."

There was an aptness in the month, January, arranged for this testimonial as McNair, because of his enormously cool and resourceful play was universally known as "The Icicle."

Brake clubs were causing trouble in Ayrshire again and in the same month three such organisations from Glasgow (though now travelling in charabancs—as the early motor coaches were known—were blamed for a severe outbreak of stone-throwing at a match between Ayr United and Rangers at Somerset Park.

Not all the violence was exhibited by the fans. There was a complaint about the practice of referees, who, after granting a foul against a player, were apparently in the habit of getting hold of them and shaking them. This was not to be tolerated in any situation.

> "The Committee, while recognising the right of a referee to check any player, feel strongly that the referee has no right to lay hands on any player and that such conduct on the part of a referee detracts from the dignity of the position."

In an equally odd case of the time a linesman, J. Johnstone of Bonnybridge, was accused of using obscene language to referee G. H. McKenzie after a game between Hibernian and Hearts, neutral linesmen being once more in vogue. The linesman challenged the unfortunate referee to fight, stating that he did not want the games anyway. As Mr. Johnstone had frequently cancelled appointments to run the line the Committee took what might be considered the long overdue step of resolving to remove his name from the referees' list and not to investigate the Edinburgh Derby charges.

A much-needed clarification of Inter-League eligibility was arrived at after the great Bobby Ferrier of Motherwell was first selected to play against the Irish League in November 1921 and then dropped for Alec Troup of Dundee because he had been born in England. There was no reason whatsoever for this, Scots had played for the Football League in the earliest days of the fixture and the very next Scottish League meeting adopted the motion "That any Scottish League Club player of proved Scottish parentage, whether born in Scotland or elsewhere, is entitled to play in Inter-League games for The Scottish Football League."

The Scottish League could be generous where generosity was required. As in any contact sport there was always the risk of serious injury or resultant illness and following the death in 1921 of the Dumbarton goalkeeper Joshua Wilkinson after a match against Rangers, it was resolved to pay the maximum amount of compensation allowable, £300, to the representatives of the deceased without admitting any liability. The cause of death appears to have been illness rather than directly-sustained injury.

The League did not take such a charitable view of the fact that the S.F.A. still clung to Saturday dates for the matches against Ireland and Wales. It was not going to make matters easier for this state of affairs to continue. Thus when the 1922 match against Wales at Wrexham fell due, Rangers and Third Lanark were refused permission to put off their respective League matches although Rangers had three players in the Scotland side and Third Lanark two. Wales were in even worse plight because shortly afterwards the English clubs pointblank refused to release players to Ireland and Wales for Saturday games and the Welsh side was perforce recruited from the four Welsh clubs (Cardiff City, Swansea Town, Wrexham and Newport County) and such non-league players as could be assembled. Representatives to the International League Board were asked to use their influence with the Football Association (who needed no convincing) and the Scottish Football Association to have the minor internationals played on weekdays.

Two related problems were facing The Scottish Football League at this time. Munitions factories had long since closed and the short-lived consumer boom was over. Too many clubs were chasing too few spectators, it was as simple as that. Two fell out at the end of season 1922–23 and were not replaced, reducing the Second Division to 20 clubs. Clackmannan, and more surprisingly, Dundee Hibs were the sides which called enough though both would return, in the case of Dundee Hibs under a different name. The Irish connection had always been seen as something of a handicap to them and the club disbanded to reform on the same ground under the title of Dundee City. This brought speedy complaints from their city rivals Dundee that the new title of the Tannadice side was potentially confusing and that if anyone had title to the name Dundee City, it was themselves as the senior club. A compromise was thrashed out whereby Dundee stayed as they were and the short-lived Dundee City settled for the title of Dundee United.

None of this solved the problem of unemployment. Football did what it could by deciding in 1922 that ground clubs could be left to decide whether the unemployed should be admitted to the ground at half-price on production of proof of unemployment and that the visiting club need not be consulted. Half price was quite enough to have paid to watch newly-elected Broxburn United who were severely censured for fielding only two first-term players in a match against St. Bernard. It was clear that there were clubs in membership of The Scottish Football League who had neither the resources nor the necessary seriousness of approach to make such membership credible. Nor were Clydebank, first of that name, much better. They committed the cardinal sin of player impersonation in that their Swan was a Stafford, rather than their geese swans. James Stafford was a registered and transferred Clydebank player, John Swan who assumed his identity was neither. Clydebank were fined £125, a great deal of money for the time, and had two points deducted. It was also agreed that where clubs had equal pointage in the championship, goal average, that is the number of goals scored divided by the number conceded, would henceforth be the determining factor.

Having got rid of two clubs through natural wastage, The Scottish Football League made the truly incredible decision to constitute a Third Division for season 1923–24. Before this happened Arbroath and Dundee Hibs (their change of name occurred a few months later) had been elected to the Second Division, being voted in ahead of East Stirling who lost League status, Arthurlie, Leith Athletic, Queen of the South Wanderers and Clackmannan, whose optimism almost became effrontery.

1920–39 THE YEARS BETWEEN

The Scottish League itself appears to have had considerable misgivings as to the permanence of the newly-created Third Division. Clubs would enter it as Associate Members, they would have no right to vote, they were obliged to play in the Qualifying Cup and if they were drawn in the Scottish Cup against any club in full membership then replays had perforce to be in mid-week. The guarantee was fixed at £15, although where drawings exceeded £40 half-gate would apply. The two top clubs would be promoted but, illustrating the grain of pessimism which ran through the whole undertaking, this was dependent on at least 16 clubs completing the Third Division programme. If only 14 or fewer completed their fixtures then one sole club would be promoted.

The following clubs were invited to membership and their town of origin is given in brackets where the name of the side does not by itself make this clear:— Arthurlie (Barrhead), Beith, Brechin City, Clackmannan, Dumbarton Harp, Dykehead (Shotts), East Stirlingshire (Falkirk), Galston, Helensburgh, Hurlford, Leith Athletic, Mid-Annandale (Lockerbie), Montrose, Nithsdale Wanderers (Sanquhar), Peebles Rovers, Queen of the South Wanderers (Dumfries), Royal Albert (Larkhall) and Solway Star (Annan). Another applicant, Arbroath United, had been rejected out of hand as it was felt that the Angus town was quite unable to support two sides, given that it had a population of just under 20,000.

The new and lowest Division hereupon made another blunder in fixing the price of admission at one shilling with a sixpenny tariff for boys. This price range was much too high for the grade of football on offer and the only beneficiaries were the junior clubs who profited greatly from this over-optimistic scale of charges.

Meantime Dundee Hibs had formally become known as Dundee United and had appointed as manager the great Third Lanark and Scotland goalkeeper Jimmy Brownlie. He received less than the respect he merited in an away game at Armadale and United complained that one of the Armadale directors had so far forgotten himself as to call Mr. Brownlie an "International pig." The game was noted for its robustness of phrases at this time, and indeed robustness of attitude towards referees. The Scottish Referees Association asked the Management Committee to try to persuade the authorities to take more drastic steps in dealing with persons found guilty of assaults on referees. The League Secretary was instructed to inform them that "in their opinion it would be most injudicious to attempt to influence the judgement of the Civil Authorities" a bureaucrat's answer if ever there was one. The League Secretary, Willie McAndrew had just been elected again to the joint office of Secretary/Treasurer at a salary of £500 per annum, tax free.

Players' wages were also making news, in particular the vexed question of what should be a reasonable retaining wage. The sum for this was fixed at £208 per annum for First Division players and £104 per annum for Second Division players but it was a mark of the poverty of many Scottish clubs that this Second Division rate was found incapable of being sustained and the fixed rate was restricted to First Division members only.

At the end of the first season's operation of the Third Division Arthurlie and East Stirlingshire had gained promotion while Helensburgh and Brechin City were last. Leith Athletic were admitted to membership of the Third Division in place of Brechin City. Theirs was to be a story of reasonable success and briefly they would be First Division members again. In the meantime the infant Division was in desperate trouble, largely because admission prices were unrealistic and clubs therefore tried to avoid them. Vale of Leven (who had taken Hurlford's place on the list of initial invitees) and Galston were both censured for operating an adults' sixpenny gate. Other small clubs were less honest and achieved the same result by having an extremely elastic conception of the term "boy."

A player's normal progression in Scottish football was through the ranks of the amateurs and juveniles to the Juniors and thence to Senior football. The Juniors were a peculiarly Scottish creation, their name being quite misleading as they numbered some fairly elderly practitioners among their players. They were semi-professional and some of the more powerful Glasgow combines such as Strathclyde and Ashfield attracted considerably larger crowds than most team in the Second Division of the Scottish League, let alone the Third. The Juniors greatly resented the system, or lack of it, by which their players could be taken away from them by Senior clubs without remotely adequate compensation and taken away moreover when the Junior club might have very important cup-ties to play. Matters came to a head in October 1924 when Second Division Bathgate sought the assistance of the League in defending an action which was about to be raised against them by the junior Larkhall Thistle. Cautious and politic as ever, the League would give no such guarantee until it had held a joint meeting with the S.F.A. so that the viewpoint of the senior organisation could be established.

The first cracks in the Third Division edifice were now appearing. Small crowds and long journeys—there were three Angus clubs and five from the extreme South of Scotland—made it impossible to pay even the derisory wages of 7/6d per week which had in some cases been agreed upon. In February 1925 Dumbarton Harp intimated that they were unable to carry on, giving ammunition to those who had maintained that if Arbroath could not support two sides it was unlikely that Dumbarton would manage it. Two months later Galston were flying flags of distress. As the end of the season was only weeks away they were urged to complete their fixtures if at all possible, which they just managed. Indeed they came out for the following season but were finally gone by January 1926. The last sides to be promoted from the Third Division were Queen of the South and Nithsdale Wanderers and as Solway Star had only been pipped on goal average, it had been a good year for the South of Scotland. Johnstone and Forfar Athletic went down, with the Renfrewshire club almost immediately in severe financial trouble.

They had exalted company. Because the First Division was essentially non-competitive, Rangers had quite often won the championship by late January with severely adverse effects on attendances, including their own. Gates of only 12,000 for run of the mill matches at Ibrox and Parkhead were by no means uncommon. Great crowds would come out to watch cup-ties but by their very nature they provided an uncertain form of income and Rangers were going through a spell when a quarter of a century would separate their Scottish Cup win of 1903 from that of 1928. Even the most prestigious clubs therefore had to watch the income flow and it should occasion no surprise that Celtic were censured in October 1925 for admitting the unemployed through the boys' gate. In his defence Willie Maley of Celtic claimed that the practice was common among all Glasgow clubs. Common or not, Celtic were peremptorily invited to discontinue it.

The League's concern with the dangers of fixed odds betting appeared abundantly justified when goalkeeper Joe Shortt of Stenhousemuir reported that he had been approached by the emissary of a Glasgow bookmaker in Larbert Station and offered the considerable sum of £50 to "let his side down" in a match with Broxburn United. Shortt immediately reported the offer and no harm was done but another player might well have been tempted.

By now the Third Division was beyond saving. In a desperate attempt to prop it up Queen's Park offered to enter their third team, (the Victoria Eleven) in the Third Division but this move foundered when the Management Committee ruled that a club could not be both a Member and an Associate Member at one and the same time. The result was that the Third Division quite simply collapsed in mid-season with fewer than fourteen clubs completing

DEAD AND GONE
Third Lanark, who were themselves defunct by 1967 in action against two Clubs who succumbed earlier. *Picture above:* Stevenson of Arthurlie saves from a Third Lanark forward at Barrhead in 1927. *Picture opposite:* In a match from the 1930s McCormack, Third Lanark's goalkeeper, saves from a King's Park forward (in stripes) at Stirling.

their fixtures and therefore no question of any promotion from it. Nor were the customary flags and badges awarded to the top clubs, although, interestingly, Helensburgh finished almost at the top and might well have attained Second Division status in a normal year. The Associate Clubs cited the large amount of travelling they were expected to do and intimated that they were not prepared to carry on. They asked that they join the Second Division clubs and that from this joint membership two Divisions should be formed on a regional basis. The League would have none of it; it was delighted that two Divisions had again come about, whether by accident or Willie Gallagher's (*Waverley's*) Machiavellian theory and contented itself with electing Forfar Athletic to the Second Division in place of Broxburn United who had withdrawn. Of the rest of the collection of dwarf stars Mid-Annandale, Solway Star and Vale of Leven found a home in the Scottish Alliance and other clubs hung on for a few years, sometimes emerging only to play in Qualifying Cup ties, before gradually they surrendered Senior status and slipped back either into the Junior ranks or in some cases into total oblivion.

The First Division's concerns were loftier but still basically financial. Vigilance was still called for to impress the notion that League matches should take priority over everything except Scottish Cup ties and international matches, and indeed even the latter were being called in question. Certainly mid-week matches against Ireland and Wales were increasingly being demanded and most members were annoyed too by the fact that Scotland now played three Saturday Amateur Internationals in addition. Since the Scotland amateur side was almost invariably the Queen's Park first eleven, this meant that on three occasions professional clubs lost out on a Saturday gate because of a match in which they had no possible interest. This would not do. The Glasgow clubs too came under fire for insisting on three Saturdays for the carrying out of the Glasgow Cup competition. A compromise was eventually reached whereby Glasgow clubs would be given League fixtures on those particular days but between Glasgow clubs, so that if they wished to defer them to a subsequent mid-week date, no team outside Glasgow would suffer loss.

The General Strike of 1926 and the protracted resistance thereafter of the Miners' Union had severely damaged the game at the lower levels in Scotland, mortally in the case of the Third Division, and even with the Second Division the wound was grievous, for football and mining districts had always gone hand in hand in Scotland. There were members of the industrial working class who genuinely could not afford to pay anything for admission to League matches. To ease their plight, Bo'ness in the Second Division had arranged, provided the visiting club agreed, to admit for nothing half an hour after the match started those unemployed who were on the parish and only received lines for provisions. Most visiting teams went along with this but in November 1926 East Stirlingshire objected.

The same club, East Stirlingshire was on less potentially opprobrious grounds over the question of linesmen which arose almost simultaneously with that of free admission. It is a measure of the financial straits even of the Second Division that, on the motion of Ayr United, neutral linesmen had been dispensed with in the matches of that Division, the total savings being £1 per game. As replacements East Stirling suggested that only club officials or directors be asked to act as linesmen. The Falkirk club pointed out that the job was given very often to a reserve player who was on the same bonus as the chosen eleven and naturally desired to do what he could to help them win. There were not wanting those to say that most directors might well exercise a bias against their own side in order to avoid having to pay out a bonus.

Some sides had by now had enough of the alleged glamour of League football. Arbroath and Nithsdale Wanderers fell due to seek re-election in May 1927 but the last-named retired voluntarily from membership. In their place came Leith Athletic, a club that many thought had been harshly treated in being excluded for so long.

There was also a move afoot to make the Management Committee the exclusive preserve of directors and committeemen, in other words to remove from office any managers or paid employees of football clubs. This motion appeared to be aimed at Willie Maley of Celtic and it became a hardy but unsuccessful annual, even when in November 1927 Mr. Maley appeared to give his critics invaluable ammunition by trenchantly criticising the referee after an Old Firm match at Parkhead—restraint in defeat was no more a characteristic of Old Firm managers then than now. The League Management Committee contented themselves with severely censuring the Celtic manager for his remarks to the officials at half-time and stating that "they deplored the fact that a member of that Committee should have put himself in such an invidious position." In another decision taken at the same time the League appeared to have learned the dangers of over-expansion when agreeing that "no Associate Members should be admitted after this date unless a General Meeting of the League resolves otherwise."

Scarcely a day passed without some Scottish League side being reported under threat. The Stirling club, King's Park, complained bitterly to the League that their gate had been ruined because a report had been published that their opponents for that Saturday, Clydebank, were selling their ground and going out of existence. King's Park temporarily stopped payment of the guarantee to Clydebank and sought guidance from the League as to whether they need pay it at all. On their part, Clydebank intimated their willingness to discharge their obligations and see the season out, even on another ground. King's Park were instructed to pay over the guarantee and Clydebank clung to life for another three years, but the situation was grossly unsatisfactory and Mr. E. H. Furst of Hearts did not lack backing in the next meeting of the Management Committee when he moved as a matter of urgency that the number of clubs in Division Two should be reduced. His proposal was that eventually, and at no great distance in time, the League should be made up of two Divisions, each of which would contain 16 clubs. He found support, but, for the moment, not quite enough.

The Scottish game was caught between the rock of finance, of business prudence, and the hard place of sentiment. No one wished to exclude a club which might simply be going through the bad patch which afflicted every Scottish club from time to time, Rangers and Celtic apart. Because of their sociological, quasi-religious and tribal development, those two clubs were largely, though not totally, insulated against chill market forces. There was no doubt however that some of the Second Division clubs were in their death throes, it was merely that the death throes were protracted. Anyone with an eye to see knew that the West Lothian clubs, Armadale, Bathgate, Bo'ness and Broxburn United had no long-term future, they could not have, for the West Lothian coal field was shrinking and the shale oil industry was on the way to disappearance. Bathgate and Armadale were re-elected for season

PERFECTLY PLAYABLE

Tommy Robertson of Dundee about to take a corner kick in a Dens Park League match of 1936. There is not a line in sight and only a few of the softer spectators have umbrellas.

1928–29 but there was a limit to the tolerance which had been extended to them. In the midst of all this gloom there is a glimpse of a more innocent age in the minute that player Danny Blair of Clyde had been ordered off in the match against Rangers "for interfering with the Referee, A. B. Williamson."

Armadale, newly reprieved, raised the question of an unemployment gate. The League dutifully canvassed Second Division opinions but Armadale's proposal for a sixpenny gate for the unemployed fell as did Clydebank's more radical proposal for a sixpenny general admission. In their submission Clydebank stressed the difficulty of competing with good-quality Junior matches which were available at a lower admission fee. The inference to be drawn was surely that a team which could not compete with Junior football was not capable of representing the Senior game credibly or effectively. Yet, as we shall see, the League consistently shrank from the necessary surgery at this time.

They were preoccupied with relations between referees and players and the press. They had recently forbade referees to comment on decisions to the press, stating that their only communication must be with the League Management Committee and, with the substitution of the S.F.A. where appropriate, that is still the channel of communication today.

Over the years the ruling bodies have taken much criticism for this procedure but it has to be said that it is eminently sensible. Referees will have bad games and in the course of them they will give decisions which are quite simply erroneous. If allowed to talk to press, radio and television afterwards they would be put into the position of justifying decisions which modern playback facilities could expose once more as wrong. Players were also forbidden in December 1928 from writing about any recent match in which they had been involved. This was to be made a condition of contract when a club signed a player. They were likewise forbidden from accepting from a Supporters Club or any outside source a bonus, payment in cash, or a gift of any kind.

Meanwhile, presented with a heaven-sent chance to reduce the Second Division to 18 clubs the League drew back. By March 1929 Bathgate could not even make the end of the season and folded up. As by that stage of the season they had not played each team that was in the running for promotion twice, it was decided that the fairest procedure was to expunge completely their playing record from the Second Division table. A month later Arthurlie went, but as they had played all the promotion-chasing clubs their record was allowed to stand.

The reformers were jubilant at the A.G.M. of 1929 but to their

THE SCRAPPY ONES COUNT TOO
Andy Black of Hearts turns away after forcing the ball just over the line despite frantic efforts from Watson and goalkeeper Culley of Hibernian. This 1936 Tynecastle match gave value for money, Hearts winning by an emphatic 8–3.

utter consternation and despair, the two fall-outs were replaced by the two small town teams of Angus, Brechin City and Montrose. In defence of this decision it was argued that there was a duty to take the game all over Scotland, but this did not satisfy those who felt that the absolute essential for a Second Division club was that it should be a credible member of the First Division if promoted. With Brechin and Montrose having populations in the 5000–6000 range, this seemed most unlikely.

There has been much concentration in recent pages on the lower divisions but that is where the potentially fatal sickness was, or, to use the old nautical term, the stokers know the ship is sinking before the captain does. In the First Division, the problem was of a different kind. Simply expressed it was that no side, not even Celtic, could mount a sustained and effective challenge to Rangers in the League. Very occasionally, as in 1926 there would be a blip and Rangers finished sixth. It was precisely the rarity of such an event which made it remarkable.

Extremely well-managed by Wiliam Struth, who had previously been the club's trainer, and helped by the absence of a maximum wage in Scotland, Rangers carried all before them. There was of course a *de facto* maximum wage which was always a couple of pounds per week above whatever the top rate might be in England at the time. Rangers used this very shrewdly to ensure that between the two wars they never allowed a player to be transferred that they were not prepared to lose. The result was that for twenty years Rangers absolutely dominated League football and this dominance should little sign of weakening in 1939.

Such an unbroken success story was very gratifying for the Ibrox club and their many supporters but it was not a healthy thing for the League itself. Almost every year from January on it was a safe bet that four or five of the ten First Division matches on the card would be totally meaningless and those that mattered would concern relegation rather than the championship. Inevitably, with only two major competitions in a season on offer, crowds suffered.

The county competitions were now being exiled to the very margins of the season. There were to be no Saturday dates for any of them, the Glasgow Cup alone excepted. Come to that, there were to be no more Saturday dates for the big Inter-League match. The Football League now intimated that matches against The Scottish League in England would be played in mid-week and they very much wished the same timing to apply when the match fell due to be played in Scotland.

In common with the other major footballing bodies, The Scottish League did not at this time look at all favourably on the efforts of outside agencies to become involved with the running of the game, however indirectly. Broadcasting of sporting events was now a commonplace but the B.B.C. was regarded with suspicion and its request to broadcast the Inter-League match of October 1929 was refused. It would be more than half a century before a stable agreement would be worked out between football, radio, and in later years, television.

Pools promoters were perfectly prepared to put large sums into football at this time but there was no willingness to take what was seen to be tainted money. Indeed the footballing authorities in England in the mid 1930s went so far as to make an attempt to suppress publication of league fixtures, claiming copyright in them and denying their use to the pools promoters. With a robust commonsense the Scottish authorities refused to join their English counterparts in this nonsensical ploy. Football League clubs were not given their fixture for the week-end until the Friday (except those who had to make long journeys, in which case they were informed on the Thursday) and the result was chaos, snatched travel arrangements and large-scale antagonising of the people who kept the game going, the supporters. Two weeks of this was enough to show the sheer futility of the notion and the Football League reverted to the publication of fixtures as normal.

In any event, there were more pressing problems in Scotland. In two successive fixtures Clydebank failed to meet their guarantee of £50 to Leith Athletic and Bo'ness. Because of the late date in the season, it was the end of March 1930, they were given another chance to fulfil their obligations and finish the championship. They were however fined £125 but by the end of May the fine and the two guarantees were still outstanding. Stretching forbearance to the limit, the League decided that if the guarantees were met by September 30, the fine would be reduced to a mere £25. Somehow the money was scraped together and Clydebank staggered out on to the field for one last season.

The B.B.C. made another attempt to cover the nation's most popular sport. It requested the League's permission to approach individual clubs with a view to having their matches broadcast. The Scottish League turned down the request. On broadcasting, all Scots would sing the same song. England was ahead in this matter and match commentaries on big games were becoming part of the normal radio diet.

At this time the Scottish League was in a legalistic and "what we have we hold" mood. It passed the following stern rebuke:

> "The Committee expressed regret at the lack of courtesy on the part of the Glasgow Football Association in fixing Hampden Park for their final tie on Saturday October 11 1930 when that ground was engaged in a League fixture without first making application for the alteration thereof."

Meanwhile the country's industrial position deteriorated, nowhere more so than in the heavy manufacturing areas of the West of Scotland and Central Scotland. Branch railway lines closed, viable seams of coal became exhausted, half-finished ships stood on the stocks, their hulls rusting. Clubs lurched from one crisis to another. It was the turn of Bo'ness to find themselves unable to meet guarantees early in 1931. The club had other debts which it declared itself to be in no position to pay off. It offered an ingenious solution for the £50 guarantee owed to Dundee United which was simply that Dundee United should forget about it and not pay a guarantee to Bo'ness when they came to visit them later in the season. The Scottish League would have none of it. Again somehow the money was found, the pattern was that a club could always surmount a first crisis of this kind, but rarely the second.

Despite having flown distress signals for the whole season, Bo'ness and Clydebank were re-elected, all the more surprising in

FIRST GOAL OF THE SEASON AT THE MARINE GARDENS

ONE OF THE 550

Jimmy McGrory on hand and knees in the hoops watches as the Leith Athletic goalkeeper Boyce retrieves the ball from the back of the net in this match at Marine Gardens, Leith in 1931, Celtic winning 3–0.

THREE IMMORTALS
Jimmy Quinn of Celtic, acting as linesman looks on as Alan Morton and Jimmy McGrory shake hands before the latter's benefit at Celtic Park on August 27th, 1934.

---

the latter case since Tom Colquhoun, their one director and administrator of proven quality, had died in January 1931 and with him went any hope of a viable club in the shipbuilding town. Their re-election was flung back in the Scottish League's face when midway through the close season, on July 1 1931, Clydebank abruptly resigned from membership of The Scottish Football League. Once again the chance to reduce numbers was not taken perhaps because an odd number of clubs would have created problems. What is certain, however, it that Clydebank's replacement was the most bizarre choice ever admitted to membership of The Scottish Football League, at least in the two top Divisions. By 25 votes to 7 Edinburgh City, an all-amateur team, were given preference over Nithsdale Wanderers from Sanquhar who had come up to the Second Division from the Third for a season and then drifted out of League existence.

The admission of Edinburgh City meant that the capital, with a population less than half that of Greater Glasgow, would be asked to support five senior clubs against the latter's six. The new admission was to prove a source of deep embarrassment to its sponsors. In eight seasons membership of Division Two Edinburgh City finished in bottom position six times and second bottom once. Moreover, in those eight seasons it conceded more than 110 goals every season except one. It is charitable to assume that the hasty circumstances of Clydebank's resignation meant that the replacement club did not come under any prolonged scrutiny. There may, too, have been something in the fact that the other amateur League club Queen's Park,—Edinburgh City were sometimes grandiloquently styled the Queen's Park of the East—were experiencing something of a revival at this time and had finished as high as fifth in the First Division in 1928-29, scoring 100 goals in the process.

The Edinburgh amateurs never threatened to do anything remotely as good and their admission became even more weird when one considers that exactly at that moment a League sub-committee which had been appointed to look into its constitution and structure had reported as follows:—

"The Sub-Committee, having considered the question of the effect of automatic promotion and relegation (which has been in effect for the last ten years) on the League as at present constituted, were unanimously of the opinion that the system has not attained its object—the development of the clubs of the Second Division, and so raise the standard thereof nearer to that of the First Division clubs. They were also unanimously of the opinion that the failure was not due to the system of automatic promotion but to the numbers of clubs in the Second Division which under no circumstances could ever become First Division clubs. In these circumstances the Sub-Committee decided to recommend to the Management Committee that steps be taken to reduce the League as early as possible to 34 clubs—18 First Division and 16 Second Division."

It was truly astounding that, faced with this unanimous recommendation from a powerful and influential sub-committee, the League should promptly burden themselves with the like of Edinburgh City, an amiable and gallant bunch of amateurs whose function was to be the chopping block of every other Second Division side and whose sole fugitive claim to remembrance was a Scottish Cup win over Hibernian, completely against the odds, in 1938. Moreover they had been allowed to enter League football with a pitch just over minimum breadth (50 yards) which they could not extend because of the existence of a sprint track at Powderhall, where they were tenants.

The game was still strangely hesitant where public relations were concerned and for every step taken forward, another went cautiously back. Thus R. M. Connell of Peter A. Menzies Advertising

CAPITAL LOSSES
Two of Edinburgh's long-gone Clubs in contention. Crighton the Edinburgh City goalkeeper touches over a header from Peter Flucker (in hoops) of St. Bernard.

Services was given permission to publish an official programme for the Inter-League match against England in November 1931 on the understanding that no liability could attach to the Scottish League by its sale or publication and that it should contain no betting or money-lending advertisements. Almost in the same breath players were forbidden to sign autographs on the field of play or, much less understandably, in the precincts of the pavilion or ground.

Referees who provided some pleasing eccentricities had to be repressed. Peter Craigmyle of Aberdeen, most famous of all Scottish inter-war referees, had paid no heed to the previous instruction that referees should not catch hold of players when remonstrating with them. He was told again. Even more individual was the practice of A. H. Leishman whose custom it was to retire behind the goalposts after awarding a penalty. As he could give no satisfactory explanation of this practice he was ordered to desist from it.

But always, it came back to money. The city and industrial clubs maintained that the S.F.A. and Scottish League were dominated by the country clubs and there was no doubt that things were not as bad in the small Angus towns, Aberdeen and Ayrshire as they

1920–39 THE YEARS BETWEEN

MOTHERWELL CHAMPIONSHIP SIDE 1932

In 1932 Motherwell, with one of the finest Scottish League sides ever, successfully shattered the Old Firm's monopoly of the league title.

were in the central belt. Clyde made strong pleas for an unemployed gate at the end of 1931 saying that on several occasions they had had to turn away from their games sufficient numbers of unemployed to have coverted a League game which had been a financial failure into a success, had there been a special gate for them. They could not move the Scottish League, even after securing the support of near neighbours Celtic. In its own defence the League would have been perfectly entitled to point out that it had on several occasions canvassed the opinions of its members on this question without securing anything that remotely approached a general consensus.

In an effort to counteract the influence of the country clubs within the Scottish Football Association the League entered into talks with that body on the question of direct League representation. The S.F.A. were not enthusiastic, pointing out that many members of League clubs were already also Council Members. The League dissented, stating that what they were after was representation directly as a body in their own right. They had eventually to settle for the right to nominate one of the Vice-Presidents of the senior body and one other.

In an effort to acquire additional revenue, some clubs had decided to cash in on the booming sport of greyhound racing. The League Management Committee was concerned about the possible tie-up with gambling and the danger that where a ground was shared, dog racing might eventually come to have priority. It therefore issued the following instructions to those clubs on whose grounds greyhound racing was taking place or was about to take place.

> (1) Where dog racing is carried on, or is to be carried on, the Dog Racing Track must not interfere in any way with the playing pitch.
> (2) Where a club uses or lets its ground, hires or leases ground, or sells its ground and hires or leases same from the purchaser, it must be a condition of such use, lease or hire that not only will the playing pitch be kept free of the racing track but that Dog Racing will not be carried on upon the ground in opposition to the League games of clubs in the district which are normally at home when the ground club is away.

In addition, League officials were given full powers to inspect all grounds where dog racing was being carried on or contemplated. This inspection showed that Armadale's playing pitch was wholly taken up with the dog track and they were ordered to stop racing at once. Less serious encroachments were reported from the grounds of East Stirlingshire, Falkirk and King's Park.

The directive to finish with dog racing marked the end for Armadale who by that time were bringing in more revenue from the greyhounds than from football. They had started season 1932–33 but within a fortnight in November both they and their West Lothian neighbours Bo'ness were forced to withdraw from the Second Division and this time there were no replacements sought. Two unlikely substitutes had volunteered themselves in the shapes of Newcastle United and Berwick Rangers but the withdrawal of two clubs gave the Scottish League the change to get the Second Division down to a more manageable 18 sides.

The League gave its crusade against animal racing (cheetahs were also being raced at this time) top priority and was quite prepared to pay the price of losing another couple of clubs if it had to. All clubs in membership were summoned to a Special General Meeting in November 1932, the circularising letter setting out the reasons as follows:

> "It is generally admitted that Dog and other animal racing and Football should not be associated in the interests of our national game which must be kept as free as possible from betting—the underlying basis of the existence of dog racing.
>
> "The first question which arises is how to eliminate Dog or other animal racing from its association with football. In this connection it would be impossible to compel clubs under contracts (legally entered into by them) to break same."

At the Special General Meeting the following rules were made:—

1. Clubs in membership of the League, except as hereinafter provided, shall not use their grounds or rent them or lease them for the purpose of being used, nor shall they lease or play on grounds which are being used for Dog or other animal racing.
2. Clubs in membership of the League who prior to August 17 1932 have entered into binding contracts to permit Dog Racing on their grounds must take all legal steps incumbent upon them to terminate said contracts (unless sooner terminated) on the date upon which they expire or can be legally terminated in the opinion of the Dean, for the time being, of the Faculty of Advocates in Edinburgh.
3. Clubs in membership of the League who are tenants, sub-tenants or joint occupants of any ground used for Dog or any other Animal Racing under any contract entered into prior to said August 17 1932 must terminate such contract at the termin-

HOW THEY DRESSED IN THE 1930s
Tubular shorts, high boots and legs like tree-trunks are the common factors for Clyde's John C. Gillies, Arbroath's full-back of Italian extraction, Attilo Becci and Hearts Andy Black.

ation thereof, and shall not renew same without the consent of the Management Committee who shall have power to grant permission for an extension if they deem it expedient, having regard to the circumstances.
4. No dog or other racing animal shall be allowed on any ground of a club in membership of the League or on any ground leased or tenanted by a club in membership of the same later than two hours prior to the kick-off and not earlier than two hours after the termination of any football match and no club in membership of the League shall advertise a football match in conjunction with a Dog or other animal Race Meeting.
5. No betting, whether by tote or otherwise shall be allowed on the ground of any club in membership of the League on the occasion of a football match.

There were those in League circles who felt that perhaps there was an element of over-kill in the anti-greyhound legislation but the extent of the threat was seen some ten years later during the Second World War when for a time it looked as though Clyde, whose ground by that time belonged for all practical concerns to the National Greyhound Racing Association, would have to vacate Shawfield in order that dog-racing meetings could be held.

At long last in the summer of 1933 there was a reduction in the membership of the Second Division to 18 clubs. The two West Lothian sides which had fallen by the way during the season, Bo'ness and Armadale, were not replaced and there would be no further change in the permanent composition of the membership of the Scottish League until after the end of the war.

The League was not having matters all its own way in skirmishes with the S.F.A. The latter body had occasioned much annoyance by continuing to sanction the scheduling of amateur internationals for Saturdays in the course of the season. This drew the following riposte from the Scottish League:— "That, as the selection of the teams for amateur internationals is almost wholly confined to players of the Queen's Park Football Club, and as this results in interference with the League fixtures and financial loss to League clubs, the S.F.A. be requested to take such steps as will avoid such interference and financial loss in the future." Nothing was done about the English or Welsh matches but the Irish game was occasionally played in mid-week before 1939.

The S.F.A. was likewise requested not to fix international venues (it was the custom in the 1930s to take minor internationals, especially the Welsh game, to provincial grounds) until League fixtures had been compiled, so that reshuffling of fixtures might not be necessary. By February 1934 only the full international match against England was reserved for a Saturday, although The Scottish League's proposal, submitted to the International Board, that players should always be made available by their clubs to represent the land of their birth met with a less than enthusiastic response from the Football League. In practice Anglo-Scots were usually released but the record of English clubs in so far as Irish and Welsh players was concerned was little short of disgraceful.

Those entrusted with the governance of Scottish football were increasingly aware that the game was spreading throughout the world and that present British dominance would not last indefinitely. In 1933 the Paris League offered a match in that city on April 24, a Sunday, but after earnest consideration of travelling arrangements the Scottish League decided that the game could only take place if the League programme for the day before was cancelled, too high a price to pay in their judgement.

Scottish teams, increasingly, were going abroad, very far abroad

98   THE FIRST 100 YEARS

T. MOONEY (AIRDRIEONIANS)

W. MILLS (ABERDEEN)

D. GRAY (RANGERS)

J. KENNAWAY (CELTIC)

J. S. SYMON (DUNDEE)

J. J. TULIP (QUEEN OF THE SOUTH)

PHOTOGRAPHS OF SCOTTISH PLAYERS FROM 1930s

1920–39 THE YEARS BETWEEN

R. BEATTIE

G. STEVENSON

B. ELLIS

P. McKENNAN

J. BROWN

W. BUCHAN

K. DAWSON

J. DELANEY

T. WALKER

CARICATURES OF SCOTTISH PLAYERS FROM 1930s

THE FIRST 100 YEARS

WELL DONE THE SECOND DIVISION
The lower Division had two representatives in the Scottish Cup semi-finals of 1938 and East Fife (in stripes) went on to beat Kilmarnock in the final. The St. Bernard's player nearest the camera in this Tynecastle semi-final is Jerry Kerr who in the 1960's was a highly successful manager of Dundee United.

in some cases. Rangers visited Austria and Germany but Motherwell comfortably topped that with visits to South Africa and Argentina while Queen of the South would shortly play in North Africa. Such matches needed to be subject to some sort of official control in order to stop Scottish sides over-extending themselves with the result that frequent defeats might damage the reputation of the Scottish game. It was therefore decided that in Europe, Scottish club sides could play district representative teams but not national teams whereas in the British Colonies (including South Africa), where the game was at a less advanced state of development, full representative sides could be met.

In the general tidying-up that was currently taking place, the League wanted something done about the Scottish Cup. For all the "romance of the ballot box" that the football reporters loved to write of, there was little to be said for sending a club like Rangers or Hearts to Blairgowrie or Lockerbie to play in front of a few hundred people, win by double figures in a travesty of a contest and run the risk of having players injured on some very rough and ready pitches. What they sought, but did not immediately get, was a First Round of 18 Second Division clubs plus six qualifiers, with the 20 First Division clubs coming in to make a total of 32 clubs in the second round.

In an interesting judicial decision in England, Lord Roche laid down that a player earning more than £250 per annum should not be classified as a manual worker and therefore did not require to be insured under the National Health Insurance and Unemployment Acts. In Scotland this affected the players of the leading clubs, first-team players with Aberdeen, Hearts, Celtic and Rangers were averaging about £7 per week as a basic wage at this time.

Despite the increasing amount of money involved, association football in Scotland had been remarkably free of financial scandal. There had been the attempt previously mentioned to suborn the Stenhousemuir goalkeeper and another such involving Montrose, interestingly bookmakers appeared to pick out smaller clubs as being less likely to attract attention. In 1935 a case arose which could have affected promotion from the Second Division. An Ayr United player, Robert Russell, was told by the Falkirk manager Mr. Robert Orr that if he turned out for Ayr United against Falkirk in a vital promotion match between the two, he would lose his everyday job with Alexander's coachbuilders in Falkirk. He accepted a payment of £3 from Mr. Orr and declared himself unfit. Falkirk won the match and Russell then admitted what he had done. The match was ordered to be replayed, with Ayr United winning and the gate was made available to the Scottish League who divided it between Ayr United and Falkirk Infirmary. Ayr passed their money on to the County Hospital, both institutions receiving £50. Russell was suspended until the end of the season and fined £10 while the Falkirk manager was debarred from any further official participation in the management of the sport.

By way of light relief the Management Committee a few weeks later for the Inter-League match with England at Ibrox "decided to refuse the gratuitous services of the Coatbridge and District Ladies' Pipe Band" and to engage the Govan Brass Band instead. In January 1937 one of the links with the very earliest days of the League was broken with the death of Mr. Alex. Lawrance of Dumbarton, the very first President of the League and a devoted exponent of the cause of amateurism.

So the last of the inter-war years passed away. The problems remained as they had been immediately after the Armistice. Too many clubs were chasing too few spectators and the vast majority of League games were meaningless. Yet the changing of the format of the League was almost impossible to accomplish. Understandably, in the votes that mattered clubs would consult their own individual interests.

THE RECORD BREAKER

Jimmy McGrory's characteristic headed goal against Aberdeen gave him the British goalscoring record on the last day of 1935.

A tiny step was taken towards reconstruction in the sphere of reserve football. There was no Reserve League as such but an organisation called the Scottish Football Alliance in which most but not all of the First Division sides participated. A reserve side could be an expensive item however, and even Celtic drifted in and out of the Alliance in the years between the wars, while frequently newly-promoted clubs would not run a reserve side in their first season of promotion in the fear that it might also prove to be their last.

The numbers of the Alliance were augumented by the presence of two small-town teams from Ayrshire, Beith and Galston. Both had been members of the ill-starred Third Division. In the early summer of 1938, a group of reformers, headed by Mr. James Lyon of Hamilton Academical, decided that the two little clubs were an anachronism and that from now on only the reserve teams of First Division clubs should be allowed to participate in the new Reserve League. This would also bring about the embarrassing expulsion of Dundee, Alliance stalwarts of long standing, who had lost First Division status in 1937.

The reformers, to be fair, did have a valid point in that the Qualifying Cup commitments of Beith and Galston in September and October, matches which were reserved for Saturdays, led to the postponement of reserve games and their subsequent piling-up at the end of the season. On the night before the meeting which would decide his club's fate, James Abbott, President of Galston, wrote thus to every club in membership of The Scottish League:

> "It is with concern that I learn from the public press of the proposals that may be brought forward at the Annual General Meeting of the Scottish Football Alliance, proposals which, if carried, would have the effect of excluding this club from participation in the suggested re-arranged competition.
>
> "I would remind you that Galston Football Club was founded in 1888 and, but for the war years, we have maintained senior football in this district ever since then.
>
> "The Club were members of the Third Division of The Scottish Football League for a period and on the dissolution of that body were for a year in the West of Scotland Amateur League. In 1932 the Club were welcomed as members of the Alliance at a time when lack of interest in that competition threatened its existence. They have faithfully carried out all obligations as members and have deservedly received the appreciation of the public.
>
> "From a pure love of sport my associates and I are keenly desirous of continuing senior football in this area and so aid in

RECORD MAKERS
The Raith Rovers forward line of 1937–38 Glen, Gilmour, Haywood, Whitelaw, Joyner. In winning the Second Division the Kirkcaldy side set up a record aggregate for a season of 142 goals.

---

the general stimulation of our national pastime. Exclusion from the Alliance would mean the end of senior football here and I appeal to your club not to support proposals which would mean for us extinction."

Alas! the dignified and brave appeal of Mr. Abbot received little support. Only Queen's Park, Clyde, St. Mirren and, understandably, the two Ayrshire clubs Kilmarnock and Ayr United, went into the lobby to cast a vote in their defence. The Alliance was disbanded and reconstituted to become the Scottish Reserve League. By 1939 Beith had joined the Junior ranks but the football enthusiast will today search vainly for the name of Galston on the active list.

In football as elsewhere the rich man was in his palace while the poor man sat at the gate. Almost the last pre-war League statistic worth recording was that pertaining to the Rangers v. Celtic match of January 2 1939. At Ibrox Park, the traditional Ne'erday match between Rangers and Celtic was watched by a crowd of no fewer than 118,561. Six-figure crowds were commonplace for Cup Finals and the England International in the Scotland of the 30s, but this was comfortably the largest attendance ever recorded at a League match in Great Britain. Rangers won the game 2–1 on their way to yet another League championship, incidentally reversing a fearful 6–2 defeat at Parkhead earlier in the season. They were simply much too good for the rest of the domestic opposition but restructuring was at hand. It would be brought about, paradoxically enough, by someone who is not known to have displayed any great interest in association football.

Chapter 6

SCOTTISH LEAGUE FOOTBALL IN THE SECOND WORLD WAR

It could be argued that the above chapter heading is somewhat misleading in that The Scottish Football League was not directly responsible for much the greater part of such football as was played between 1939–45, but the period has suffered a totally unjustified neglect since from the regional leagues emerged several ideas which were to be of permanent importance, among them summer football, the idea of a League Cup and a differential points system for home and away wins.

On September 2 1939 a full programme of Scottish League matches was played, those teams which had far to travel showering quickly and diving onto their bus or train in an endeavour to get home before the first night of the wartime blackout. Clubs had played five matches of The Scottish League First Division programme before the lights went out for the same number of years. As always, minds went back to the previous war but few of the experiences of 1914 would be particularly valid 25 years later.

From football's point of view there were two crucial differences from the previous conflict. The first was that whereas conscription had only applied fully to the last six months of the Great War, as people still thought of it, it would now operate from the outset. Indeed, on September 2 every Liverpool player save one was already with the Territorial Army and all men would have to register for military service on attaining their twentieth year. The other new factor was that of airpower and on the declaration of war football grounds, together with any other venue where large crowds might assemble, were ordered to be closed by the Government.

On September 6 1939 the Scottish Football Association suspended all football and players' contracts were consequently declared void. Clearly this affected star footballers, who were full-time, more than the ordinary professional who had another

Price—One Penny

OFFICIAL PROGRAMME
ST BERNARDS FOOTBALL CLUB
SEASON 1939-1940

ST. BERNARDS v. QUEENS PARK — September 2nd 1939

If Diana Wynyard offered you a cigarette, it would be a De Reszke – of course!

Ask for MINORS
10 for 4½d - 30 for 1/1½d.
Cork tipped mild Virginia—or plain tipped, whichever you prefer. De Reszke Majors, extra large, 10 for 6½d.

LAST POST
The programme issued for the St. Bernard's v Queen's Park match of September 2nd, 1939, the last ever Scottish League match played in by the Edinburgh Club.

THE RANGERS FOOTBALL CLUB LTD.
No. 382
Ground - IBROX STADIUM, GLASGOW

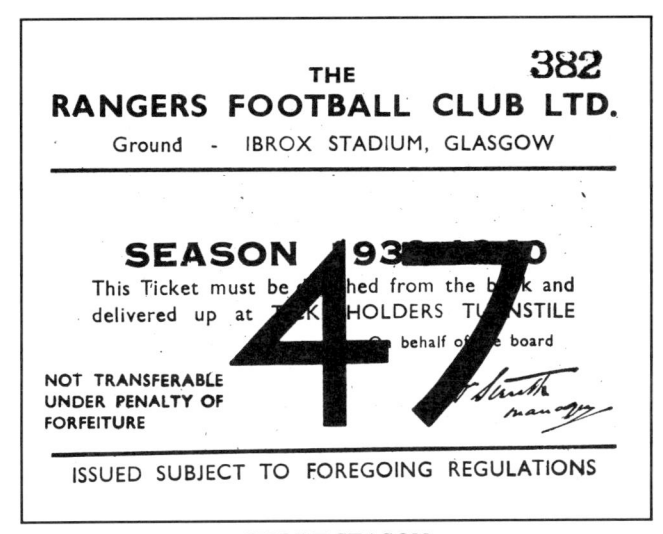

SEASON 193 — 0

This Ticket must be ...hed from the b...k and delivered up at ...K HOLDERS T... NSTILE ...behalf of ...e board

NOT TRANSFERABLE UNDER PENALTY OF FORFEITURE

ISSUED SUBJECT TO FOREGOING REGULATIONS

SHORT SEASON
Rangers season ticket holders saw only five League matches in season 1939–40 for their thirty shillings, before war put a stop to official League Football. Later, war-time Regional Leagues were hastily arranged.

civilian occupation. Both Old Firm clubs would be severely criticised for their microscopic contribution of leading players to the forces—of those 22 players who wore first-team jerseys in September 1939 and whose claim to such were unchallenged, only Willie Thornton and David Kinnear of Rangers and George Paterson and Willie Lyon of Celtic would end up in uniform—but in their defence it has to be said that their stars could have been unemployed for months in awaiting the call to service. Instead, most found themselves in reserved occupations, some indeed had taken full-time jobs there shortly before the outbreak of war.

The total closing down of grounds was an understandable panic reaction. Soon the Government, aware that boredom could lead to anger, was prepared to countenance a restart. On this point, not for the first time, the two legislative bodies found themselves with opposed viewpoints. The S.F.A. announced itself as quite happy to see an indefinite programme of friendly matches while the League declared that it was not remotely interested in such a proposal, there would be League football of a sort or there would be nothing. The Government, mindful of the part that football had played in recruiting and fund-raising in 1914 was anxious to see the game get under way again.

The sport was of course no longer self-governing. The country was divided into safe and unsafe areas and in the latter crowds

THE EVENING DISPATCH, TUESDAY, JANUARY 4, 1938.

Tommy Walker at Home

THE WELL-OFF PROFESSIONALS
Top flight professional footballers could make a comfortable living in the 1930's. In the picture above Mr and Mrs Tommy Walker admire their latest acquisition, a 1938 radio while the picture opposite shows Rangers massive centre-forward, Jimmy Smith contemplating his pride and joy, the new car.

---

would be severely restricted. This led to astonishing anomalies such as the fact that the crowd at Parkhead for a Celtic match would be set at 10,000 whereas Shawfield, scarcely half a mile away, could take 20,000 because half of the ground was geographically in Lanarkshire. The final say on crowd size would rest with the local Chief Constable.

On September 23 1939 various friendly matches were played and preparations made for the resumption of League football on a wartime basis. It took another month for this to happen and the Glasgow clubs were accused of dragging their feet in order to utilise the intervening Saturdays for their own local Glasgow Cup ties. In the end two Regional Leagues, West and East, were formed under Scottish League auspices each of 16 clubs. Six clubs therefore were invited to drop out of football for the duration of the war, perhaps with the unspoken hope that they might not take up the struggle again once the war was over. These first casualties of Hitler's War were Brechin City, Montrose, Forfar Athletic, Edinburgh City, Leith Athletic and East Stirlingshire. The exclusion of Leith Athletic was particularly wounding. It had been decided that two of the three smaller Edinburgh clubs had to go. Edinburgh City stood no chance, but since it was deemed impossible to differentiate between the claims (or lack of claims) of St. Bernard and Leith Athletic the toss of a coin determined that the former would play in wartime football and the latter would not.

It will be seen at once that Angus had suffered particularly severely from this curtailment of clubs and the county was very opposed to Regional Leagues right from the start. It will be as well to mention now the composition of the two divisions.

Regional League West	*Regional League East*
Airdrieonians	Aberdeen
Albion Rovers	Alloa
Ayr United	Arbroath
Celtic	Cowdenbeath
Clyde	Falkirk
Dumbarton	Heart of Midlothian
Hamilton Academicals	Hibernian
Kilmarnock	St. Johnstone
Morton	Dundee
Motherwell	Dundee United
Partick Thistle	East Fife
Queen's Park	Dunfermline Athletic
Queen of the South	Raith Rovers
Rangers	King's Park
St. Mirren	St. Bernards
Third Lanark	Stenhousemuir

The great weakness of the geographical division of the country into west and east is immediately apparent. The large-scale eastern clubs, Hibernian, Heart of Midlothian and Aberdeen were cut off from the profitable fixtures with the West of Scotland giants. Inherent flaws in the system were compounded by the fatal delay of a month in getting under way and by the savage early winter which followed a quite magnificent autumn when most of the grounds had stood empty on sunny Saturday after sunny Saturday. Angus, with three clubs out altogether and the other three deprived of their most lucrative fixtures, was especially resentful and as early as November 28 Arbroath were talking about withdrawing from the Eastern section of the wartime league.

More serious was the plight of the two big Edinburgh clubs and Aberdeen. Not even the immediate reduction of wages to £2 per week with a maximum bonus of £1 could keep them solvent. Heart of Midlothian had in 1939 declared a dividend for the very first time in the club's history but in the first three months of wartime football they never once attracted as many as 8000 spectators and often played to gates of 1500, a state of affairs which could not possibly continue.

The bitterness of League clubs was compounded by the action of the S.F.A. in announcing that they would no longer assume responsibility for the insurance of players. They justified this on the argument that as there were no internationals or cup finals to bring in revenue, nothing could go out. The League clubs found this a less than tenable line of reasoning. They pointed out that currently the S.F.A. had £30,000 on call which had largely been earned by the efforts of players with League clubs. The question was asked, acidly, how much money the S.F.A. would have earned from a Scottish Cup Final between, say, Nairn County and Burntisland Shipyard. The S.F.A. was not to be embarrassed into changing its stance and the best it would do was to offer to pay insurance for those players incapacitated over the close season, an offer which was rightly regarded as less than generous.

As early as December 1939 it was clear that the new set-up offered no permanent solution. Alec Irvine, Chairman of Hearts, fired this warning shot across the League's bows although he seemed to be offering re-assurance "We are determined to give the experiment every chance. There is no talk of our closing down, as has been reported in certain quarters." Nevertheless, the Edinburgh club were insistent that they would have to play next season in the same league as the great Glasgow duo.

Not even the common threat presented by Hitler could get League and Association to run in harness. The S.F.A. were keen to organise some form of Emergency Cup, a *volte-face* from their early insistence on friendly war-time football. They were prepared, with much justification, to include all 38 League clubs in the draw and to organise it on the lines of a League Cup. They omitted to consult the League however and on being taken to task over this, S.F.A. President Douglas Bowie said that the running of the Cup was purely a matter for the S.F.A. and that they saw no need to consult anybody about it.

As the world moved on into 1940 new bodyblows struck the beleaguered game. Things appeared to be heading back towards comparative normality when 40,000 spectators attended the first Old Firm match of the war on New Year's Day, the game having been transferred to Ibrox which had a higher safety limit for crowds. The week before, two special football trains had run to Hamilton for the Rangers match, the first since the outbreak of war. But the savage winter weather finally put paid to the Regional Leagues when, of 48 matches scheduled for a three week period in late January and early February, only three actually went ahead.

A few days later the war claimed its first casualty when on February 6 1940 Cowdenbeath closed down. When only six out of 50 shareholders attended an emergency meeting called to keep the club going, there could be but one outcome. Their playing record was expunged and from now on some club would have a blank Saturday. Arbroath considered following suit but decided to honour their commitments for that season although making it plain that they would not participate in a similar set-up in season

1940–41. Heart of Midlothian and Hibernian re-iterated that they too would be missing if the clubs were organised on the same principles as the Regional Leagues had been.

And yet, on the military front, nothing had happened for the first six months. It was therefore unfortunate that on the very day when a proposal was made that promotion and relegation should be restored for next season—even Cowdenbeath expressing an interest in that—the war should begin in earnest with the German invasion of Scandinavia. The idea of a league with two divisions of 14 clubs (St. Bernard, Cowdenbeath, King's Park and Stenhousemuir were favourites to be jettisoned) vanished for good with the lightning invasion of France and the Low Countries. The question now was, would there be any football at all in August 1940?

Meantime at least the War Emergency Cup would go ahead but with only 31 entrants since the eminently sensible plan to allow Leith Athletic or Edinburgh City to take part, both still in being although not currently in League football, was turned down. In a departure from established cup tradition ties would be played on the home and home basis in the early stages and although the Cup was technically an S.F.A. affair, unlike its peacetime equivalent the entrants were drawn exclusively from clubs in membership of the Scottish League.

There were other arguments against the re-introduction of promotion and relegation in any league sytem. If clubs were allocated to First and Second Division on the state of affairs pertaining in August 1939 then Queen's Park, with their enormous ground unkeep, and Morton and Airdrie, who had done well in the first season of war-time football which had given them the chance of playing leading West clubs, would suffer greatly. In addition, Cowdenbeath and Arbroath, both First Division members in 1939 had announced that under no circumstances would they function in August 1940.

One thing was certain, there had to be a change in the formation of the league for the first year of the war had brought horrendous losses. Celtic were £7155 down on the season's workings, Hearts £2555, Ayr United £2654 and Motherwell £1212. In the Eastern Section even East Fife, with the cushion of a Scottish Cup win recently behind them dropped £2317, Alloa, Dundee United, who reached the final of the Emergency Cup and Rangers were almost alone in declaring a profit. Clubs began to economise, St. Mirren and St. Johnstone going to the extraordinary lengths of sacking their managers and trainers.

Another thing was certain; any league football played would not be under the direct auspices of The Scottish Football League. On

June 6 1940 that body accepted the recommendation of its own Management Committee that it should close down for the duration of the war. Clubs could, if they wished, form local competitions but the League although giving any assistance it could, would undertake no official responsibility for them. Many people, including the highly respected *Waverley,* sports-writer of the *Daily Record*, had been very scathing about the League's well-intentioned desire to go back to something approaching a peacetime structure.

"Any attempt to run football as though nothing was happening in the world outside would be sheer lunacy. Carrying on with a Second Division containing clubs more suited to Junior status than to Senior has been a costly business."

He, like others, clearly saw a one division wartime league as a blueprint for the eventual resumption of peacetime football.

But would that one division come about and who would make it up? This is perhaps the place to look at the various attitudes of clubs towards wartime football. As might be expected it ranged from the consistently enthusiastic to the totally apathetic. In the first camp and pre-eminently, were Rangers. From the declaration of war their attitude, totally commendable, was that they would do everything in their power to make wartime football as credible as might be. Dundee United, Dunfermline Athletic, the two Edinburgh sides and Aberdeen were anxious to keep going, always with the proviso in the case of the last three that they were allowed some access to Western opposition. Airdrie, Dumbarton and Morton, all beneficiaries of the first season of war-time football were also keenly committed to the continuance of the game.

In the other corner were Celtic, whose attitude throughout the wartime years was tepid in the extreme. Setting their faces against the employment of guest players—not for them the Stanley Matthews, Matt Busbys or Frank Swifts, even when freely available—they made surprisingly little effort to retain their own pre-war star players, very few of whom were required for military service. Indeed on one celebrated occasion in 1942 Morton came to Parkhead with three members of the famous Celtic Empire Exhibition Trophy forward line in their side. St. Johnstone and Dundee, the latter a highly influential club in East of Scotland circles, were just as lukewarm and the unenthusiastic approach of the two last-named clubs was to lead to the cessation of football in the Midlands and North-East of Scotland for an entire year.

The new league set up for season 1940–41 had still a geographical description but was now called the Southern League. Falkirk, Heart of Midlothian and Hibernian joined it and since the number of clubs was restricted to 16, Albion Rovers, Airdrie and Dumbarton were invited to withdraw. They displayed a natural indignation but were saved by force of circumstance. Almost alone, among Scottish clubs, Kilmarnock had their ground requisitioned—it was used as a fuel store—and had to withdraw from consideration. Ayr United did not answer the original letter of invitation and eventually, after an acrimonious Board meeting which led to the resignation of chairman and vice-chairman, declined to participate. It was felt better to omit Queen of the South since travelling to Dumfries in the winter months might prove difficult with a reduced train service.

The Southern League which started in August 1940 was therefore composed as follows:—Airdrieonians, Albion Rovers, Celtic, Clyde, Dumbarton, Falkirk, Hamilton Academical, Heart of Midlothian, Hibernian, Morton, Motherwell, Partick Thistle, Queen's Park, Rangers, St. Mirren and Third Lanark. But what about the East of Scotland?

The notion has gained ground that wartime football was prohibited by the Government in this area. That was not the case. It is true that there were restrictions which particularly affected the Forth Bridge and Tay Bridge areas but these would merely have limited the number of supporters who could have travelled with visiting teams and lack of transport would have had the same effect anyway.

It has to be said that Perth, Aberdeen and Dundee went without football in 1940 chiefly because of the stance taken by Dundee and St. Johnstone. The Perth club had lost over £2500 in 1939–40 and they now pre-empted further discussion by formally vacating their ground at Muirton Park, thereby saving rates and rent. Dundee were also keen to close down and made singularly little effort to carry on. Their fellow-townsmen Dundee United, who had just had their most successful season ever, losing narrowly and undeservedly to Rangers in the War Time Cup Final, were desperate to maintain momentum, to the extent that they even considered playing as Juniors and applied for membership of the S.J.F.A.

Just for a few weeks in the summer of 1940 it looked as if there might be a league of sorts in the East of Scotland. Dundee United and Dunfermline Athletic, both very enthusiastic, persuaded the clubs, Dundee, East Fife, Raith Rovers, King's Park, Stenhousemuir and St. Bernard to try for a Midland League but even although the S.F.A., in an unprecedented action, offered to guarantee the constituent clubs against loss, the idea foundered on the lack of keenness of the potentially most powerful club, Dundee. Ironically, Leith Athletic closed down, not because they wanted to but because they had not been asked to join. King's Park who had made a very small profit in 1939–40 were also greatly in favour of such a league but eventually the little Stirling club bowed to the inevitable and through their Managing Director, Tom Fergusson, who would later be celebrated as the founder of Stirling Albion, let it be known that if the scheme failed they would dispose of their equipment and go into abeyance.

It was time to tidy up the game. Because Scotland had paid £2 per week when England was only paying £1.10.0d there had been cases of Scots and Englishmen, working or stationed in the North of England, coming to Scotland to play at week-ends. More serious were the allegations of under the counter payments by Scottish clubs themselves and on the face of it it was odd that international Andy Black should prefer King's Park to his own club, Hearts. It was even odder that returning Anglos, their contracts voided by war, should show similar self-denial. Thus Willie Buchan, a most distinguished ex-Celt, turned out for the humble Stenhousemuir and stars such as Bill Shankly also played with lesser-known clubs such as King's Park. It had clearly been a widespread trend and Waverley was moved to say "There must be no under-the-counter stuff such as was prevalent last season." The S.F.A. therefore decided that Anglo-Scots and English players working or serving in Scotland must henceforth be properly transferred, even for short periods.

In the summer of 1940 invasion seemed imminent. St. Mirren had their ground taken from them temporarily and were allowed to play out of Ibrox although they incurred severe losses in so doing. Less sympathy was extended to Clyde when they informed the Southern League that their landlords, a greyhound company, might require Shawfield Stadium on Saturday afternoons. They offered to play their home games at nearby Rosebery Park, the ground of Shawfield Juniors, but were left in no doubt that this proposal was totally unacceptable to other clubs in membership of the league. Fortunately an accommodation was reached which preserved the use of Shawfield for Clyde on alternative Saturday afternoons.

There was no such thing now as the full time player. Players trained when and how they could, sometimes travelling to games overnight from their unit or shift in a factory and taking the field without sleep. David Meiklejohn, the celebrated Rangers player and Scottish internationalist, made the bizarre and drastic proposal that games should be limited to a duration of sixty minutes only, because players were not sufficiently trained to go the traditional ninety minutes distance after war work or service. The

Southern League, which was finding it hard enough to attract spectators to matches of the traditional length, saw a vision of empty terraces and hastened to discount the idea.

There was no formal reserve football although Rangers and Queen's Park kept second elevens in being to play friendly matches. The S.F.A. kept the game alive in those areas where league football had temporarily disappeared. More than 6000 spectators turned up at Stark's Park, Kirkcaldy early in 1941 for a representative match between the Army and the S.F.A. The success of such ventures led Waverley to write in the *Daily Record* "I am more than ever puzzled to understand why the clubs in the Midlands and East turned it up so easily."

Some Midlands clubs were already asking themselves this. Dundee United, Aberdeen and Dunfermline called a meeting in March 1941 which 17 non-functioning sides attended, including Dundee and St. Johnstone who indicated that nothing had happened to make them change their minds about war-time football. Among the clubs present were Cowdenbeath whose supporters now offered to run a team and be responsible for the financial side of things. Although the club had been fined £500 for quitting the Regional East League prematurely in 1940, this would not have prevented them joining the proposed North-Eastern League.

Attention shifted back to the Southern League. Its structure allowed for only 30 league matches per year as against 38 First Division matches pre-war. Moreover, there was no longer a Scottish Cup, which could mean four or five more fixtures had gone. To fill the gap the Southern League Management Committee now took a decision which was to rank among the most important ever taken in Scottish football. It was decided that there should be a League Cup with four sections of four clubs, each of which would play the others home and away. From the four section winners would come the semi-finalists. The notion was brilliantly successful and would prove to be a staple ingredient of post-war Scottish football.

The problem might well have been to devise a competition that Rangers would not win. They had taken the War Time Emergency Cup in defeating Dundee United and had won the Regional League play-off by defeating Falkirk, winners of the Eastern Section. Many of the Press were uneasy at what they considered to be scandalously partial refereeing however. There had been disputed decisions in Rangers favour in both matches and when Dumbarton were equally dissatisfied with the handling of a league match at Ibrox, *Waverley*, a normally phlegmatic writer, was moved to reply to a plea from Mr. R. Lindsay, Chairman of Dumbarton, "You are right in saying that Rangers don't want favours from referees but they certainly get them. I appeal to the S.F.A. to let it be known that so far as whistlers are concerned, all clubs are equal."

Rangers would go on, without benefit of referees let it be said, to win the Southern League championship for the five years of its existence with the original membership. They had no credible challengers until the last two years when Hibernian came close. The great weakness of the Southern League was the total lack of challenge from Celtic who almost seemed to have given up. It was abundantly not the time for their Chairman Tom White to say, as he did in February 1941, "Post-war players should all have civil jobs as well. The game would be healthier for it." Even if the sentiments were correct the timing was badly adrift.

Other clubs were more forward in discovering talent. On April 28 1941 there were groans from the comparatively small numbers of Hibernian supporters at Tynecastle in an end of season match when the Easter Road forward line was announced as containing two members of the Junior clan. Junior, Newman and Trialist were names which figured with great frequency in the wartime team lists, A. N. Other being now less popular with the virtual disappearance of amateurism. The concern of the Hibernian supporters was groundless for their team won 5–3 and the two unnamed Juniors turned out to be Bobby Combe and Gordon Smith, two of the most gifted players in the history of the club.

And for season 1941–42 there was to be a North-Eastern League. Aberdeen, Dundee United, East Fife, Dunfermline Athletic, Raith Rovers, St. Bernard, Leith Athletic, and Rangers would comprise the membership. Rangers would run their second eleven and it was their agreement to take part which tipped the scales and made such a league viable. This move was not universally popular and there was a counter-move from the Southern League to prevent Rangers joining the North-Eastern League on the grounds that a club could not be a member of two different leagues at the same time. The real reason for the opposition was that Rangers reserves playing at Ibrox could be competition for other Glasgow clubs. An unnamed Ibrox source (usually an indication that it was the manager, Mr. William Struth), described this opposition as "a pathetic admission by certain people of their inability to field a team capable of attracting public interest."

When this move seemed likely to succeed and Rangers participation in the new league hung in the balance, the remaining North Eastern clubs played a trump card. They threatened that they would not allow any of their players to play for Southern League clubs in the Summer Cup for, with the active encouragement of the

Government, football had become a year-round sport. This was a real blow for no fewer than four Aberdeen players were on loan and two from Raith Rovers. Further, the North Eastern clubs stated that they would invite a Scottish Command side to take over the last place and therefore military players would be unavailable to Southern League clubs.

Faced with this double-edged weapon the Southern League clubs saw sense and accepted as gracefully as might be. Certainly Rangers were highly popular in Fife, Dundee and Aberdeen, heartlands of the Scottish game which would no longer be starved of football. The Southern League saved face by extracting a promise that they would at all times field their strongest side in that competition, something which the Ibrox club would no doubt have done anyway.

In June 1941 the suspicion of under-the-counter payments to players became certainty when St. Mirren were fined £100 for illegal sums given to internationalists Jimmy Caskie of Everton and Leslie McDowall of Manchester City. Both players were also fined and debarred from again playing for St. Mirren while no fewer than five of the seven directors were suspended from any further involvement with the game. In the light of many other suspected instances the general feeling was that St. Mirren were extremely unfortunate to have been dealt with so severely.

That month of June 1941 in some respects marked a turning point, both in the war itself and in the smaller world of association football. Russia was invaded and from then on total German victory became much more improbable and the threat of invasion dwindled to nothing. People were coming out to football again. Hearts, Third Lanark and Celtic all made a profit, Celtic indeed turned a £7000 loss into a gain of £2365.

There were still difficulties and the material side of things would get harder. When Clyde complained to Morton in early June 1941 that the grass at Cappielow was too long for a Summer Cup tie there, the groundsman, Hugh Howat, explained that at each cut the blades of the mower had been chipped by shrapnel lying on the pitch, Greenock having been heavily bombed a few days before.

Albion Rovers were having trouble in fielding a respectable side and talked of closing down. Dundee were suggested as a possible replacement but this aroused much hostility because of the Dens Park club's lack of commitment to wartime football. How, it was asked, did they propose to travel to Glasgow when apparently travelling to Fife had been beyond them? Queen of the South, forced out of the league through no fault of their own, were felt to be a much better choice but in the end Albion Rovers decided to carry on and survived the war reasonably comfortably.

There were some telling events going on, if one looked carefully at the restricted coverage of wartime newspapers. Leith Athletic and St. Bernard would find it harder than the other North Eastern clubs to surmount their year's inactivity. The latter club advertised in the press for good young amateur players but there were very few of those about and Queen's Park had by far the best of them. There was a more poignant tale. In August 1941 Celtic fielded their great Exhibition forward line against Hearts. The five names, Delaney, McDonald, Crum, Divers, Murphy, were engrained in the hearts and minds of every Scottish football follower. Celtic lost, the five did not play well, and on the evidence of one game two of them were dropped and the five passed into history. Still, the fact that Celtic had decided to operate in the coming season with 20 players instead of the 14 of the previous one was an indication that perhaps their interest and appetite for the game were reviving.

The first evidence of that revival was unfortunate. There was large-scale rioting at a Southern League game between Rangers and Celtic at Ibrox in September 1941. The Lord Provost, Sir Patrick Dollan, well-disposed to the game in general although a scourge of mid-week football, was sweeping in his condemnation:

> "The Chief Constable has powers to prohibit games between Celtic and Rangers until the end of the war and I have informed him that if he cares to exercise that power he will have the support of all citizens. Every latitude has been allowed these clubs and I'm indebted to them for their considerable support for War Funds, but I would rather do without financial aid than obtain it at the price of good citizenship and the winning of the war."

Undoubtedly, the trouble had been caused by Celtic fans initially but refereeing was still a matter of considerable concern. Sandy Adamson, veteran sports reporter of the *Glasgow Evening News* writing on a Rangers match of the previous month said "Then came one of those dreary penalty awards to Rangers and the next thirty minutes were hard to endure." *Waverley* was forthright as ever:— "I have often wondered why referees stood so much questioning of decisions by Rangers players." So too, evidently did the S.F.A. War Emergency Committee.

That body had in the first place punished Celtic Football Club by closing Parkhead for one month forcing them to play their home games at Shawfield. In the third paragraph of their judgement, however occurred the following:

"That in view of the increasing prevalence of players showing dissent at referees' decisions—which the Committee considered too much in evidence on the part of Rangers players on September 6—referees are to be informed to deal firmly with dissent, whether by word, deed or gesture and any referee who fails to obey is to be immediately removed from the referees' list."

It is interesting to note that the Rangers inside-forward Alec Venters, sent off against Hibernian three weeks later and suspended for four months was thought to have been treated rather leniently!

There was more than one league in Scotland again and the North-Eastern competition was proving a great success. Although Rangers sometimes found it difficult to reach Aberdeen—they had to pick up a player from the Pittodrie terracing to complete their ranks for a cup-tie in November 1941—the second leg at Ibrox drew 14,000, although Rangers entered it three goals down. Their first team, at neighbouring Love Street that day, played to a mere 5,000. This is explained by the fact that Aberdeen, a mixture of pre-war favourites and distinguished Servicemen, were highly attractive opposition whereas Rangers swept everything comfortably before them in the Southern League and their fixtures lacked the greatest of football's ingredients, uncertainty.

The spring of 1942 was taken up by another great cup debate, this time as to whether the North-Eastern sides should be included in the League Cup. This was opposed on the grounds of travelling difficulties, although at that time of the season, late February, kick-offs could have been later. These objections were met. Aberdeen and Dundee United agreed to be drawn against each other in the first round to reduce the risk of long journeys for the South-Western clubs. Rangers met the difficulty of their having two teams in the competition by promising that anyone in their second eleven would have had to have played at least seven games for the North-Eastern side. The opposition changed tack and now said that Leith Athletic and St. Bernard would be no attraction.

There seemed to be two genuine grounds for opposition for which the above reasons were used as smokescreens. There was a reluctance, based on jealousy, to give Rangers two bites at the cherry, and there was a disinclination to upset a format of sixteen clubs in four sections which was very easy to run. The North-East clubs were furious when by 10 votes to 6 the Southern League clubs voted to leave the League Cup as it was. They passed the following resolution:

"The North-Eastern clubs regret the unsportsmanlike and unfriendly attitude of Southern League clubs. We refuse to accept as sincere the reason given for their refusal to participate in any competition which included teams in the North-Eastern League."

Any sympathy which one might have felt for the North-Eastern clubs was completely dissipated by their announcement on April 29 1942 that the two smaller Edinburgh clubs, Leith Athletic and St. Bernard, would not be invited to renew their membership for season 1942–43. They had struggled manfully to fulfil their obligations and this rebuff meant the end of the road for St. Bernard, Cup winners in their time. They made their last appearance in May 1942 and within a couple of years their ground had been sold. In their place and that of Leith Athletic came Hearts and Hibernian Reserves, hardly increasing the number of footballing outlets. At the same time the Glasgow and District Reserve League was set up, another stage in the slow inching-back towards normality.

The equipment position was anything but normal, however and it was perhaps as well that clubs did not know that fully another seven years of privation awaited them as the war moved into the autumn of 1942. All clothing, including sports gear, was now rationed and the clubs and Scottish Football Association, unable to function on an inadequate official allocation, were reduced to appealing to supporters to help out from their own personal clothing coupon ration. For the match against England at Hampden in April 1943 the Scottish side were exclusively kitted out (all except goalkeeper Jerry Dawson) from the pre-war jerseys of the great Scottish inside-forward, Tommy Walker. This prompts the irreverent thought that similarity in build to Walker might have been one of the first considerations in the Selectors' minds.

Transport was also causing grave difficulties. In an endeavour to lessen traffic on the railways and leave them clear for essential services, the Government ran an "Is Your Journey Really Necessary?" campaign and instructed the railways that cheap train fares should no longer be available for sporting occasions. Clubs could only obtain a bus for their players if they had an official permit and Celtic found theirs withdrawn in November 1942, at exactly the same time that the S.F.A. and Southern League agreed that the requirement to have a new ball for each match could be dispensed with until the end of the war.

The first day of 1943 brought a record defeat of Celtic by Rangers, 8-1 being the result of a Southern League match. The famous Parkhead club had floundered helplessly since parting with

IN UNIFORM
Sergeant Tommy Walker of the Signals calls home in a wartime broadcast from the Far East.

manager Willie Maley early in 1940. This was a decision which could be justified in terms of age, Maley was then well over 70, but his successor Jimmy McStay, himself a famous Celtic player, never seemed to regard himself as anything more than a temporary

TWO GREAT CAPTAINS
Matt Busby, who played much of his war-time football in Scotland, introducing Field Marshal Montgomery during a war-time international. Four Scots nearest the camera are (*l to r*) Delaney (Celtic), Duncanson (Rangers), Dodds (Blackpool) and Walker (Heart of Midlothian).

appointment and was unable to galvanise his Board into taking war-time football seriously.

Rangers carried almost everything before them. They won the League Cup on corners from Falkirk in a match which despite being played in May was cursed with such abominable weather that the wonder was that the game was completed. On the same day in the Mitchell Cup tie at Kirkcaldy between Raith Rovers and Aberdeen, the refereee had to abandon the match early in the second half when several players were on the point of collapse. It was the most spectacular May storm seen for many years but it could only be alluded to in the most guarded terms in newspaper accounts, in case such meteorological detail might assist the enemy.

Yet despite all difficulties, football was strengthening from month to month. Spectators were coming back and clubs moving into profit. In season 1942–43 Partick Thistle made £1804, Third Lanark £540, Hibernian £1076 and even Dumbarton revelled in a modest £98. The war was now in its fourth year, something highlighted by the fact that Hibernian now had no fewer than 30 players in the Forces. Even Motherwell, the majority of whose playing staff worked in the mines or heavy industry, nevertheless had 13 men away with the colours.

The North-Eastern League continued to be a seed-bed for ideas. With only eight members it ran its league in two separate series for 1943–44 and it decided that in the second of these, away wins would be rewarded with three points and away draws with two. Hibernian Reserves had dropped out and were rather disappointingly replaced by Falkirk Reserves, disappointingly in that the chance was lost to bring back one of the several clubs who had been out of football since 1940 but were eager to resume.

The Football League clubs, which had paid their players thirty shillings a week since the outbreak of war, now raised this sum to £2 which had always been the going rate in Scotland. This increase would help to solve the problem of the guest player, for there would now not be so many North of England Scots coming across the border in search of the extra ten shillings for their endeavours.

A GOOD BLOOD LINE
An early photograph of Tommy Gallacher with Queen's Park in 1942. Son of the famous Patsy of Celtic he later won a League Cup medal with Dundee. His nephew Kevin made his reputation with the other Dundee Club.

The summer of 1943 saw a brief check to the juggernaut success of Rangers. They lost 1-0 to St. Mirren in the final of the Summer Cup, a tournament which had been proposed by Harry Swan of Hibernian in 1941 and had gone from strength to strength, assisted by another of the Government's self-denial campaigns, Holidays at Home. Among the other rewards for winning, St. Mirren were allowed to meet Aberdeen at Hampden Park, the Dons having won the North-Eastern Cup competition. This was the first time for four years that Aberdeen had met a side in Glasgow at first-team level.

At this stage of the war, Winston Churchill was talking about "not the beginning of the end but the end of the beginning." The extremely carefree and cavalier ways of war would no longer do, in particular where the signing of players was concerned. There would therefore be an end to Service players turning up casually on week-end leave and playing for the

QUEEN'S PARK AT FULL STRENGTH
Three stalwarts home on war-time leave in 1945, (*l to r*) K. Chisholm, later to play for Leicester City in the 1949 F.A. Cup Final, R. Brown, Scotland International Goalkeeper and later National Team Manager, and David Letham, President of The Scottish Football League 1981–1985.

club of their choice. Hence forth, to be eligible for a temporary transfer a soldier, sailor or airman would have to be posted to a unit in the district where the club was located for which he wished to play.

This was a more orderly procedure and pleased the administrators. Less pleased were the spectators who had taken as one of the few consolations of war the chance to see such as Tommy Lawton and Stan Matthews play for Greenock Morton and the famous England goalkeeper, Frank Swift join Anglo-Scottish internationalists Willie Buchan and Alex Herd at Hamilton.

The employment of guest players had been a vexed question. Some clubs, such as Celtic and Partick Thistle would have little or nothing to do with imports from England. Celtic even turned down the services of Matt Busby, who ended up with Hibernian for two seasons. There his intelligent prompting brought on such players as Willie Finnigan, Gordon Smith and Bobby Combe and made the Edinburgh side a real power in the years immediately following the war. Other clubs, such as Dumbarton and Airdrie were able to field full internationalists for the first time for many years. The Scottish game was the undoubted gainer from this and in the North-Eastern League Stan Mortensen, a young Blackpool player, and Albert Juliussen, a Wearsider, demonstrated for

Aberdeen and Dundee United respectively why the English game was currently well ahead.

The year 1944 opened with a threat to Dundee Football Club. On January 25 it was reported that a syndicate of Dundee businessmen had made an offer for Dens Park with the aim of turning the ground into a greyhound racing stadium. The bid came to nothing but appears to have concentrated minds wonderfully in Juteopolis, as *Scottish Sport* had invariably referred to the Tayside city. By mid-April it was announced that Dundee had made application for membership of the North-Eastern League for season 1944–45. It had been hoped that St. Johnstone might join them but despite favourable conditions, not the least of which was that Perth as a garrison town was liberally endowed with players from the south, St. Johnstone declined the opportunity to restart. There is no doubt that this was to cost them heavily after the war.

King's Park were more enterprising. The Stirling side, although without a ground since the destruction of Forthbank by a German bomb in 1941, were willing to begin playing again, but their application was rejected, presumably on the grounds of their homelessness. With Dundee in harness the North-Eastern League looked as though it might stand at an awkward nine clubs but Arbroath were prevailed upon to resume operations in August 1944 and so matters settled.

Clubs were beginning to take thought for the future. Even Rangers, with the largest staff in Scotland were feeling the effects of four years non-stop football, with seasons that had lasted for eleven months without a break. They withdrew from the Second Eleven Cup of 1944 and intimated that they would likewise be unable to participate in the Summer Cup that year, a decision which was also taken by Celtic. Their places in the tournament would be taken by Raith Rovers and Dundee United, sides which without being anything like the same box-office attraction, would nevertheless have a certain charm of novelty in the West of Scotland.

One by one the old names crept back. Kilmarnock were not yet in a position to run a first team because their ground had been requisitioned in 1940 and had not yet been handed back to them. They did however manage to run a Glasgow and District Reserve League side in 1944–45 and played their home matches at Blair Park, the ground of neighbouring Hurlford Juniors. This meant that 24 of the pre-war 38 Scottish League clubs were now active in some shape or form.

There was a momentary flutter at the Annual General Meeting of the Southern League in the summer of 1944 when applications to join were received from Aberdeen and the newly-resurrected Dundee. There was a good deal of sympathy and support for the Aberdeen application as it was felt that there had been every effort made to keep things going during the war at Pittodrie. The same could not be said for that of Dundee. There was a widespread feeling that the Dens Park club would have to work its passage back to the top flight.

Even those clubs not quite ready to resume were taking stock seriously. St. Johnstone now served notice on Rangers that they would expect financial compensation for the services of Willie McIntosh, a free-scoring forward who had been on loan to the Ibrox club for three years. If terms could not be agreed, then they would transfer McIntosh to one of two other clubs, Hearts and Partick Thistle, who had expressed an interest. Elsewhere clubs were exploring the possibilities of retaining popular guest players on a permanent basis once hostilities were over. The war had now dragged on for five years and although casualties among footballers were markedly lower than in the 1914–18 conflict, this meant that many players had effectively lost more than half of a footballer's brief career. There would be many new faces when official League football eventually got under way again.

Dundee soon gave notice that their absence during the war years had been a distinct loss to Scottish football. Within days of their return to competitive football they attracted a crowd of 13,000 to their first home match, a record for a North-Eastern League fixture, and topped that immediately afterwards when 15,500 attended the first Tayside Derby for four years. The North-Eastern League was, in its last season, continuing an imaginative experiment by which an extra point was awarded for a win recorded away from home.

The end of the war was now in everyone's mind. St. Johnstone at last signified that they would resume in August 1945. That was in January of that year and the following month Kilmarnock and Ayr United both stated that they would resume full-scale operations, Kilmarnock being at last free to resume occupancy of their ground, Rugby Park. In March 1945 Alloa, who had been toppled from their hard-earned First Division place by the war, and Cowdenbeath also indicated that they would be playing after the summer. Cowdenbeath launched a drive which it was hoped would bring in £4000 to help them restart. Each supporter was to be asked to contribute £1 per head and it was calculated that a 50% response from their normal 8,000 gate would bring in the required amount.

There remained that handful of small League clubs which the Scottish League frankly hoped would go away. At a meeting of the

Forfarshire Association, exactly half of whose members were destined for the axe if the large clubs had their way, Provost John Lamb of Arbroath reflected their fears in these words:—

> "If the teams to comprise the First and Second Divisions postwar are selected irrespective of their positions in the pre-war Leagues then there will be a storm of indignation. There is only one sporting way to reduce the number of clubs in the post-war Divisions if that is deemed imperative. Let the clubs fight it out on the football field. Then those that go up will have something to be proud about while those who go down may have regrets but will have nothing to grumble about."

And so, the last few months of the Second World War raced to a close. Wartime football in Scotland ended as it had begun, with Rangers winning both the Southern League championship and the Southern League Cup. The Ibrox club had monopolised the championship and all but monopolised the Southern League Cup. They would now have to meet rather more serious challenges. The game in Scotland had survived, even if only just at times. The six years immediately past had not been all loss. Some prominent Anglo-Scots had been seen again in the colours they originally wore. Spectators had been exposed to real greatness in the shape of the war-time England team which, even allowing for the unavailability of top-line Scottish players—this has been much exaggerated, the bulk of leading Scottish internationalists did not serve abroad—had begun to hint at a vast gap in standards opening between the two countries.

The North-Eastern League, with its innovatory ideas of a pool of a stated proportion of gate money and its awarding of extra points for draws and victories away from home, had played a crucial part in keeping football alive in large areas of Scotland between 1939 and 1945. And finally, there had been the additional bonus of being able to see many foreign players, members of the European forces in exile, who were to demonstrate that the Continentals were catching up on their masters fast, and might indeed have already surpassed them in ball control if not yet in shooting power. Some of the Polish players in particular would stay on to make a name in Scotland, men such as Alfie Lesz of St. Mirren and Feliks Staroscik of Third Lanark. Most of the pre-war Anglo-Scots went back south but a few, such as Gordon Bremner of Arsenal and Torry Gillick of Everton remained to grace Scottish fields, in their cases with Motherwell and Rangers respectively. Only one thing could be said with any certainty about Scottish football in 1945 and that was that it would not be a carbon copy of those last few days of the 1939–40 season.

Chapter Seven

THE POST-WAR YEARS

In many respects season 1945–46 was even more strange than the six that had gone immediately before. Preparations were made for it in the belief that it would be another wartime season. Germany and Italy had surrendered in early May 1945 but there remained Japan and the defeat of that nation would, people thought, require a bloody and full-scale campaign with many of those Servicemen now no longer needed in Western Europe having to switch to the Pacific theatre of war.

Two divisions were to operate in Scottish Football, once more under the control of The Scottish League, and to mark the fact that they bore no direct relations to those of 1939 they were called A and B Divisons rather than First and Second. As a reward for meritorious wartime service Aberdeen were transferred to Division A and both Kilmarnock (who had fielded a reserve side in the previous season) and Queen of the South emerged from compulsory wartime closure. In B Division the fresh starts were Cowdenbeath, Ayr United, Stenhousemuir, Alloa and St. Johnstone. The full composition of the Divisions was as follows:—

A DIVISION:— Aberdeen, Clyde, Celtic, Falkirk, Hamilton Academical, Heart of Midlothian, Hibernian, Kilmarnock, Morton, Motherwell, Partick Thistle, Queen's Park, Queen of the South, Rangers, St. Mirren and Third Lanark.

B DIVISION:— Airdrieonians, Albion Rovers, Alloa, Arbroath, Ayr United, Cowdenbeath, Dumbarton, Dundee, Dundee United, Dunfermline Athletic, East Fife, Raith Rovers, St. Johnstone and Stenhousenuir.

Assurances were given that these groupings would only be temporary but almost immediately, with the astonishingly sudden surrender of Japan only a few days into the new season, post-war reconstruction of the League became a matter of urgency. There would have to be a re-shaping and this would have to be done by the legislators quite deliberately as promotion and relegation, which would normally have managed this for them, was not in operation.

Moreover there was the question of those small clubs which had

EASY, MARSHAL!

Players were desperate to resume serious football in 1946, no-one more so than Archie Kelly of Hearts who had the misfortune to injure a shoulder and crack a post in this Tynecastle meeting with Kilmarnock.

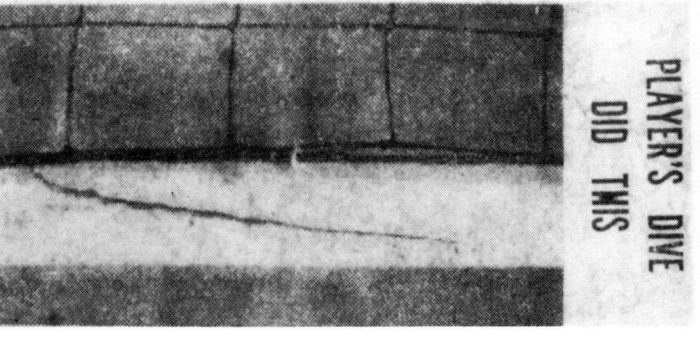

been forced out of League football in 1939–1940 but which had been revived without exception, much to the chagrin of some leading Scottish League officials, and they were now looking for a field of operation. All the 38 clubs in Scotland had survived the war save two. St. Bernards have already been mentioned and their ground, Royal Gymnasium had been sold from beneath the feet of at least some of their committee in September 1943, although even at that there were those who entertained hopes of an amalgamation with Leith Athletic or perhaps a certain independent existence. The very last act in the chronicles of this famous old Edinburgh club would be to enter for the Qualifying Cup of 1946 although they did not actually take part.

The other casualty was the Stirling side, King's Park, whose ground, Forthbank, had been destroyed by almost the only bomb dropped on the town during the war. To most people's surprise, King's Park were not reconstituted, (they could at least partially have been recompensed) for the destruction of their grandstand owing to enemy action). Instead a new club, Stirling Albion was formed, which was going to have to fight very hard indeed to secure membership of The Scottish Football League. As King's Park, its re-admission would have been automatic so perhaps the change of name signified something of the pre-war indebtedness of the old Stirling club.

In the meantime the question remained of what to do with those clubs who were *bona fide* members of the Scottish League but had not, for whatever reason, been included in either of the two divisions. The solution arrived at was to form an Eastern League with Dundee Reserves, Dundee United Reserves and the remaining small clubs, Stirling Albion, Montrose, East Stirlingshire, Edinburgh City, Leith Athletic, Forfar Athletic and Brechin City in membership. The small clubs accepted this demotion with reasonably good grace; they had been assured, after all, that these allocations were merely temporary.

The fear that they might not be began to emerge quite soon. Those who had wished to reform Scottish football and who argued that the peculiar population distribution of Scotland would never allow automatic promotion and relegation to work successfully, were vigorous in their contention that there would never be a better time than in the immediate aftermath of the war. Their opponents were equally vocal in their assertions that a club could only be expelled from The Scottish Football League for proven breach of rule. The spectators, coming back in increasing numbers from the Forces were much more interested in the re-appearance of pre-war favourites. Now that the likes of Peter McKennan of

From the Gymnasium to Old-Meadowbank

HAVE STAND WILL TRAVEL
In the 100 year history of The Scottish Football League, the travelling grandstand is not unknown. When St. Bernard's folded in 1945 this one made the short one-mile trip to Old Meadowbank, Leith Athletic acquiring it.

Partick Thistle, Jimmy Mason of Third Lanark, Tommy Walker of Heart of Midlothian, Willie Thornton of Rangers and George Paterson of Celtic could once more be seen on Scottish grounds of a Saturday afternoon, they were not too involved for the moment with the finer points of League re-construction.

In this they were mistaken. The decision arrived at would largely determine how many of these players would continue to play in Scottish football and for how long. Rangers won this interim Division A and Dundee, to nobody's great surprise, took the Division B title. These successes were gratifying for the clubs concerned but in the long term comparatively unimportant. What was important was the structure of the Divisions for 1946–47, and matters were not helped by the wreckage and confusion of the larger world outside.

There would be no quick return to what citizens of the 1930s would have recognised as peacetime conditions, that process would in fact take almost ten years. Till the middle 1950s building permits would be hard to get, petrol would be severely rationed, food rations more meagre than during the early stages of the war and mid-week football almost restricted to the public holidays on which it had been permitted between 1939–45 as the country lurched from one fuel crisis to another.

THE POST-WAR YEARS

It is interesting to consider the different approaches taken by the Football League and Scottish League towards post-war reconstruction. The Football League had agreed that in the interests of equity and fairness, season 1946–47 must be exactly what season 1939–40 would have been without war. Astonishingly, in view of the number and intensity of attacks on English football grounds, every one of the 88 clubs had survived to take up its appointed place.

The Scottish solution was far different. In the early months of the winter of 1946 the air was thick with talk of a Super League which would be confined to 14 or at most 16 clubs. Ground capacity would determine who should be invited to join the elect and thus Queen's Park would be included at the expense of other clubs with a more distinguished playing record. There would be no automatic relegation from this league and the impression was given that new clubs would have to make a very strong case to be voted in as replacements.

The scheme came to nothing since it was always improbable that the majority of League clubs would vote for what in effect would have been a slow death. Clubs would accept Second Division football so long as there was a prospect, however remote, of a First Division spot if they performed well enough on the field. The Super League died stillborn but the Scots were far from emulating the English pattern of an exact return to the pre-war situation. To do so would have been to re-instate Cowdenbeath, Ayr United, St. Johnstone and Alloa to the First Division, or Division A as it would be called for the next 10 years or so. With the exception of the last-named club, none of them had been exactly committed to the cause of wartime football and there was undoubtedly an element of retribution in the allocation of clubs. It was pointed out that Cowdenbeath had been out of league football for five years but so too for that matter had Queen of the South. There had been some thought that B Division might be expanded to 16 clubs but this did not happen, instead a C Division was formed which was made up of the Eastern League teams and various reserve sides. There was a sop to the "minnows", as they began to be called, in that if C Division were to be won by any one of them promotion to B Division would follow.

The wisdom of that provision was seen in that Stirling Albion who attracted crowds of 8,000 to their new ground, Annfield, won promotion almost straightaway and after a couple of years further embarrassed their detractors by going up to Division A in one of the most spectacular ascents in the history of Scottish football. The fact that they were unable to consolidate in the top flight and

HOW CAN YOU BUY
WILLIE WADDELL?

(with apologies to the composer of
"How Can You Buy Killarney?")

An Englishman landed in Edmiston Drive,
And watched Willie Waddell with critical eye,
"How can I buy him?" he asked Mr. Struth,
And Bill he replied, "I'll tell you the truth."

Chorus:
How can you buy all the Cups that we've won,
And how can you buy Mrs. Thornton's son,
How can you buy our big Georgie Young?
 And how can you buy Willie Waddell?
nature bestowed all her gifts with a smile,
The right foot, the left foot, the "noddle,"
When you can buy all these wonderful things,
 Then you can buy Willie Waddell.

2nd Verse:
"I'll give Thirty Thousand," the Englishman said,
"And also a star," Mr. Struth shook his head.
"You can give Thirty Thousand, stars, moon and sun,
But you still can't have Waddell, there's only one."

A SONG FOR A WINGER
This parody of a popular song of the late 1940's extols the footballing skills of Willie Waddell, Rangers international winger who later became their manager.

---

shuttled frequently between the two Divisions, A and B, should not be allowed to detract from the very real magnitude of their achievement.

Stirling Albion were a success. At the other end of the scale the perennially optimistic Edinburgh City had drawn thirty shillings as gate money in an Eastern League match against East Stirlingshire or, put another way, approximately 60 people had thought it worth their while to attend. Such a state of affairs could not possibly continue. Over the next ten years the small clubs would fight a most skilful and prolonged battle to achieve proper League status once more. They would win, but it would be too late for Edinburgh City, by then out of existence after a brief and equally unsuccessful flirtation with Junior football.

The twenty years after the war were perhaps the most competitive in the history of Scottish League football. In that time the championship would be won by Rangers, Celtic, Heart of Midlothian, Hibernian, Aberdeen, Dundee and Kilmarnock. Of these, Hibernian and Heart of Midlothian would win it more than once and Dundee should certainly have won it more than once. The return to professional wages was deeply damaging for Queen's Park who from 1944–47 in the absence of attractive paid alternatives had put together a side capable of taking on the best in Scotland. Now, losing half their side in each of three successive seasons, they were unable to maintain their place in Division A and with a brief flurry of an exception in the mid 1950s their days among the top Scottish clubs were over. They just managed to stay up in the first post-war season but could not repeat the performance the following year. In contrast Dundee did not seem to have suffered greatly from their self-imposed wartime hibernation. They came up in 1947, and with an astute mix of English and Scots players finished a strong fourth in 1948. They should have capped a remarkable recovery by winning the League in 1948–49, for they were easily the best footballing side in Scotland at the time but nerves got the better of them on the last day. They lost 4–1 at Falkirk, missing a penalty in the process, and so allowing Rangers—who rarely if ever lost in that type of situation—to nip in and take the championship by defeating Albion Rovers by the same score at Coatbridge. Dundee had profited greatly at this time by their association with George Anderson, their Managing Director, who had formerly been connected with Aberdeen.

With the League Cup, growing in success every year, very much in mind it was felt that the optimum formula for Scottish football was two divisions, each of sixteen clubs. Accordingly, Division B was expanded in 1947 by the promotion of Stirling Albion who had won C Division and the election of Leith Athletic who were destined to have but one more season in the mainstream of Scottish football. It is singular to reflect that of the four permanent casualties sustained by Scottish football since 1945 (if we consider Stirling Albion a straight replacement for King's Park) no fewer than three of them have been Edinburgh clubs. Stranraer applied for membership but geographical remoteness ruled them out.

In June 1947 a very rare event indeed happened. The Scottish Football League was in need of a Secretary for Willie MacAndrew was retiring after 48 years as Secretary/Treasurer. His connection went right back to the very earliest days of the League when Abercorn, Port Glasgow and Linthouse were members and St. Bernards a First Division side. His calm, phlegmatic demeanour had defused many a volatile situation at League meetings but he now moved into retirement, having stayed on to give some sort of continuity over the war years. In his place came James F. Denovan from Dumbarton, invariably known as Fred and under whose secretaryship the League was to make considerable advances.

The five years following the Second World War saw crowds of unparalleled size flock to Scottish football matches. The crowds

JIMMY MASON
One of the last of the classical Scottish inside forwards, his frail physique masked a surprising strength on the ball.

were by no means confined to the big clubs, Queen of the South on several occasions attracted more than 15,000 people to their compact Palmerston Park and Queen's Park and Kilmarnock had 28,000 at Hampden for a B Division match. Most staggering of all, though not strictly a League concern, was the 87,000 who turned out to watch a Glasgow Cup final between Celtic and Third Lanark at Hampden Park in 1948 although it has to be said that Cup Finals were as rare for Celtic supporters then as they would be commonplace twenty years later.

Leith Athletic dropped out of Division B in 1948 and were replaced by East Stirlingshire whose stay was to be equally brief. The small clubs were not making the best case for inclusion—at least on a playing basis—and their cause was not helped by a decision of the League Management Committee to operate two divisions of Division C, North-East and South-West, which effectively meant that for one of the small clubs to gain promotion, it would have to finish above such as the reserve sides of Aberdeen, Hearts, Rangers and Celtic. This would certainly make the attainment of promotion more difficult, which of course was exactly the idea. The re-arrangement of Division C worked to the advantage of Stranraer who, suddenly less geographically inaccessible, were admitted in May 1949. They had earned their admission, for the year before they had held Rangers to a solitary goal in a Scottish Cup tie on their own Stair Park. At the same time Forfar Athletic replaced East Stirlingshire in Division B.

The latter team came up with an ingenious proposal at the Annual General Meeting of 1950. The ingenuity lay not in the idea that B Division should go up to 20 clubs by the admission of Brechin, Montrose, Leith Athletic and themselves, that was the standard motion from the small clubs, East Stirling had the wit to recognise that 32 clubs consitututed the ideal basis for the League Cup and 36 would present difficulties. They therefore proposed that the four newly-admitted clubs be excluded from the League Cup as should in subsequent seasons the four clubs which finished in the four last places in Division B. Ingenious or not, there was little support for the motion on its being canvassed around and it was withdrawn without actually being put to the vote.

As an indication that football had a heart East Stirlingshire had been granted permission to present their players with electric clocks to mark their winning of "C" Division. There had been some confusion over official medals and the club was determined that this kind of success, which came rarely to Firs Park, should not go unrecorded.

At a higher level the Scottish League was unhappy with its

LAWRIE REILLY
This quick silver centre-forward was a great favourite at club and international level. One of the famous five of Hibernian, his penchant for scoring late goals for Scotland won him the title of "Last Minute" Reilly.

number of representatives on the S.F.A. Council and wanted these to be increased to twelve. The S.F.A. offered nine and the League was inclined to accept this but not the S.F.A. notion that the additional members should come as far as possible from clubs not already represented on the Council. The League argued that it should be free to nominate what it considered to be its best men, no matter whence they came, but in this as in the question of numbers the S.F.A. carried the day.

At this stage the League championship had developed the pattern, which it would sustain for the next five years or so, of being a two-horse race between Rangers and Hibernian. One reason why this should be so was contained in the news that nine Rangers players had been given benefit payments (which meant they had been with the club for at least five years) and Hibernian made similar payments to only one player fewer.

Hibernian had felt themselves strong enough in October 1948 to withdraw a request for postponement of a League match against Partick Thistle although they would have been entitled to this under rule as three of the Edinburgh club's players had been selected for the international match with Wales. The League's note on the subject indicated that times were still abnormal:—

"The League was pleased to hear that the application had been withdrawn and the necessity of playing a mid-week game in these troubled times avoided."

Canny stewardship, not without occasional flashes of generosity, continued to be the hallmark of League administration. It was left to clubs to decide whether they wished to operate a special gate for Old Age Pensioners at a reduced rate but where they decided in favour of this, care was to be taken to prevent abuse of the system. The B.B.C. had begun to run a regular Saturday evening sports programme and were paying the League £150 per annum for the right to broadcast commentaries. This sum was given by the League to the Players' Benevolent Fund. Individual clubs were due another £115 for making facilities available to the Corporation and the League suggested that the clubs might care to donate these fees in like manner to the same objective.

The autumn of 1949 had seen considerable crowd trouble at the first two Old Firm matches of the season, one at Ibrox, the other at Parkhead. In each instance Celtic had expressed themselves very unhappy with the referee and they now asked that the next two scheduled games against their old rivals should be postponed indefinitely, to allow tempers to cool. The Scottish League did not accede to this request nor did they endorse Celtic's wish that in future Old Firm matches should be handled by a non-Scot.

Four years had now elapsed since the end of the war and gradually those who had played League football before 1939 were disappearing. In an attempt to salvage something for those who had in some cases lost six years from an already short career, a case based on the enormous crowds attending matches, the Players' Union asked for a sum of £30,000 to be raised to institute a Provident Fund for players. This would be done by way of a levy on all matches and a player would get a sum equivalent to 10% of his yearly earnings.

A similar scheme was being canvassed in England but official reaction in Scotland was unsympathetic. Mr. Robert Kelly (later Sir Robert) of Celtic denounced the scheme as harebrained and said that comparisons between Scotland and England were useless. He pointed out that 84% of Scottish players were part-timers and questioned why such a fund should be created for players who had other employment. Individual cases of hardship were treated more compassionately, the League donating £50 to the benefit fund of Billy Campbell, the Morton international wing half-back compelled to quit the game by serious illness.

Nothing pleased The Scottish Football League better than the occcasional assertion of its own mind where the S.F.A. was concerned. During the war clubs had gone back to the old system of paying referees and linesmen directly. The S.F.A. now proposed that it or the League should be responsible for paying the requisite fees and thereby avoiding the embarrassing scenes which had sometimes taken place when a referee went to receive payment from a club which felt that it had been badly done by. On this occasion the League did not take the enlightened view. It informed the S.F.A. that it did not think the change necessary, the League Secretary adding that his masters meant to continue the present method.

It was a time of much discontent. Celtic submitted a letter saying that their wing-half, Robert Evans, did not desire to be considered for Inter-League and International honours "for very good and personal reasons". These were that a section of the Scottish crowd at international matches had barracked him severely and indicated other preferences for his position. The Management Committee while deploring this occurrence and well aware that such incidents had happened, nevertheless decided, as they were bound to do, that the player if selected must comply with the rules of the League in this respect and make himself available for selection.

Players and their representatives were beginning to question the established order of things. In particular they were unhappy with the Retain and Transfer system, whereby a player could effectively be tied up by his present club provided that they had made him timeously a recognised minimum wage offer. The small scale of permitted benefits £650, later raised to £750, after five years and taxable, contrasted most unfavourably with the £14,000 tax free awarded to the Test cricketers of the day, such as Cyril Washbrook and Denis Compton. The discrepancy was all the more marked in Compton's case because he was also a professional footballer of repute and but for his summer game he would have been in receipt of a miserly £750 less tax.

The Players Union occasionally overstated what was in essence a very good case. To say that where a player was dissatisfied with his lot and appealed to the Management Committee he was appealing to the very people who had put him in his original situation was only half the story. Where appeals against transfer fees on the heads of unhappy players were concerned, the Managmenet Committee had a very good record in reducing these to less fanciful and more realistic sums.

No matter how drastically reduced on appeal however, such appeals were time-consuming and time is never on the side of the professional footballer. His only viable alternative was to opt out of the League system altogether and find a non-league club and it is true that at the time these paid good wages. They were however all in England and such a step at a time of national housing shortage almost inevitably meant prolonged separation from one's family.

Players were right to be aggrieved. It was not that their weekly wage was terribly low, relatively speaking. Most Scottish footballers in First Division sides were making between £10–12 per week and they were doing well by the standards of most of their watchers. But if we take the average attendances for leading League clubs in a season as late as 1956–57, Rangers averaged 36,000, Hearts 24,500, Celtic and Hibernian 18,000. A top-liner in a variety show in a Glasgow theatre at that time, playing to a maximum weekly capacity of 12,000 would expect and receive a salary well into three figures.

The players could have done better had they but taken legal advice which was offered to them. The grotesque differences between the benefits of footballers and cricketers alluded to just now stemmed from a case which reached the House of Lords in 1927, *Reed v Seymour*. Their Lordships held that Seymour, a Kent cricketer, need not pay tax on the proceeds of a benefit match because the money realised was in the nature of a personal gift, a token of esteem. On the other hand, the benefit paid to a professional footballer was a payment made by the football club out of their funds as part of a contractual obligation, and as such attracted taxation. The trick was to have a benefit organised by a self-standing committee, independent of the player's club, but although Bob Thyne of Kilmarnock had exactly such a benefit around 1951, it would take almost another twenty years before footballers and their representatives realised how valuable it would be to have a "token of esteem" from admirers rather than the discharge of a contractual obligation by their present employers.

The whole fabric of British professional football was thought to depend on the maintenance of the Retain and Transfer system and its unquestioned acceptance by the players themselves. There were signs that this acceptance might be of limited duration. Acting on behalf of two East Fife players, Allan Brown and George Aitken, both internationalists, the Scottish Professional Footballers Union threatened that unless both players got their wish and were placed on the Transfer List they would take the matter to the Court of Session.

In the end that was unnecessary. East Fife fought a spirited and bitter delaying action but eventually both players went south, Aitken after a brief stop-off with Third Lanark. This solved the

142　　　　　　　THE FIRST 100 YEARS

WILLIAM McNAUGHT
(Raith Rovers)
This classical exponent of full-back play exhibited his skills in the comparative obscurity of Stark's Park. In an age when backs were primarily long kickers, his astute use of the ball was a revelation. He was a powerful influence in the development of the young Jim Baxter.

BILLY HOULISTON
(Queen of the South)
Like Willie Sharp, Houliston played all his football in Scotland. His interpretation of centre-forward play was vigorous rather than thoughtful but it earned him a place in the Scotland side which won 3–1 at Wembley in 1949.

personal problems of the players but left unresolved the deeper question. This was quite simply, how could the Scottish game be kept credible if its star performers were continually creamed off to the South? At the moment the situation was contained, if only just, because of the existence of maximum wage in England but if that were to go, and there were signs that it was under heavy fire, the lure of England might prove totally irresistible. If in addition the Scottish League were ever to devise a more competitive format, so that players of the leading Scottish clubs could not rely on bonuses which nine weeks out of ten were almost automatic, that would further exacerbate the situation. In a well-intentioned attempt to alleviate matters the League sanctioned the payment of talent money to championship sides. The winners of A Division could be paid up to £1000 for the whole side and £500 was allotted to the winners of B Division.

The dice were being loaded against the small clubs. The unspoken though dreaded possibility was that both sections of C Division could be won by clubs eligible for promotion, say, East Stirlingshire and Brechin City. To guard against such an event promotion would only be awarded if the Management Committee was satisfied that the ground of any such club was suitable for holding B Division games.

There were 38 league clubs in League membership with almost as many ideas on what shape the Divisions should take. Thus, at the A.G.M. of 1952 East Fife had a proposal for two Divisions of 20 and 18, East Stirlingshire wanted 16 and 22, Stenhousemuir, more forward-looking, wanted 16 and two 12's on regional distribution and Stirling Albion a staggering 42 club League, not as bizarre as it first looked when the Stirling club went on to explain

THE POST-WAR YEARS

WILLIE SHARP
(Partick Thistle)

In a 17 year spell at Firhill Willie Sharp personified the good club man. He played for the Scottish League and is the scorer of the fastest goal recorded in Scottish League football, scoring after 7 seconds versus Queen of the South in 1947.

that this would allow senior clubs to be located in the new towns of East Kilbride, Cumbernauld, Livingston and Glenrothes, towns which were either projected or in the actual building. Failure to act on this last proposal was to mean the loss of many thousands of potential supporters to the game over the next twenty years.

The chance to put teams in to grow up with the new towns was not taken but the most famous of old town rivalries continued to cause much trouble to the game's rulers. After large-scale disorder at the Old Firm match of New Year's Day 1952 at Parkhead the Glasgow magistrates made the following recommendations:

1. That the clubs should no longer meet on New Year's Day.

2. That Celtic and Rangers matches should in future be all-ticket and that a crowd limit consistent with safety should be imposed.

3. Such a figure should be determined by the Chief Constable.

4. That Celtic F.C. should construct numbered passageways at Parkhead to facilitate the work of the first-aid services and of the police.

5. That no flags should be exhibited liable to cause offence to the followers of one side or the other.

The League Management Committee made a reasoned if defensive reply. They rejected the first point and said that the conditions of the second were already met. Celtic would co-operate with regard to the construction of numbered passageways and the League kept its sting in the tail for the final point. Which flags, it enquired innocently, did the Magistrates have in mind? The Committee knew perfectly well that while the flying of the Tricolour of the Republic of Ireland excited animosity, so too did the use of the national flag, the Union Flag, when flaunted as a party or sectarian emblem. Nor was the Scottish League convinced that the Magistrates were doing all that they might. "It was their (the League's) firm conviction that the Magistrates could assist considerably by proper use of the powers with which they were invested". Their reply went on to say:

HARRY HADDOCK

WILLIE TELFER

DOUG COWIE

JIMMY GABRIEL

BILLY STEVENSON

BERT McCANN

SCOTTISH PLAYERS OF THE 1950s
Harry Haddock (Clyde), Willie Telfer (St. Mirren), Doug Cowie (Dundee),
Jimmy Gabriel (Dundee), Billy Stevenson (Rangers), Bert McCann (Motherwell).

"So far as the New Year's Day fixture between the clubs is concerned the Management Committee cannot agree that the arguments advanced by the Magistrates are sufficient to warrant any re-arrangement of the fixture. An examination of the records down the 50-odd years of this fixture reveals that there have been very few incidents of any kind on a New Year's Day. Another factor which weighs with the Management Committee is that this fixture is regarded as part of Glasgow's New Year celebrations and is eagerly anticipated by many thousands of law-abiding citizens. It was also felt that in acceding to this recommendation the Committee would simply be yielding to a very small proportion of the vast football-loving public by giving them the satisfaction of having disrupted club fixtures which over the years have been traditional in the Scottish League calendar."

Strong stuff, but the League had under-estimated the strength of the "very small proportion" or for that matter the increasing annoyance of the citizenry as a whole and the time was fast approaching when this most ritualistic of matches would no longer take place on the first day of the year.

Meantime attendances were still buoyant and how could they fail to be with forwards such as Conn, Bauld and Wardhaugh of Hearts, and the entire Hibernian forward line of Smith, Johnstone, Reilly, Turnbull and Ormond? Rangers, although inherently relying on a supremely well-marshalled defence, had also players of considerable distinction in their front line of whom Waddell, Gillick and Thornton were best-known. It is significant that all the above players, with the exception of Johnstone of Hibernian, played out their footballing days in Scotland and even he came back north eventually. More than that, Scottish football made perhaps its most breathtaking acquisition from England when Billy Steel came back from Derby County to join Dundee at the unheard-of transfer fee of £17,500.

Relations with the S.F.A. were prickly at this period and there were two causes for this. Following on the trouble at the Parkhead match on New Year's Day, Celtic had been commanded by the S.F.A. to desist from flying the flag of the Irish Republic on match days. When they refused they were told that they would be expelled from membership of the Association. The club's directors made it perfectly clear that the club would go into oblivion rather than comply, being perfectly sure that a club could only legitimately be expelled from the Association for proven breach of a rule embodied in the Constitution and in that Constitution there

BILLY STEEL

His transfer from Derby County to Dundee in 1950 for a then record British transfer fee (£17,500) did much to inject confidence to the Scottish game. Strong, stocky and skilful, Steel helped Dundee to two consecutive League Cup successes.

was not the remotest mention of flags. The determination of Celtic to go out of existence if necessary sent a shudder of apprehension through the other League clubs—it is significant that throughout the whole matter their most staunch supporters were Rangers—and there was considerable resentment in League circles at what was taken to be the high-handed attitude of the S.F.A. The League was annoyed that it had not been sufficiently consulted, had not been consulted at all, and in a terse note requested that "Before any such action be taken in future an opportunity for consultation with the League be given". In the end the S.F.A. backed down, as Robert Kelly of Celtic had always known they would.

The other cause of tension was the increasing conflict between clubs and country on the subject of international matches. These last were proliferating greatly, even if still far from the one a month rate of the 1980s. Club managers were not paid to promote the Scottish international team's fortunes nor did their own careers depend upon its success or lack of it. Their duty was to do the best they could for their own clubs and therefore public criticism of them was sometimes misplaced, if vociferous. A noted case arose in April 1953 when Rangers insisted on playing two of their staff, George Young and Sammy Cox, against Airdrieonians on the Wednesday night before the two were due to appear against England at Wembley.

This meant that the players would have to travel south independently, which the S.F.A. declared to be unacceptable. Despite that, the two Rangers players turned out for their club and matters were not improved when Cox was injured early in the international although there was no reason to connect the two events. Increasingly, the money would be in club football and the accommodation of international committments would become harder, not easier. The Scottish Football Association asked that in future no League matches should be arranged within the four days prior to a Saturday international. The Management Committee stated in return that while they were very willing to co-operate they would not bind themselves to a hard and fast rule because of the many difficulties created by postponed matches.

In that year of 1953 another well-known name left the Scottish League scene. The composition of the reserve Leagues, as C Division was known in everyday speech, was increasingly causing concern. For the major clubs in the North and East the reserve teams were becoming a horrendous drain on finances. As early as August 1952 Aberdeen had given warning that they would not fulfil mid-week fixtures at Stirling, Kirkcaldy and Leith. They were warned of serious consequences if they did not and played under

WILLIE BAULD (*Heart of Midlothian*)
Thoughtful, intelligent, in some ways ahead of his time, "the King" won League, League Cup and Scottish Cup medals with the fine Hearts side of the late 1950s. He is indelibly associated with the others of that inside trio, Alfie Conn and Jimmy Wardhaugh and like them died comparatively young.

protest. But just as disenchanted with the set-up were Leith Athletic themselves and in July 1953 they intimated that they would not participate in Division C (North and East) the following season although they wished to retain their membership of the Scottish League. They were informed that this was not possible and expelled under Rule 45 at a Special General Meeting on Friday August 28 1953. They lived on for a year or so, appearing for Scottish Cup-ties, and then sank beneath the waves. They deserve a passing sympathetic salute because, like St. Bernards, they had been deprived of promotion to the First Division in the days before automatic promotion and relegation. Their going, and the increasing dissatifaction with C Division, brought the continued League existence of the other small clubs into question.

Away from C Division, gates were still generally good however and the Scottish Professional Footballers' Association not unreasonably wished a share of this prosperity for their members. They now put in a claim in the autumn of 1953 for playing and close season wages of £9 and £7 per week for full-time Division A players, £6 and £5 for part-time Division A players, £4 and £3 for Division B players and £2 throughout the year for Division C players. They also wanted Union representation at appeals against any disciplinary sentence and a proportion of transfer fees to be set aside to supplement the Players' Benevolent Fund. The Management Committee, aware that the players were in a very weak position in that, in a career as short as that of a footballer time is never on the side of a striking player, intimated regretfully that if the players wanted to go on strike so be it. The League did relent to the extent of allowing Union representation at any final hearing. The Players Union came back the following year and were equally unsuccessful with claims for two year contracts and benefit entitlements of £250 per year of service, the first being rejected as "not practicable" and the second because "the economic position of clubs did not justify a change in the present rate" although there were at least a dozen clubs who could well have afforded this.

Meanwhile a new and long-running vexatious question had arisen. What should be the League's attitude towards television? The mid-50's saw a succession of highly-successful televised English floodlit friendlies, particularly a series of matches involving Wolverhampton Wanderers and although competitive floodlit football was not yet permitted it would assuredly come. The four national associations agreed that while there would be no blanket ban on matches as such, matches in mid-week at least, there would be restrictions on viewing where necessary and these principles would be applied to floodlit matches as well. The B.B.C. did not help by badly over-playing its hand early in the proceedings with the transmission of a match between France and Germany in October 1954 against the wishes of the footballing authorities. The Scottish League was faced, not for the first time, with the task of doing the best it could for all its members, a difficult assignment given their wide disparity in wealth and aspirations. At the top end of the scale the big clubs were now beginning to look towards Europe while in Division C Berwick Rangers and East Stirling could be censured for not having hot water available to the opposition at the end of matches. Entertainment Tax too was creaming off much-needed money from the game and both League and Association advised all clubs to contact their local Member of Parliament with a view to bringing pressure on the Chancellor of the Exchequer to have Entertainment Tax removed from at least the first 5000 spectators. This was at the suggestion of Dunfermline Athletic and the effect of this proposal, if successful, would have been to exempt the majority of B Division clubs from paying any Entertainment Tax at all.

Football was increasingly seen as a major attraction for television and in May 1955 the Scottish League Secretary received the following letter from the B.B.C in Glasgow.

CONFIDENTIAL

Dear Mr. Denovan,

At the recent meeting which Mr. Peter Dimmock, Mr. George Runcie and Mr. Peter Thomson had with you and Mr. Kelly, Mr. Dimmock promised to give you in writing a short *resumé* of our proposals for six experimental Television Outside Broadcasts of six League games during 1955/56. I now put these proposals on paper for you.

In seeking the approval of your Management Committee and clubs we are most anxious to stress that with such co-operation we are sure that the potential shop-window of B.B.C. Television can do nothing but good for League Football in Scotland. We sincerely believe that by giving viewers, and particularly the younger viewer of today who will be the turnstile-paying fan of tomorrow, an occasional taste of League football on a Saturday afternoon, attendances will in the long run improve.

We would like to suggest the following arrangements this coming season:—

1. The agreement to be "non-exclusive" so far as commercial television is concerned.
2. A maximum of six "live" transmissions during the season of

the last half-hour of League matches. The selected matches would be decided, with the Clubs' agreement, between the League Management Committee and the B.B.C. The location would not be announced in the *Radio Times*, as is the case with sound broadcasts. [*sic*]

3. If a similar arrangement is negotiated with the English League we can opt out of network and televise the Scottish games on the same day.

4. In return for this agreement we would be prepared to film or telerecord a certain number of League matches throughout the season for transmission in the late evening. This would, however, be contingent upon agreement being reached in Paragraph 2.

5. In return for the arrangements outlined in Paragraph 2 above we would pay a sum of Two Thousand Five Hundred Pounds (£2500) to The Scottish Football League to be disbursed in any way you think fit.

In conclusion may I say how certain I am that controlled television can only be in the best interests of viewers and League clubs alike.

Yours sincerely
(*Signed*) George Runcie
for Gordon Gildard
Head of Scottish Programmes.

The clubs did not see this as a great opportunity, for on being given the chance to make a response only 3 of the first 28 received were favourable. Certainly Robert Kelly of Celtic, referred to in the letter, was an implacably wary sceptic where televised football was concerned and not without reason. The interests of broadcasters and football legislators would seldom be found to be identical over the next 35 years and the situation was complicated by the fact that in Scotland two clubs between them attracted almost 70% of the footballing support.

Some kind of accommodation would clearly be worked out eventually but the summer of 1955 was more important in that it brought about the first major re-organisation of The Scottish Football League since 1946. Oddly enough it had its motivation chiefly in the dissatisfaction of certain major clubs with the provision which the League was making for Reserve Football, whereby reserve teams had to play in one or other of the C Divisions. This had simply not worked, even although Celtic, with commendable unselfishness, had volunteered to play in the North-East Division to help out that weaker section.

The Management Committee suggested two B Divisions of

11 and 10 clubs respectively, moving up the five excluded small clubs, Berwick Rangers, Brechin City, East Stirling, Montrose and Stranraer, but there was little enthusiasm for this. Berwick Rangers almost got 18 and 19 through at the Annual General Meeting but failed by one vote, 24–13 to obtain the necessary two-thirds majority. At a critical stage of the meeting Mr. Thomson of the Berwick club revealed that several sides had intimated their intention not to run a reserve side in C Division the following year and these included such notables as Rangers, Hearts, Hibernian, Aberdeen, Clyde, Partick Thistle and St. Mirren. This altered the complexion of things and at a recalled General Meeting the decision was taken to go to two Divisions of 18 and 19 clubs. In parenthesis it should be said that Aberdeen had taken the league title for the first time in their history in 1955 and that after a year of working the extended Divisions as A and B there was a welcome return to the more accurate and meaningful descriptions of First and Second for the campaign of 1956–57. Two of the small promoted clubs certainly justified their rise in the world, Brechin City finishing a highly-respectable sixth and Stranraer twelfth in the first season of enlarged Divisions, namely 1955–56.

Where floodlit football was concerned, and it with television would be the main issues of the middle 1950s, the League exercised a prudent circumspection. To allow innovation, yet to retain control, these had to be its watchwords. A Special General Meeting was called on December 23 1955 to deal with floodlit football matches with the result that permission was granted for matches to be played under floodlights in those competitions already authorised subject to the following conditions:

1. That prior consent has been obtained from the body under whose direct auspices the match is to be played.
2. That both clubs concerned have mutually agreed.
3. That emergency lighting is available and has been approved by the responsible authorities.
4. That the fullest co-operation has been assured with local police and transport departments.

Recognised competitions were one thing but the Scottish League would have nothing to do with Johnny-come-lately tournaments. Thus those Scottish clubs, Heart of Midlothian, Hibernian and Partick Thistle, who had agreed to take part in a floodlit Anglo-Scottish league were ordered to withdraw. It may be noted that quite a few of the scheduled matches went ahead anyway, but as friendlies, to which no exception was taken. Having spotted a gap in the fence, however, the Management Committee hastened to repair it by the introduction of a new Rule 67 which decreed that "No club in full or associate membership of The Scottish Football League shall play in any competition which has not received the approval of the Management Committee."

There would be complaints about inadequacy of floodlighting at some grounds, others would be slow to instal them, Hampden for instance was without lights until 1961, but the benefits of lights to a winter game in a northern land were enormous. Apart from the relief from the necessity to stage games before sparse crowds on mid-week afternoons, kick-off times on a Saturday could go back to a regular three o'clock, with beneficial results to gates, and this at a time when attendances were beginning to dip. There were now two television companies wooing Scottish football as in 1957 Scottish Television entered the lists.

Any over-familiarity by referees or departure by them from the most orthodox of paths was dealt with by severe reproof from the League. One of their number, Willie Brittle, was censured for having joined in the applause for a particularly fine piece of play in one of the matches he was controlling, an understandable reaction on the referee's part and a very human one too and yet there was justice in the League's magisterial rebuke, for aloofness ranks high among the attributes of a referee.

It could hardly be said that footballers were being lavishly rewarded. Bonus payments, at £3 for a win and £1-10-0d for a draw in the First Division were only a pound and ten shillings more respectively than in 1939. The Hearts side which won the Championship in 1958 (it would do it again in 1960) was not over-

---

PASSING THE CEMETERY OF DALRY
ON A MATCH DAY

1. Think on us, seein' thir tall stanes
   Of us, the awners o' but banes
   Ablow the ground o' Auld Dalry
   When "Penny all the Half-times!" cry.

2. Think on us, as ye tread that street
   How we lie here wi' faulded feet
   When Herts as bricht as hips and haws
   The blast aboot their jerseys blaws.

3. Rangers' licht blue or Celtic's green
   Would be a sicht for oor sair een
   But Herts alane oor herts could haud
   in the cauld cley that we are clad.

4. Oh merry merry hae we been
   All along the gress sae green,
   Aneath yon lean and lappert sky
   "Hey, hey, Herts' ba'!"—to hear that cry!

5. Oh big and bigger growes oor gate
   you're no shut oot if you come late
   An' you should hear us making oor mane
   On this side o' the Coffin Lane:

6. *Oh to be stridin up Dalry*
   Wi' a wind that flaffs the flags sae dry
   And onwards to Tynecastle green
   When we had Walker and his men!

Extracted from *A Cinema of Days*, James T. R. Ritchie, The Albyn Press, Raeburn House, 32 York Place, Edinburgh.

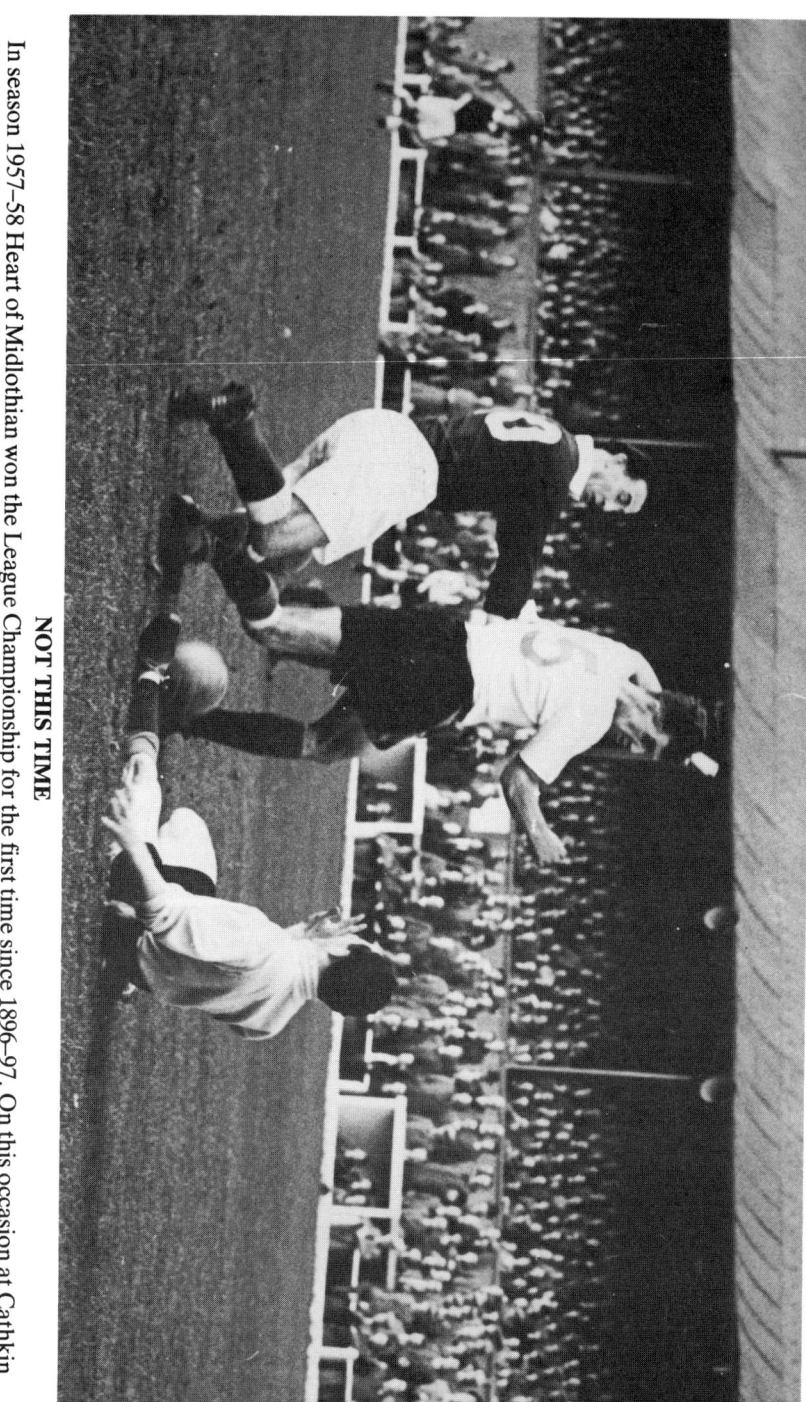

NOT THIS TIME

In season 1957–58 Heart of Midlothian won the League Championship for the first time since 1896–97. On this occasion at Cathkin Park Jimmy Wardhaugh of Hearts was thwarted by the combined attentions of Billy Lewis and Jocky Robertson of Third Lanark.

liberally paid with a talent payment of £550 to the entire team. Benefit payments were more substantially improved by £100 to £750 after five years' service, although these were not mandatory and clubs could and did plead poverty on occasion. The League showed itself willing to co-operate with the S.F.A. in staging matches between League and Scotland elevens as the basis for international selection.

The Scottish Cup semi-final of 1958 in which Hibernian defeated Rangers 2–1 in a mid-week replay had an odd League sequel. Scot Symon, manager of Rangers, approached the League saying that there had been a request that the referee appointed to handle the next home game, against Raith Rovers, should be changed, on the advice of the police. The referee was Mr. R. H. Davidson of Airdrie who would go on to hold high office with the Scottish League and he had had charge of the semi-final, in which he had disallowed a Rangers score late on in the game. On contacting the police the League were informed that they had made no observations whatever on the choice of referee and the incident ended with Rangers being censured.

Rangers were not the only club at odds with referees at this time. John S. Thomson, the firebrand chairman of Morton, was also embroiled with them. He was a Catherine Wheel of a man, throwing out ideas continuously, some of them very original but with an unhappy gift for antagonism so that all too often the source of the idea, rather than its intrinsic merit, was what received consideration. He had, for example, forbidden linesmen to run on the touchline at Cappielow Park because in his view it cut-up the pitch dreadfully. He had been in bother for remarks made about the same R. H. Davidson in the *Weekly News* of February 28 1959 and he further threatened, in August of that year, to send carbon copies of his match reports not only to the referees directly but to the Press. In a glacial phrase he was informed by the Management Committee that "he would do well to reconsider."

As a matter of courtesy the Football League sought the opinion of their northern neighbours on what their reactions would be if the Football League were to include Scots-born players in the forthcoming Inter-League game. They were informed that they had complete discretion in the matter and were welcome to avail themselves of any Scots who might happen to be playing in the Football League at the time. As a result Denis Law and Dave Mackay would both wear Football League jerseys before too many months had elapsed.

Television had now been in operation for almost two years in Scotland as far as the regular transmission of football was concerned and it was time to have a look at its operation in conjunction with the S.F.A. As a result of a meeting in the spring of 1960 the following were declared to be their joint thoughts:

1. Excerpts from matches for late night viewing were not considered harmful.
2. Live television could be permitted but only under the strictest control. In relation to these two items the view was expressed that the fees for these facilities were too low.
3. Sports programmes on television on Saturday afternoons were having a serious effect on the game. In this connection the Management Committee thought that a meeting with the B.B.C. was essential.

On this last point the footballing authorities were not destined to make much headway. Whatever was being shown on television on Saturday afternoons it was not Association Football, the F.A. Cup Final and the Scotland v England matches excepted, and there was no reason to suppose that the various Rugby Unions, Athletics Associations and race tracks would arrange their schedules to avoid the inconveniencing of Scottish football. Nevertheless success was achieved on two fronts, matches were not to be recorded for excerpts at full-time (4.40 p.m.) on Saturday afternoon and live Saturday night transmission, which had been a real possibility in England, was also knocked on the head.

The Scottish League already had one club in its ranks, Berwick Rangers, which was technically English and there was now an attempt to join by another. Gateshead, dismissed from the Football League very unjustly in the opinion of most people, applied for membership of the Scottish League in 1960 but were turned down on the grounds of distance.

The month before the rejection of that application in 1960, Scots had seen perhaps the most far-reaching match ever to be played at Hampden Park, the unparalleled European Cup final between Real Madrid of Spain and Frankfurt Eintracht of Germany with the Spaniards winning by 7–3. Not even the Scots' marvellous talent for self-deception could blind them to the fact that here was a game played at a different level and that these players had displayed a degree of skill quite alien to us. In all fairness those at the match had at once recognised this and the President of The Scottish Football League, W. W. Terris, seized the occasion of the A.G.M. to deliver the following heartfelt remarks:

"As previously mentioned this is The Scottish League's 70th Annual General Meeting and not on that account alone but

THE POST-WAR YEARS

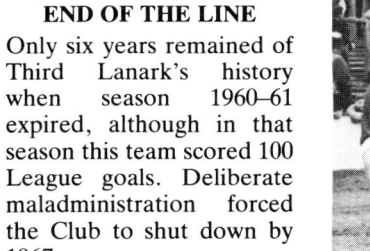

THIRD LANARK — Season 1960-61
Back Row (l to r): McGillvray, Caldwell, Robertson, Reilly, Robb, Cunningham
Front Row: Goodfellow, Hilley, Harley, Gray, McInnes.

END OF THE LINE
Only six years remained of Third Lanark's history when season 1960–61 expired, although in that season this team scored 100 League goals. Deliberate maladministration forced the Club to shut down by 1967.

more particularly because of other factors I feel that a bit of stock-taking would be opportune.

Football has for some time past been a valued Scottish heritage but not of course, particularly in more recent years, a heritage exclusive to Scotland.

If anyone was in doubt about it previously, we have had, in the course of the last few weeks, convincing evidence that we have been lagging behind our counterparts in other parts of Europe through failing to realise and exploit the progressive possibilities in the game and that state of affairs is manifest at both club and national levels. It is no consolation to us in Scotland that our neighbours south of the border are in pretty much the same plight as ourselves and as matters stand at present, our international games with the other Home Countries do not provide the yardstick to measure either our or their standing in the world of football that they once did.

A representative section of the Scottish football public had the pleasure last week of witnessing Club football of a standard greatly surpassing even the best that they are in the habit of seeing here and having seen for themselves the excellence attained by these foreign exponents of the game, they have every right and reason to clamour for something better than the standard of play provided by their own Scottish clubs.

The progress made in recent times by some countries which only took to the game of football years after we did has been phenomenal. Singularly enough, there is nothing phenomenal about the method by which that progress has been achieved. It is a method older than the game itself, hard work! In every competitive sphere it has been proved again and again that the one and only way to excel is to work hard. The progress made by Continental clubs is a direct challenge to us and it would be out of keeping with Scottish character to shirk such a challenge.

The view appears to be held in some quarters that some form of reconstruction of the Leagues would cure all the ills besetting Scottish football but I hope no one will be deluded into believing that reconstruction alone would yield that result. There is no substitute for hard work.

All those connected with the game in Scotland—players, trainers, managers, referees, linesmen, directors, and last but not least legislators are in a position of trust, a trust which imposes upon them the moral responsibility of setting about rectifying matters. Any improvement in the standard of play must start at club level but that does not justify cherishing such recurring controversial issues as "Club or Country?" We should concentrate rather on a "Club AND Country" approach.

If the challenge to which I have referred is seriously taken up, the possibilities are enormous and I feel that club managements are already prepared to play their parts in restoring Scottish football to its former pre-eminent position."

Wise and stirring words but, as if to demonstrate immediately the other side of the Scottish character, much of the rest of the meeting was taken up by a lengthy address by the aforementioned John S. Thomson of Morton. In the course of it he criticised severely the administration of Scottish football in terms which necessitated the Chairman's repeatedly calling him to order. Mr. Thomson then proceeded to expound his own ideas for the complete re-organisation of the game and concluded that if no heed were paid to them, commerical interests would be prepared to give him the necessary backing. At this meeting a chance to begin the restructuring of Scottish football was missed when an application for membership from Inverness Clachnacuddin was turned down. There were not many towns in Scotland with a population of 30,000 and a hinterland of nearly 80,000 looking for a chance to play League football.

What would these new footballers, charged with regenerating the Scottish game, be paid? There was no maximum, there never had been with one brief ill-fated exception, but the health of the game could not be measured by what the stars were getting—the professional game is not dissimilar to the entertainment business in that because the star of a West End production is very highly paid then all is not necessarily well with those on Equity minimum rates. Footballing minimum rates in 1961 were set at £624 for full-time players in the First Division and half that for part-timers. In the Second Division £156 was deemed a fair retaining offer. But from now on, clubs would have an additional source of income as at last the decision had been taken to avail themselves of the pools money which for long had been available.

Pools money had been on offer since as far back as the 1920s but had always been indignantly spurned as tainted gold, with the occasional involvement of bookmakers in attempts to rig individual matches being cited as proof. Now it was felt that the machinery of control was sufficiently well-established to make the acceptance of such money safe. It was to be allocated on a pointage basis and before ten years the amount available had climbed to more than £300 a point. This source of income, at a time when even the largest clubs were finding it almost impossible to subsist on turnstile returns, was an absolute life-saver for the smaller Second

Division clubs although in a curious way it provided yet another disincentive for promotion. A Second Division club, say East Stirlingshire or Stenhousemuir, was clearly much better off finishing a respectable third in the Second Division with 46 points than it would have been coming bottom of the First Division with 15 points. The solution to this problem would be found in the mid-1980s when, under a new system of financial distribution, every club was awarded a basic equal sum and the remainder thereafter depended on the club's place, not in a 10 or 14 club League but on a 38 club ladder.

Two major developments were taking place at this time in England which were to have a profound effect on the standard of Scottish League football. The concept of the maximum wage was done away with and Johnny Haynes of Fulham became the first £100 a week player. This had obvious implications for Scottish clubs as there were approximately 16 English clubs who could look at this wage scale as against perhaps six in Scotland. Even more far-reaching was the ending of the retain-and-transfer system, so long believed to be the keystone of organised professional football. Legal observers had openly thought that this system, as operated in football, was contrary to natural justice and would not survive the first determined attack made on it in a court of law, and so it proved. All that was needed was a good test case and a most able stalking horse was found in the person of George Eastham of Newcastle United who wished to move south to Arsenal for personal reasons.

His club refused to contemplate such a move and Eastham raised an action [*Eastham v Newcastle Utd. and others*] which was to become a test case for the professional footballers of Great Britain. As many lawyers had predicted, the High Court, after a protracted legal battle, decided in his favour in the summer of 1963. They found for him on two points, the first of which was that the rules governing the retain-and-transfer system were *ultra vires*, that is, the powers were not conferred on the company (Newcastle United) by its Memorandum and Articles of Association. The second ground was that the retain-and-transfer system was unlawful because it was in effect a restraint of trade.

This decision changed the whole relationship of professional footballers with their employers. It led to the system of option contracts whereby a player signed for a club for a number of years and the club had the option to renew the contract for the same period of time. The option must be on terms at least as favourable, unless by mutual agreement between club and player. If the club did not wish to take up its option the player was free to sign for another club without any transfer being required.

These two developments would have made it very difficult for Scottish clubs to resist the magnetic pull of the south but there was a third and even more damaging one. Provision was made by the Football League that a 10 per cent levy would be imposed on all transfer fees over £500. Of this 10 per cent, half was payable to the Football League and the other half to the player being transferred, provided that he had not demanded a transfer or, through misconduct, virtually forced his club to get rid of him. The effect of this new system was stark. The two top Scottish clubs, Celtic and Rangers might conceivably match English wages but the top Scots player could now acquire a substantial capital sum by moving to England for he would make £7500 on a transfer fee of £150,000. He could invest this money and let it work for him, an important consideration in such a risky occupation as professional football.

In the welter of legislation, and remembering that this is a history of The Scottish Football League and not of individual clubs, it is necessary to turn aside and recognise two performances, one by an individual, one by a provincial club. The championship was moving around with gratifying frequency and in 1962 it was won by a Dundee side which could fairly claim to be the best pure footballing team produced in Scotland since the war, a claim which their performance the following season in the European Cup would go far to substantiate.

Included in that championship side was a player, Gordon Smith, who was winning a championship medal with his third different club, having already accomplished this with Hibernian and Heart of Midlothian. The most graceful of right wingers, he had gone to Easter Road in 1941 and was freed in what could reasonably have been seen to be the twilight of his career in 1959. City rivals Hearts at once snapped him up and he won a championship medal in 1960 to add to the three he already owned. Hearts let him go after two years and surely now he was finished at top level? Not a bit of it, he was a crucial component of the Dundee championship side and in the very autumn of his footballing days played in a European Cup semi-final. His achievement in winning Championship medals with three different clubs, and none of them Rangers or Celtic, has got to stand as the greatest individual accomplishment in the entire history of Scottish League football. Unfortunately, English predators were almost immediately to break up this fine Dundee side and the club drifted back towards a comfortable semi-obscurity,

The winter of 1962–63 was one of the most severe on record with hardly a match taking place in the months of January and February. The cash flow problems of clubs was acute, particularly if there was no revenue coming in from the Pools Promoters' Associ-

GORDON SMITH (*Hibernian, Heart of Midlothian, Dundee*)
There has never been a more graceful Scottish player than Gordon Smith and his exemplary attention to fitness ensured that the outside-right played at top level for 23 years. He holds the unique record of winning a League medal with each of the three Clubs named above.

SEEN AT AYR RACES
The three Shankley brothers (note the pre-war spelling) Johnny (ex Morton and Alloa) Bob (Falkirk) and Willie (Preston North End). Bob and Willie would subsequently each win a national championship as managers of Dundee and Liverpool respectively.

ation. The latter organisation were in an equally perilous position and so the device of the Pools Panel was introduced, whereby, given a certain number of postponements on a Saturday, a collection of eminent former players would meet in a London hotel and solemnly issue lists of how they thought these matches would have gone if played. Surprisingly, the punters seemed quite happy with this state of affairs and the money accruing to the clubs was of inestimable value, especially now that the tax authorities had agreed that interim payments could be made in the course of the season. So bad had the weather been that goalkeeper George

Niven of Partick Thistle sustained a broken hand in a New Year Holiday fixture and resumed in March without having missed a competitive first team match.

Inevitably there were strident and immediate cries for a change in the playing season, arguing from the exceptional rather than the normal. A suggestion that the season should run from March–November was defeated by 25–12 at a League Special General Meeting on February 25 1963. This proposal was altogether too radical but there was a feeling that some fine tuning could be done and that at least the beginning of May should be part of the normal season. With the commitment of the Pools Promoters Association to Australian fixtures during the summer it would not be a simple matter of altering the season unilaterally and there were those, considerable in number and influential, who thought the answer lay in the provision of covered accommodation for spectators and undersoil heating for grounds rather than in any major tinkering with the football calendar itself.

The structure of the Divisions continued, as always, to cause concern. The odd number of clubs in Division Two (19) was irksome and St. Johnstone succeeded at the Annual General Meeting of 1963 in securing compensation of £50 when a club perforce had an idle Saturday. Increasingly the idea of three divisions was gaining ground although Celtic's proposal of 16–16–5 + reserve sides stood no chance whatever. The very name Third Division raised frightening folk memories and the small clubs were not going to put themselves in a position where a mere handful of them could be cut off swiftly and unobtrusively. The real dilemma was what to do with clubs which performed an extremely useful service in bringing League football to remote localities but whose own ambitions were extremely limited. Was it right that such organisations could control League policy when that body had to satisfy the much more ambitious aspirations of the big city clubs?

Rangers did not think that it was and on May 28 1964 the Ibrox club dropped a bombshell by proposing the adoption of a new rule, Rule 68:

> "It shall be competent for a resolution to be submitted to a meeting of clubs in membership of the League to the effect that the League be wound up and a person appointed as Liquidator thereof for the purposes of such winding-up, such person shall have full powers to realise the whole assets of the League pay the liabilities thereof and divide the free proceeds equally among the clubs in membership of the League at the date of the passing of the resolution for winding up. Such resolution shall

only be competent at the Annual General Meeting or at a Special General Meeting called for that purpose and such resolution shall only be carried if voted for by two-thirds of the members present. Twenty one days notice in writing must be given to the Secretary of the intention to submit such Resolution for Winding Up which shall be printed and forwarded to the clubs in membership of the League at least fourteen days before the meeting for consideration thereof."

This was a powerful new development, hinting at the possibility of the big clubs, despairing of internal restructuring, breaking away and beginning from scratch. It was a threat of the greatest magnitude to the smaller clubs and an interim interdict was applied for and granted in the Court of Session against Rangers F.C. and Others. For the moment the matter could not be further considered but it was clearly not going to go away. In all the stir that these proceedings caused, a chance was lost to equalise the numbers in the Second Division and in so doing gain a foothold in rugby country when the application of the well-doing Gala Fairydean for League membership was rejected.

What Rangers wanted to do was to dissolve The Scottish Football League of 37 clubs and reconstitute it as two divisions of sixteen. It has to be said that in many people's view this was the optimum number for Scottish football and it would certainly have been ideal for the running of the League Cup, eliminating any need for the ninth section with its awkward number of five clubs and subsequent play-off. Out would go Stenhousemuir, Albion Rovers, Berwick Rangers, Brechin City and Stranraer. But for the happy circumstance of having spent a recent year in the First Division East Stirlingshire would certainly have been threatened, for the elimination list was based on gate receipts over the last few years.

The condemned clubs had not been circularised about the initial meeting which might well have decided their fate. Jim Weir of Stenhousemuir made the point that small clubs were equally important as fixtures on pools lists as any meeting of the big clubs. In the previous season Stenhousemuir had received £1225 in pools money which was certainly the equivalent of five or even six League gates at their ground, Ochilview. It was Stenhousemuir who led the fight against the extinction of the little clubs and an interim interdict was gained in the Court of Session by solicitor Robert Turpie, who was also a Stenhousemuir committee man.

Rangers were however given permission to introduce Rule 68 which if agreed would effect the desired change. The case went to the Inner House of the Court of Session on appeal where Lord Avonside's earlier decision in favour of Rangers was upheld. On November 7 1964 Rangers withdrew from the action in the Court of Session as did the five [by that time actually four] defending clubs in exchange for an assurance that they would not be excluded from the present League or any new league to be formed. The small clubs had had the support of Robert Kelly of Celtic throughout.

Brechin City then proposed their amendment which would have allowed reconstruction but would guarantee all clubs in League membership senior football at some level. This amendment was carried comfortably. There was a nice tail-piece to this episode. One of the five clubs involved was not a limited company (no more were Stenhousmuir) and at one stage in the proceedings it appeared possible that the committee members of that club would become personally liable for the very heavy legal expenses incurred if the action went against the small clubs. They therefore perforce withdrew from the proceedings with great reluctance and rather shame-facedly.

Some time later they made most honourable amends when they donated the proceeds of a transfer fee to their four colleagues so that the latter would not be left to bear the entire burden of the legal costs. For the moment the small clubs had managed to repel boarders but those who wished to effect major surgery on Scottish League football had also learned a few lessons and there was no doubt that next time they would be better prepared.

Chapter Eight

THINKING ABOUT CHANGE

About this time a significant forward step was taken with the completion of negotiations for the purchase of the present suite of offices which the League occupies at 188 West Regent Street, Glasgow. The offices had a remarkable history and their story is in miniature the development of Glasgow itself as the decorative scroll opposite makes clear.

By December 1964 attendances were plummeting. They were 289,000 down from the previous season by the end of November, more than half the absentees being recorded in the League Cup despite the fact that there had been an Old Firm final. By the end of the year the figure had mounted to 435,000 and this was indeed perturbing. The Management Committee of The Scottish League has often been accused of inaction but equally often it has been ahead of its members, too far ahead for good ideas to gain acceptance. It now wrote to all the clubs proposing three divisions for season 1965–66 of 14–12–12 which would have necessitated the election of one new club.

Dear Sir,
Reorganisation of The Scottish Football League
With attendances at League matches continuing to fall at an alarming rate, the Management Committee have been giving the matter serious thought and they are now firmly of the opinion that a further effort should be made to alter the structure of the League commencing season 1965–66 in order to place matters on a more solid footing.

From a survey of the attendance returns the conclusion to be drawn is that as conditions now exist, big leagues stultify competition. Many clubs find themselves engaged in meaningless matches almost before the season has run half its course.

With a view therefore to increasing the competitive element of the competitions, the Management Committee feel that a re-allocation of all the clubs in membership into three divisions

168   THE FIRST 100 YEARS

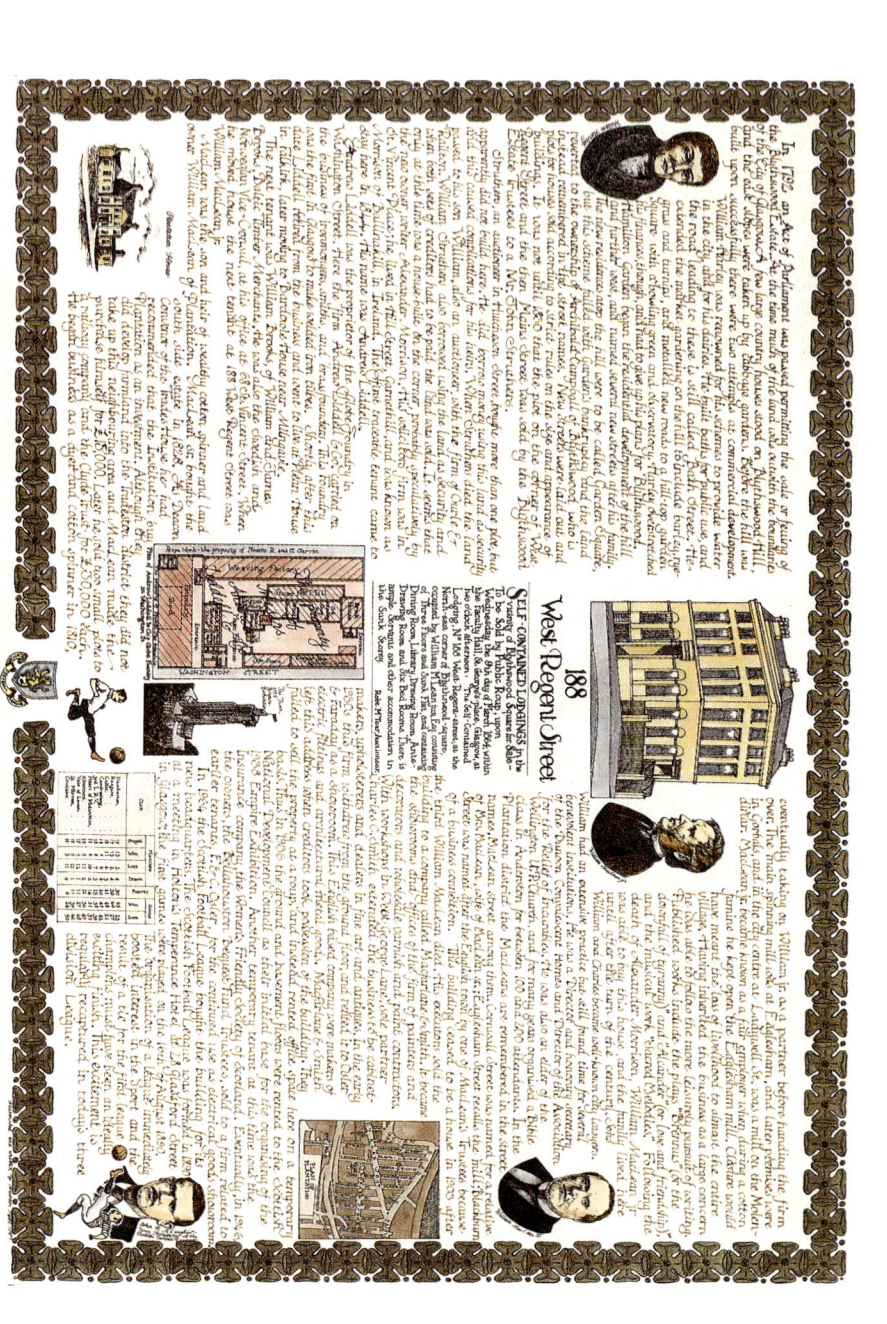

League Plaque giving history of building.

THINKING ABOUT CHANGE

with promotion and relegation of two up and two down would stimulate greater interest.

The suggestion of the Management Committee is that the First Division should consist of 14 clubs, the Second Division of 12 clubs and the remaining 11 clubs, together with one other club to be elected to membership, should constitute the Third Division.

Previous efforts by the Management Committee to re-organise the League have always ended in failure because of the uncertainty in the minds of Club members as to what division they would find themselves in. With this in mind, the Management Committee has studied the problems from an economic basis. As a result of long and careful thought the Mangement Committee decided that attendances at League matches over the past three seasons should provide the basis.

The formation of the three divisions would therefore be as follows:

FIRST DIVISION	SECOND DIVISION	THIRD DIVISION
Aberdeen	Airdrieonians	Albion Rovers
Celtic	Arbroath	Alloa
Dundee	Ayr United	Berwick Rangers
Dundee United	Clyde	Brechin City
Dunfermline Athletic	East Fife	Cowdenbeath
Heart of Midlothian	E.S. Clydebank	Dumbarton
Hibernian	Falkirk	Forfar Athletic
Kilmarnock	Hamilton Academical	Montrose
Morton	Queen of the South	Queen's Park
Motherwell	Raith Rovers	Stenhousemuir
Partick Thistle	Stirling Albion	Stranraer
Rangers	Third Lanark	New Club
St. Johnstone		
St. Mirren		

With the reduction in size of the various leagues, another short competition would be introduced. In this regard the Management Committee envisage a competition closely akin to the League Cup with all clubs participating.

Another matter which the Management Committee has considered is the duration of the playing season. The Management Committee feel that the season should be extended into the month of May. Adoption of this suggestion would provide more scope for playing-off postponed matches. As is well-known many matches have under rule to be played off the following mid-week, often in adverse weather conditions and with no profit to show therefrom.

Also resulting from an extended season, the co-operation of the

Scottish Football Association might be sought whereby the Scottish Cup competition be re-scheduled. In this connection you will find a plan showing how the competition could be arranged if the Management Committee's recommendations met with approval.

Another matter to which the Management Committee gave their consideration was the question of guarantees in the Second and Third Divisions. Their recommendation is £200 for the Second Division and £150 for the Third Division.

In order that the clubs should have an opportunity of discussing this whole matter, the Management Committee has decided to call your chairman or a representative of your club to an informal meeting. Your representative attending the meeting should have the authority to indicate to the Management Committee whether your club is in favour of the foregoing proposals.

Should the indications be favourable the Management Committee will then proceed to convene a Special General Meeting.

The informal meeting will be held at 6 Park Gardens, Glasgow on 22 March 1965.

> Yours faithfully,
> James F. Denovan
> Secy.

The move failed, it was bold, imaginative, but just a little premature and its time was not yet.

The observant reader will have noticed, tucked away among the list of First Division clubs a name that has not cropped up before, that of E.S. Clydebank. The background to the emergence of this club and its brief existence is one of the most fascinating chapters in Scottish football history and can fairly be described as the first attempt to set up a football franchise on the pattern which baseball employs in the United States of America.

The creation of an entirely new club to Scottish football, E.S. Clydebank, had a remarkable background in every respect. In June 1957, two West of Scotland businessmen, Jack Steedman (later to be President of The Scottish Football League) and his brother Charles, became directors of East Stirlingshire Football Club when they bought just over 50 per cent of the shares for approximately £1000. They had boundless enthusiasm, a great capacity for hard work and considerable knowledge of football. Almost immediately East Stirlingshire were transformed from a side whose only objective had seemed to be a mere survival in the Second Division to a go-ahead organisation which might one day aspire to promotion.

That day came at the end of season 1962–63 when East Stirlingshire became a First Division side for the first time in more than thirty years in finishing in second place to St. Johnstone. Enthusiasm at Firs Park Falkirk was high and gates were comparatively good, reaching 7000 in those tense closing weeks. Competition in the First Division was too intense for the little club however and after a miserable season in which only 12 points were garnered from 34 matches, East Stirlingshire returned to the Second Division in the shortest time possible. Attendances fell off sharply.

It was this experience which convinced the Steedman brother that the club would have to be relocated. By chance there was an alternative site ready and waiting. Clydebank Juniors were susceptible to the idea of a merger with East Stirlingshire and there had of course been a history of League football in the shipbuilding burgh. In April 1964 the four directors present at a Board meeting of East Stirlingshire agreed that the club should move through to the West coast.

By a constitutional quirk the fact that the Steedmans owned more than 50 per cent of the vote did not make their triumph certain. An Extraordinary General Meeting to block the move was cancelled and some of the brothers' shares transferred to people in Clydebank. The ferocity of local reaction was astonishing and totally unlooked for in an area that had no great history of consistently supporting the club. Importantly, East Stirlingshire had acquired considerable survival skills in their days in C Division and it was now decided that the East Stirlingshire Shareholders Protection Association, rather than the Supporters Club, would bear the burden of the fight as shareholders could be said to have a more immediate interest in the outcome.

There were public meetings and demonstrations but none of them were in time to prevent the move to Kilbowie Park, Clydebank, where the new side, with the cumbrous title of E.S. Clydebank, made its first appearance on August 8 1964. To most people it appeared that in the face of this *fait accompli* the old club would simply die. It did not.

A Glasgow solicitor, Robert Turpie, who had been over this course before having counselled the five small clubs threatened with extinction in 1955, was engaged to act for the Firs Park club. An action to overturn the removal of the club to Clydebank was embarked upon in the Court of Session before Lord Hunter and he found in favour of East Stirlingshire on the grounds that the shares which had been transferred to those people in Clydebank should under Article 13 of the club's Articles of Association have been offered in the first place to the other directors.

It was a famous victory and East Stirlingshire were back at

Falkirk by August 1965, rapturously received by a crowd of over 3,000, a level of public interest that was not sustained for very long. Crowds dwindled and East Stirlingshire sank back to an undistinguished place in the Second Division. Clydebank meanwhile began life as a separate entity in the Second Division the following season 1966–67 and have been good enough, even although only marginally better-supported than East Stirlingshire in the long run, to have played Premier Division football on more than one occasion and to have become a noted nursery for players of quality.

So, who was right, the East Stirlingshire Shareholders Protective Supporters Association or the Steedman brothers? Perhaps in a strange way they were both right, for the whole episode illustrates the conflict between business and sentiment which is forever at the heart of Scottish football. The Steedmans, dedicated football men though they were, wished to apply the commonsense principles of business to the situation; the viewpoint of the East Stirling supporters and shareholders could be summed up thus: "If you want a League side in Clydebank, fine, but start from scratch. The proper and only place for East Stirlingshire Football Club is the town of Falkirk."

So East Stirlingshire survived and so too did the other small clubs whose disappearance was the stuff of annual predictions. The little fellows proved to be quite exceptionally hardy and when the next casualty occurred some two years later the victim would be a much more prominent name in Scottish football, Third Lanark. The two events can be linked because there was a suggestion that the Glasgow club might also consider re-location although in the event this came to nothing.

What made the disappearance of Third Lanark particularly regrettable was the fact that in footballing terms the club had experienced something of a golden age in the early 1960s. In season 1960–61 it had finished in third place in the First Division and in the process scored 100 goals, always a comparatively rare performance in a Scottish League First Division programme and particularly when it was achieved over 34 matches as against the 38 of pre-1939. There had been a League Cup Final appearance in 1959 and the Third Lanark forward line of Hilley, Goodfellow, Harley, Gray, McInnes tripped off the tongue just as easily as that of Henderson, McMillan, Millar, Brand and Wilson for Rangers or Smith, Penman, Cousin, Gilzean and Robertson for Dundee.

Third Lanark had the misfortune to have a chairman, William G. Hiddleston, who saw Cathkin Park more as a site ripe for commercial development than as the setting for Association Football, First or Second Division. The composition of the share-

CLOSING DOWN SALE
Cathkin Park in 1969, derelict after Third Lanark had ceased operations. The new stand had been functioning for less than three years.

holders within the club whereby a comparatively large number of people each owned a mere handful of shares, made the company ripe for take-over. In the three years from 1964 players were sold for much less than their market value—Jimmy Goodfellow astonishingly was given a free transfer—the ground was not maintained, players were paid tardily and then in silver, there was no water for showers after the match, transport to away games was unavailable and there was a host of unbelievably petty annoyances of a similar nature. It is hard to resist the conclusion that the object of all this was to make Third Lanark such an unattractive club to play for that no player would willingly come to Cathkin Park.

This was certainly the conclusion arrived at by Mr. John Moncrieff Turner and The Honourable Henry Shanks Keith, Q.C., the Inspectors appointed by the Board of Trade to enquire into the affairs of the Third Lanark Athletic Club Ltd. They found evidence of failure to keep statutory records, irregular share transfers, entries for payments made to players which the same players strenuously denied ever having received. In addition a "Hi-Hi" (from the nickname of the Club) Lottery was recorded as having a weekly prize of £200 but there were almost no confirmations of any pay-outs being made.

In a scathing Summary and Conclusions the Board of Trade

THE GREATEST OF ALL SCOTS MANAGERS
Jock Stein, who guided Celtic to a European Cup win and nine consecutive league championships, seen in contemplative mood towards the end of his career.

THINKING ABOUT CHANGE

Inspectors left no doubt that they considered William Hiddleston almost totally responsible for the appalling state of affairs which they found and they went so far as to say that the deterioration coincided with his return to the Board of Directors in December 1962. He had then re-emerged as majority shareholder at an Annual General Meeting, a fact which prompted the immediate resignation of the then manager, the former Rangers and Scotland defender, George Young. The Inspectors wrote in paragraph 132 of the Report:

> "It seems clear that Mr. Hiddleston, for reasons which are obscure, made up his mind to secure practical control of the Company. In this he eventually succeeded and thereafter the Directors of the Company consisted entirely of people acceptable to him, who were not likely to, and did not, oppose him. In the end of the day, Mr. Hiddleston, with the acquiescence of the other directors, took the conduct of the Company's affairs and the management of its finances entirely into his own hands (with some assistance from Mr. Lough.) Mr. Hiddleston's determination was not matched by his ability or by his financial probity. There followed an entirely justifiable lack of confidence in the Company's management on the part of the shareholders and of persons dealing with the Company. Eventually the Company's affairs fell into a gross state of confusion and mismanagement."

There were some people out Cathkin way who would have disagreed only with the opening sentence of the Inspectors' Report in that they thought they knew perfectly well why Mr. Hiddleston should wish to obtain control of the Company and that he had realised that Cathkin Park would make an ideal site on which to build houses. The ground was sold to a building firm and in spite of all efforts to mount a rescue operation Third Lanark did not appear for season 1967–68. Then with a twist worthy of fiction two things happened; planning permission for building was refused and within another month William Hiddleston died suddenly, thereby almost certainly frustrating impending criminal proceedings against him.

The result of his handiwork was that one of the founder members of The Scottish Football League had vanished from the face of the earth and this was to begin the process of weakening all but the two big clubs in Glasgow. Over the next 25 years the other city clubs, Partick Thistle, Clyde and Queen's Park would prove themselves largely incapable of retaining First Division status, even First Division status in the reconstituted three-division system.

All that is to move further ahead than one would at the moment

FRANK BEATTIE

A strong-running wing-half with a devouring stride Frank Beattie was unlucky in being Jim Baxter's contemporary. He played in several Kilmarnock sides which finished as league runners-up but when it seemed that the ultimate honour might elude him he skippered the Ayrshire side to their only title success on the last day of the 1964–65 season at Tynecastle.

wish to go. Let us return to 1965 and an entry in the Management Committee minutes for August 1965 which baldly stated that the Scottish League side in the forthcoming match with the Irish League at Ibrox Park in September would be in the hands of Jock Stein, recently-appointed manager of Celtic. Stein, with a unique record of triumph at three different clubs, Dunfermline Athletic, Hibernian and Celtic, would eventually pose severe problems to Scottish football by the very nature of his unrelieved and prolonged success but that would still be ten years off.

In January 1966 it was decided that, with effect from the beginning of the following season, one substitute per side could be allowed in competitive matches. This did not pass without vehement opposition from the traditionalists who were ready with tales of heroic feats performed by ten or even nine men. So forthcoming were they with such accounts that the listener could have been pardoned for wondering why managers retained the traditional preference for fielding eleven players at the start of a match. Football now had to compete in the entertainment business and, increasingly, spectators did not want to see a match distorted from the earliest stages through injury.

There had been an attempt to test the market for summer football and a competition by the name of the Summer Cup had been run in 1964 and 1965. The public response was tepid partly because the Old Firm declined to take part and because the first final was afflicted with bad luck in that the outbreak of a typhoid epidemic in the city of Aberdeen caused a postponement of the final, since Aberdeen were one of the competing clubs. When only eleven acceptances were received for the 1966 Summer Cup it was decided to abandon the competition.

The Scottish League continued to press for increased representation on the Council of the Scottish Football Association so that their pre-eminent position in Scottish football might be properly reflected. The era in which several clubs had won the league championship was coming to an end. Those who liked to see the honours go round enjoyed Kilmarnock's triumph over Hearts in the last League day of 1965, a triumph all the more meritorious in that the Ayrshire club had come very close in three of the preceding four years and finally, faced with the task of beating Hearts at Tynecastle by at least 2-0, proceeded to do exactly that. The neutral did well to enjoy the spectacle because fifteen years would elapse before the next success of a club other than Rangers or Celtic. The latter were about to enter on their great period of ascendancy which would see them take nine championships in a row. It was a wonderful performance and no praise can be too

RONNIE SIMPSON
(Queen's Park, Third Lanark, Newcastle United, Hibernian, Celtic)

His story is almost too strange to be factual. He played senior football for 24 years, starting at 14 with Queen's Park. Outstanding ability compensated for lack of height and he would stop shots with any part of his body. Two F.A. cup medals with Newcastle brought him to Hibernian and then in his mid 30s to Celtic. The rest is football history, Lisbon in 1967 and a first cap at the age of 36, and all this from the son of a Rangers centre-half!

Special commemorative envelope to mark Celtic's feat of nine consecutive championships.

extreme for either the players or their manager, Jock Stein. It has to be said, however, that this long unbroken spell of domination was not necessarily to the game's advantage, any more than the lack of any sustained challenge to Rangers had been between the wars. As Celtic continued to win the championship effortlessly, not in quite such a flamboyant and marvellously cavalier way towards the end of the nine year period, uncertainty of outcome vanished and attendances dwindled. Celtic's attendances actually declined more steeply than those of League clubs in general.

The clubs still clamoured for reorganisation and then, when the Management Committee made a suggestion, rejected it. That long-suffering body proposed three divisions of 16–12–12 in the spring of 1966 which would have entailed the admission of three new clubs. To compensate for the reduction in numbers of League games an additional competition, open to all, would be played and given the name of the Spring Cup. The package attracted a fair amount of support but not enough, 17 clubs voting in favour while 20 were against the idea.

Inevitably, Scottish League football was insular from time to time and obsessed with its own problems exclusively. It was important that the Scottish club game should be highly regarded in Europe and good performances in the various European competitions were by far the best way to achieve this. The Scottish standing was never higher than in 1967 when Celtic won the Blue

KILMARNOCK'S FLAG
Willie Waddell, Kilmarnock manager congratulates Bertie Black after the dramatic last-day championship win at Tynecastle in April 1965. Other players in the picture are (l to r) Jackie McGrory, Frank Beattie and Jackie McInally, father of the Scottish internationalist, Alan McInally.

Riband of European competition, the European Cup and Rangers came very close to winning the final of the Cup Winners' Cup against Bayern Munich a little later that year. These successes were even more valuable in a way than those at international level because they showed what could be done by players who had stayed in Scotland and whom the supporters could see every week, a point which Jock Stein was quick to make.

The progressives thought that even more could be done with a streamlined organisation. In April 1968 at a Special General Meeting Rangers secured a 29–7 majority for their suggestion of four years previously, Rule 68, which said that it would be competent in certain circumstances for a club to propose the dissolution of The Scottish Football League. At the same time however a clever Brechin City motion became Rule 69 by the same margin, as its wording did much to allay the deepest-seated fears of the small clubs:

JIM BAXTER (*Rangers*)
If ever a player became an instant legend it was Baxter. In five short years at Ibrox "Slim Jim" set Scottish Football by the ears. His style was cultured, elegant and taunting as when he destroyed England at Wembley in 1967. Never a dedicated trainer, his career was shorter than it should have been.

"Any resolution to wind up the League shall be incompetent which has the purpose or effect of winding-up the League and the re-forming of a new Scottish national league within three years to the exclusion of any club in membership with satisfactory rights of promotion to the highest grade in any such new League (unless such excluded club or clubs shall agree to such exclusion) and any such Resolution, if successful, shall be reversed in the event of these circumstances arising within the said period."

Such changes as were made took account of modern thinking. Hearts successfully proposed that where two or more sides in the championship were equal in points, goal difference rather than goal average should be used to separate them. Had this been in effect in 1965 Hearts and not Kilmarnock would have won the championship. Dundee United, believing that commitment was required from promoted clubs as well as temporary footballing ability, demanded that it should be compulsory that promoted clubs should run a reserve team.

By this time the total amount of pools money available in a season was in excess of £200,000 but the best way of distributing it had not as yet been devised. There were anomalies in a system which gave Celtic £4860 for winning the First Division while Motherwell, Second Division champions, received £5760 and this disparity also affected the respective bottom clubs, Arbroath making do with £1440 while Stenhousemuir were rewarded with £1620. The disappearance of such inequities would have to await the creation of the ladder system already mentioned.

There was a lot to learn about marketing. It was 1969 before the clubs agreed not to play League matches in opposition to the Scottish Cup Final. The following summer, in May 1970, Fred Denovan, whose unflappable good humour had defused many a tense situation in the League councils, died suddenly and was replaced by the Assistant Secretary, Tommy Maule, who had long experience of League matters.

Meantime, the other three Glasgow clubs were suffering severely from the almost total domination exerted by Celtic and Rangers and one of them, Clyde, plagued by uncertainty over the future of Shawfield Stadium and badly affected by rehousing which cleared the great majority of people from the club's own natural catchment area, decided that the time had come to leave the city. Their plan was breathtaking since it involved nothing less than their assuming the identity, to all practical purposes, of Hamilton Academical.

The Scottish football world was rocked by the news, made public on August 29 1970 that Clyde would take over Hamilton Academical Football Club with effect from September 19 of that year and that the latter had already resigned from the Scottish Football Association and the Scottish League. The odd timing was to ensure that the change-over took effect before the commencement of League matches as the season had of course started as usual with the League Cup fixtures.

The new team would be called Strathclyde Academical and straightaway the first snag was encountered as a club name could not by rule be changed in the course of a season. Clyde based their case on depopulation. At the beginning of that very season, in August 1970 only 1500 had turned out for a Saturday match against Dundee United and only 1100 for a mid-week match against one of the country's leading clubs, Hearts. The vice-chairman of Clyde, Tom Clark, father of Scottish international goalkeeper Bobby Clark of Aberdeen, explained the situation thus:

> "We're sound financially and are not interested in selling good players. But we can carry on only so long and it might have been a slow death waiting and hoping that something would turn up. Glasgow appears only interested in Rangers and Celtic. Hamilton is a town to itself and we can identify ourselves with it."

That was not the question, the question was, "Could Hamilton identify itself with Clyde?" and the signs were that it would not. The immediate Hamilton match against Raith Rovers had been cancelled but four of their ex-directors got together, sought an interview with the Town Council, got an extension of the lease for Douglas Park from the Town Council and decided to carry on. The next week's fixture against Albion Rovers was fulfilled and the proposed merger collapsed. Once again it had been demonstrated that while a football club can grow naturally within a community it is almost impossible to graft it on anywhere.

It was at this point that sponsorship began to become a major source of revenue for Scottish clubs. On August 18 1970 the draw was made for a British Cup, the sponsors as yet unknown. The Scots clubs forward were Heart of Midlothian, Dundee, Dunfermline Athletic, Morton, Motherwell and Airdrieonians. The new competition was seen as a highly credible rival to what was then perceived as the weakest of the European competitions, the Fairs' Cities Cup. Enthusiasm for it in Scotland was high. The Managing Director of Morton, Hal Stewart, widely-respected for his commercial acumen, delivered his thoughts in these words: "Why fly behind the Iron Curtain and lose money when there are lucrative fixtures to be picked up within a few hundred miles?" John Harvey, manager of Hearts, was even more taken with the new competition: "I see the new tournament becoming more important than the Fairs Cup which has been a financial loss to several clubs."

From the start the new competition, soon adopted by Texaco, the oil company, struggled because of the attitude of leading English clubs. Manchester United turned down an offer to participate and Arsenal, not sharing the opinion of Messrs. Stewart and Harvey, opted for the Fairs Cup. Texaco had put up a generous £100,000 by way of sponsorship and in the first round Scottish clubs did well, important in that it pre-empted any snide criticism from the South. Over two games Airdrie defeated Nottingham Forest on penalties and in the process became the first ever Scottish club to participate in a penalty shoot-out. Motherwell performed the same service for Stoke City, Morton beat West Bromwich Albion and Hearts defeated Burnley. Only Dunfermline Athletic and Dundee failed to progress to the next round. The first round scores made good reading for Scottish breakfast tables:

TEXACO CUP 1st Round (Aggregate Scores) 1970–71

Airdrieonians 4 v 4 Nottingham Forest
(2–2, 2–2). Airdrie won on penalties.
Morton 3 v 1 West Bromwich Albion
(2–1, 1–0)
Motherwell 2 v 2 Stoke City
(1–0, 1–2). Motherwell won on penalties
Heart of Midlothian 5 v 4 Burnley
(1–3, 4–1)
Dundee 1 v 2 Wolverhampton Wanderers
(1–2, 0–0)
Tottenham Hotspur 7 v 0 Dunfermline Athletic
(4–0, 0–3)

Despite these gratifying results the storm cones were already hoisted. Burnley had fielded a makeshift side for their return match at Tynecastle and despite Hal Stewart's brave words he had transferred the young but vastly promising Joe Jordan to Leeds United on the very eve of the second-round tie against Wolves, although the £7000 on offer for winning the trophy would have recouped at least half the transfer fee.

In the second round Motherwell struck a telling blow for domestic football by disposing of a strong Tottenham Hotspur while Heart of Midlothian defeated Airdrie. The semi-finals were then seeded so that there would be a Scottish–English or a Scottish–Irish final. Heart of Midlothian reached the final where they went under to Wolverhampton Wanderers but the competition was not destined to attain any great age. Its effective deathblow was the decision by the Union of European Football Associations to assume responsibility for the Fairs' Cities Cup

THINKING ABOUT CHANGE

which then became the U.E.F.A. Cup. Henceforth its fixtures took priority over those of the Texaco Cup and thus the latter was killed off in short time.

The Texaco Cup had extended over the season but in late 1970 plans were laid for a brief pre-season tournament the following August which would involve the four highest scoring sides from each of the two Scottish Divisions. The smaller clubs were delighted with this development, the big two, forever circling each other warily, were less so. Neither Jock Stein nor his opposite number, Willie Waddell was anxious to start the season with a defeat which involved the loss of a trophy however new, and Celtic chairman Desmond White was even less enthusiastic. In an interview in the *Celtic View* of August 4 1971 he left the reader in no doubt of his feelings on the subject:

> "Let's deal first with the Drybrough competition. To our mind it is quite unimaginative and offers nothing to the clubs that most need a financial lift. The rewards will go to those who need them least.
>
> There is another aspect that worries us. With the Home Internationals running into June and the Drybrough matches beginning at the end of July the close season is virtually non-existent. This is a dangerous development. Football all the year round must be inimical to the true interests of the sport. You can get too much of a good thing. Even a child will tire of strawberries if he is fed them all the time—and you can scarcely catalogue Drybrough's in football's strawberry class.
>
> The Texaco Cup on the other hand provided football of a high competitive standard against English opposition. This type of game always stimulates the interest in Scotland. Celtic are not opposed to additional matches on a blanket-negative basis. What we are against is football at a sort of semi-stagnation level which is detrimental to the game's interests."

Plain speaking and very typical of Desmond White's approach to the game's problems. On the topics of over-extension of the season, meaningless games and for that matter exhaustion of the players he was very largely right. But while Scots were always interested in matches against English clubs the converse was simply not true. English eyes were on Europe and any matches against Scottish clubs would be distinctly second-best, although weakened sides would be fielded to provide an alibi in the case of defeat. This put Scottish teams in an intolerable position. If they won, their victory was devalued. If they lost, it confirmed the notions of English superiority which the English already held.

Celtic gave further proof of their aversion to such competitions as the Drybrough Cup when they served notice in May 1971 that they would oppose the League rule which made it mandatory for all clubs to take part in all League competitions.

In a strange reversal of roles from the previous season, Dumbarton attempted to take over Clyde who a mere twelve months before had been prepared to do the same office for Hamilton Academical. This was widely seen as a device to obtain First Division football for Dumbarton by the back door and the notion found little or no support. The new Scottish League Secretary, Tommy Maule, said, "If Clyde were to take over Dumbarton there would be no problem about retaining First Division status. But if Dumbarton, as seems to be the case, want to take over Clyde, they have no chance of gaining First Division membership by such a move."

Robert Robertson, chairman of the Hutcheson Engineering Group which would have financed such a bid, said that Alec Jackson, the manager of Dumbarton had been instructed by the Dumbarton board to approach Clyde and open negotiations. It would be a straight cash settlement subject to the League being agreeable to a Dumbarton/Clyde combination being given first-class status.

Clubs were going to have to look at new ways in which to make a living. Pools money had by now risen to £100 per point which was gratifying, but attendances were falling. Season 1970-71 had seen a drop of 143,000 in aggregate attendances and interestingly, the side showing the most steep decline were Celtic whose sixth consecutive championship success was seen by 47,000 fewer than their fifth in matches at Parkhead.

Despite Celtic's expressed reservations the Drybrough Cup duly took place and became Scotland's first sponsored tourney purely for Scottish clubs. It was in essence a spin-off from the similar Watney Mann competition in England, Drybrough's being a subsidiary of that company. The method of selection of clubs, the four highest scorers from each Division, seemed not unreasonable but it did not receive a wholly favourable press. Alex Cameron, chief sports writer of the *Daily Record* noted that, "In my view, to try to achieve finalists with the widest appeal to please the sponsor gives a competition a phoney look."

Yet something had to be done because on Saturday April 24 1971 only 39,000 spectators had watched 16 league games. Was the type of football being played to blame? No less a player than the great Gordon Smith, who knew what he was talking about when it came to Scottish league football, thought that it was. He clearly thought the worth of the individual player was being under-

THINKING ABOUT CHANGE

KENNY DALGLISH (*Celtic and Liverpool*)
As durable as he was skilful, Dalglish scored 100 goals in both Scottish and Football Leagues, played 100 times for Scotland, won League medals and Cup medals in both countries, lifted European Cup medals with Liverpool and made the transition to highly successful Manager at Annfield astonishingly easily. He was that great rarity among footballers, a highly creative player who was a clinical finisher.

regarded: "After all, a final score is a fact and a fact is a dull thing, whereas a movement by Finney or Matthews is an end in itself. That, says the true spectator, is enough, I have had my money's worth."

The League and clubs were often accused about this time with being obsessed with the notion of reconstruction but the problems facing the game were vast and not to look to see if there might be a better way would have been a gross dereliction of duty. The game now faced opposition from individual participant sports. Few people worked on a Saturday so the half-dozen really big clubs could take large travelling supports with them. This especially affected clubs such as Partick Thistle and Clyde who had formerly picked up large numbers of Old Firm supporters when Rangers and Celtic were far out of town. Other sports were willing to use the showcase of Saturday afternoon television and even people well-disposed towards football were prepared to spend at least the occasional Saturday at home watching the Grand National or a Rugby Union International. There was a feeling that League football had become all too predictable. In his *Scottish Football Book No. 18* of 1972 the veteran writer Hugh Taylor in his editorial said, "To be blunt, the First Division has become a farce. Celtic are so far out on their own that they can win the flag without looking round."

Increasingly they were winning it with fewer people looking on. Jock Stein talked of amalgamation although it has to be said, with less than his usual degree of clarity and insight: "Amalgamation seems to me to be the only answer. But amalgamation must be in the interests of the big as well as the small clubs. The S.F.A. and the League could help." He did not specify how they could help and it is hard to follow his reasoning here. It is much more likely that Dundee for example can either support two football teams or none. Support is not suddenly going to emerge for some hybrid team bearing the name of Dundee City. What would in all probability happen is that the dedicated supporters of the existing Dundee sides would simply withdraw from the game. There is absolutely no evidence of a re-distribution of the 10,000 or so Third Lanark supporters among the other Glasgow clubs. They either abandoned football or transferred their attentions to Pollok, a local Junior team in the south side of Glasgow.

By January 1973 the alarm bells were ringing loud and long. An informal meeting was called by Tom Hart, chairman of Hibernian, to discuss the drop in attendances which, with only half the season gone, were 190,000 down in the First Division. Hearts had seen 45,000 vanish, Rangers, in a very bad trough by their standards,

60,000, but Celtic on their way to acquiring their seventh championship in a row had lost an astonishing 71,500 spectators. Moreover, even the most successful clubs in Scotland were unable to hang on to their players. It was deeply worrying when Celtic saw a player such as Lou Macari leave for Manchester United and even more so that he gave as one of his major reasons for going south the goldfish-bowl nature of the game in Scotland. It was now that Ian Archer of the *Glasgow Herald* made his famous remark: "We are fast reaching the stage where the only talented players inside Scotland will be those who also suffer from homesickness."

Celtic, the two Edinburgh clubs and both Dundee sides all attended Tom Hart's meeting but Rangers declined their invitation. The meeting recommended changes in Television and Radio contracts for League matches and a revision in allocation of payments from the Pools Promoters Association which would favour the larger clubs. In addition, the visitor's share of the League gates should be reduced to 20 per cent (the big clubs had for years argued that equal division of gates meant that they in effect subsidised the rest of the League), there should be amended and improved terms for sponsorship of the League Cup and Drybrough Cup and the League Cup should return to its old format. The various changes in the convoluted history of the League Cup demand and will receive, a separate chapter.

Rangers, who had stayed away from this meeting, called one of their own a fortnight later and this time it was the turn of Celtic to abstain, feeling that it followed too closely on the one at Easter Road. The Ibrox meeting was less radical, contenting itself with the suggestion that no points at all should be awarded for a goalless draw, that £1000 should be given to the season's leading scorer and that there should be awards for the best player in every position. The last-named point had been tried and worked very well in American baseball and could very easily have been just as successful here but the chance of a worthwhile experiment was lost.

Clubs were not always realistic in what they would like to see done. On March 19 1973 at an S.F.A. meeting Desmond White of Celtic in opposing a radio broadcast of a semi-final of the Scottish Cup said that radio was disastrous to other clubs playing on the same Saturday and that Scottish Television was trying to establish regular sports programmes on Sundays, a day when in the future important matches might be played.

> "Live spectators come first, and while we regret that the elderly and the sick should be deprived, we must not pander to the lazy and indifferent and encourage an armchair audience."

It was not as simple as that. The footballing authorities were right to be suspicious of live T.V. but everything pointed to the fact that increasingly the radio audiences were at matches and followed events from other grounds on their transistor radios. The instantaneous cheers or groans as a hated rival went behind or ahead was eloquent testimony to that. If broadcasting was stopped so too would all kinds of invaluable trailers come to an end, "puffs" for matches and information on matches on and off in winter. If broadcasting fees were dispensed with, would sufficient numbers come back through the turnstiles to compensate for their loss? Above all, what would happen to trackside hoardings and boards once advertisers found that there was going to be little or no televised coverage of important matches? The Broadcasting media and football were inter-dependent and the sooner both realised that the better it would be. Drawing breath, the Management Committee tried again.

If the game had become negative and stereotyped, something should be done about it. An experimental offside rule was introduced for the Drybrough Cup in 1973 whereby the 18-yard line would be extended to both touchlines and offside would only apply within these areas. Flushed with its notion, the Management Committee proposed that this should apply to all competitions in season 1973–74.

Not for the first time, the Management Committee had got ahead of the members. It was pointed out that the S.F.A. and not the League controlled the conditions under which the Scottish Cup would be played and there were other, greater, snags. Such an experiment could only be tried domestically and how would Scots in European matches fare when asked to revert to the traditional offside law? Come to that how would Home Scots adjust to the altered situation in international matches? It was argued that players did this fairly easily in the different types of professional cricket and counter-argued, unanswerably, that cricket was not football. The experiment was thus confined to the Drybrough Cup and, for one season only, the League Cup. As neither competition was taken particularly seriously at that time, the lessons learned from them were discounted. The whole episode showed the difficulty of introducing any really radical reform to the game.

By the 1970's industry had come to terms with the notion of A.C.A.S. and Industrial Tribunals and it seemed as if football might well have to do so too. In April 1973 the Scottish Professional Footballers Association appointed the 25 year old Gordon Dunwoodie as their Secretary and he at once identified his main target for attack. He threatened to appeal against sus-

CITY PARK
Good enough for Edinburgh City when they were Scottish League members but not for Ferranti Thistle who had to change both name (to Meadowbank Thistle) and ground (to Meadowbank Stadium).

pensions "which deprive players of their livelihood without proper representation and are therefore contrary to natural justice." It was decided that the S.P.F.A. should wait for a case involving a full-time player to arise. The Association's most recent recruiting drive had been very successful so that now only Rangers, Berwick Rangers, Brechin City and Queen's Park (whose players as amateurs had no concern with the aims or objects of the S.P.F.A.) were not represented in their ranks.

The main features of the Annual General Meeting of the League in 1973 were the overwhelming rejection of the proposed offside amendment and Ayr United's success in getting agreement that in bad weather, a game could be postponed the day before it was due if the two clubs were separated by more than 100 miles. For the first time ever, League fixtures could be cancelled where necessary on the Saturdays before World Cup Qualifying matches. Clubs were also empowered to field two substitutes in matches under League auspices although it remains the case that this is an entitlement rather than a compulsion.

Sponsorship was not easy to attract, partly because firms such as Drybrough understandably resented the trenchant criticism of their own competition and partly because The Scottish Football League could only offer limited exposure in British terms. There was great chagrin when the tobacco company John Player declined to sponsor the League Cup in the summer of 1973 but it was pointed out that Scotland was a limited market and most national companies in Scotland were controlled either from England or abroad. The whisky firm, Bell's of Perth, were later approached with more success.

The League had got itself into a bonny tangle over television. A maximum of twenty minutes was allowed for filmed matches on Saturday nights but there was still opposition to Sunday transmission. There could be mid-week showings after 10 p.m. and any English games must also be restricted to 20 minutes. For transmission of any European games the approval of the Television Sub Committee had to be obtained.

In May 1974 a new Associate Member joined The Scottish League when Ferranti Thistle's application was successful. The interested follower of the Scottish game will seek in vain for the name Ferranti Thistle on any League table. It was decided that it was not fitting that a League side should directly reflect industrial involvement and the name was changed to Meadowbank Thistle as, for the first time in twenty years, Edinburgh had more than two Senior clubs. The new club not only needed to change its name but also its ground, since City Park was adjudged unsatisfactory for League football. The newcomers therefore had to take up residence at Meadowbank Stadium which, while better equipped, has proved less than totally satisfactory as a ground at which to watch football.

The election of Ferranti/Meadowbank had come as a considerable surprise as there had been other applicants, namely Ross County, Forres Mechanics, Gateshead United, Hawick Royal Albert, Elgin City and Inverness Thistle. Had only one Highland applicant gone forward that might have been enough to swing it but distance and poor road communications were cited as a reason for not admitting any team from the north. Some five years later the A9 road was improved out of all recognition and that argument would have held no validity. It is unlikely that this was the real reason for preferring Ferranti anyway. They were regarded as choppingblocks and a fertile source of pools pointage but although they struggled badly at first, the club worked wonders with the slenderest of resources and in the mid-1980s would come very close to gaining Premier Division status.

By now, the summer of 1974, the member clubs, having frequently rejected modest proposals for reform, threw caution to the winds and agreed to a radically new set-up. There would be a Premier Division of just 10 clubs with two up and two down. There would be a First Division of 14 clubs and a Second of the same number. To those who asked "What's in a name?" the answer was

A MEETING OF TWO GREATS

Jock Wallace greets a badly-injured John Greig who had come on as a substitute for Rangers championship-winning match at Easter Road in 1975. On the right is Sandy Jardine who had come off to let Greig make a token appearance.

"Everything". There would have been fierce opposition to the Divisions being called First, Second and Third Division. Memories of the 1920's were still searingly vivid fifty years later and East Stirlingshire, Montrose, Forfar Athletic, Brechin City and Queen of the South had no wish to renew acquaintance with a Third Division. To make sure that the new Second Division could not be lopped off neatly at a convenient date, the small clubs insisted that it must contain at least one third of the clubs in membership of The Scottish Football League.

Clubs would be given a year in which to find the level at which they would be competing and season 1974-75 was designated for the grading process. The top ten sides in the First Division would form the Premier Division, the next eight in the First Division (old style) and the top six in the Second Division (old style) would make up the First Division (new style) and the remaining fourteen clubs would form the Second Division (new style).

It reads rather more complicatedly than in fact it was. The last season under the old regime was noteworthy for the fact that Rangers under their manager, Jock Wallace, took the title away from Celtic after their outstanding manager, Jock Stein, had guided the Parkhead club to the flag for nine consecutive years. There were those among the Celtic support who saw the new structure as a deliberate attempt to stop Celtic winning but in truth, although success automatically guaranteed European entry for Celtic, there had been a marked diminution in their gates despite their unbroken run of triumphs.

The ten sides in the Premier Division would play each other four times, the sides in the other two division would meet on the traditional two occasions. To make up the number of games for them, important from a pools money standpoint, there would be a supplementary competition to be called the Spring Cup. After a season's work the clubs stood as follows for the League matches of 1975–76:

PREMIER DIVISION:—Rangers, Hibernian, Celtic, Dundee United, Aberdeen, Dundee, Ayr United, Heart of Midlothian, St. Johnstone, Motherwell. FIRST DIVISION:—Airdrieonians, Kilmarnock, Partick Thistle, Dumbarton, Dunfermline Athletic, Clyde, Morton, Arbroath, Falkirk, Queen of the South, Hamilton Academical, East Fife, Montrose, St. Mirren.
SECOND DIVISION:—Clydebank, Stirling Albion, East Stirlingshire, Berwick Rangers, Stenhousemuir, Albion Rovers, Raith Rovers, Stranraer, Alloa, Queen's Park, Brechin City, Meadowbank Thistle, Cowdenbeath, Forfar Athletic.

The thinking behind the creation of the new League set-up was logical enough. There would be two up, two down between each of the divisions. There was the hope and the wish that every team in the Premier Division would be a full-time side, for there had been those who wanted to make this a condition of entry. Clubs would also be expected to field a team in the Premier Reserve League. As to the two lower divisions, there was the notion that small clubs which had shied away from promotion to the old-style First Division would not now take fright at the idea of moving from Division Two to Division One. Scottish footballing folklore was plentifully supplied with stories of small Second Division clubs which, on the brink of promotion, had lost their last four matches to inferior opposition or mysteriously transferred their star centre-forward at a critical time.

In the famous case of the bribery of the Stenhousmuir goalkeeper in 1926 (or rather, the attempted bribery) counsel for the bookmaker involved in the case had sought to cast doubt on the Larbert club's commitment to promotion. He received no very positive answer from the then club secretary, Malcolm Roughead, who on his appearance in the witness box and being asked if Stenhousemuir might decline to accept promotion if they won it on the grounds of expense, could do no better than stammer, "That has not been settled by our Committee."

The mundane matter of fixing guarantees was attended to and they were set at £1000 for the Premier Division, £500 in the First Division and £200 in the Second Division. The top four clubs in the League would be seeded in the League Cup of the following season. Attendances had continued to fall, not helped by ill-luck such as was evinced in the miners' strike of 1973–74. This led to a prohibition on football under floodlights which meant that games had to kick-off at 2 p.m. in November and December, with a bad effect on gates. In the emergency, permission was sought and won to play competitive football on Sundays, but although this dispensation was introduced with a great flourish of trumpets, the notion of Sunday football never really established itself. For the spectator it seemed to have little more than curiosity value, while there were objections from neighbouring residents. The police did not like the notion of Sunday duty and adjusted their charges accordingly. Football folks were scarcely more enthusiastic. Players resented having inroads made on their week-end and managers had to keep an edgy squad motivated for an additional day. More decisive than all these perhaps was the implacable opposition of the Pools Promoters Association whose massive operation was geared to matches being played on Saturdays and for whom a move would cause such severe dislocation that any club wishing to change its fixture to a Sunday had to give six weeks' notification of its intention to do so.

Very tentatively, therefore, Scottish football entered upon a new era which, it was hoped should mean fewer meaningless games for the supporter and a fair chance that League title races might be protracted until the last month of the season. Nobody imagined that the major surgery would effect an instantaneous and total cure. Some thought the patient past saving but the League were to show very soon that they had taken the advice of Shakespeare and plucked the flower, safety, from the nettle, danger.

Chapter Nine

THE PREMIER DIVISION THE 1970s

It would have been too much to expect that the new League structure would be found to be correct in every particular right off the reel and it took some time for the public to warm to it. From the outset it was apparent that it would be difficult to maintain Premier Divison status. Two clubs went down from ten and, as it was extremely difficult to envisage any situation in which Celtic or Rangers would be involved in relegation trouble, effectively the other clubs stood a one in four chance of relegation. Over the years there has been a tendency for the gap between the Divisions to increase. Thus, of the clubs who made up the Second Division (new style) in its first year of operation, only Clydebank have ever managed to achieve the heights of the Premier Division and that but briefly.

In that very first season Dundee United only remained in the Premier Division—so for that matter did Aberdeen—because their goal difference was better than that of their neighbours up the road, an ironic twist when one considers their excellent records in the top stream thereafter. The experiment of a 26 match League programme for the other two divisions was anything but successful, and the Spring Cup failed to excite much public support. It was won by Airdrie, who defeated Clydebank in the final after extra time, but the League itself, in not having the trophy engraved originally, had perhaps some pre-vision that this was not a tournament which was likely to endure. So unpopular was it that the First and Second Divisions clubs adopted a motion from Albion Rovers in May 1976 that the clubs in these divisions should meet each other three times. Inevitably this led to inequities in the fixture list as a club might meet a strong rival twice in away matches and only once at home but the fact that clubs were very willing to accept this points to the proof that the 26 match programme had been ill-conceived.

Rangers had won the first of the Premier Divisions, as they had won the last of the old-style First Divisions but the real beneficiaries of the Premier League would in the rather longer term prove to be Aberdeen and Dundee United, the New Firm as they came to be called. Both sides seemed to thrive on meeting the Old Firm four times in a season and at different times Aberdeen and Dundee United established a remarkable ascendancy over Rangers and Celtic respectively. From the very beginning there was pressure to increase the numbers in the Premier Division to 12 clubs but agreement could not be secured for clubs to meet each other three times in a season and to undertake a four-meeting programme, which would entail 44 matches with 12 clubs was to give a considerable hostage to the Scottish weather.

On the legislative side there was a feeling that the Management Committee would reflect the realities of the new order with four Premier Division representatives and three for each of the other two divisions. The bulk of clubs outside the Premier Division thought that matters would be best served by three representatives from each of the three divisions.

Television fees continued to increase though not as fast as the League would have wished. The B.B.C. were now paying £550 for each of 34 recordings of 20 minutes with Scottish Television being charged £825 for each 30 minute excerpt from 40 matches. Both networks would pay £1700 for the privilege of screening highlights of the League Cup Final. Matters were somewhat strained at this time because individual clubs were allowed to exclude the cameras from their grounds, a rather strange procedure one might think in view of the fact that the television sub-committee was empowered to negotiate for all clubs in membership. Hibernian, under their chairman, Tom Hart, were particularly intransigent and on several occasions turned camera crews away on the day of important League matches. It is interesting to note that the then Secretary of the Scottish Football Association, Willie P. Allan, held in reserve the right to switch the venue from Easter Road should a similar situation arise in a Scottish Cup tie under the aegis of the S.F.A. The television companies, particularly Scottish Television, showed remarkable forbearance in a situation whereby their contract with the League was largely ineffectual. There was for instance no television coverage of Celtic's championship win at Easter Road on the last full day of season 1973 although given Robert Kelly's earlier and vigorously-expressed reservations about television (by no means totally ill-founded) Celtic could hardly complain too vociferously of their exclusion from the nation's screens.

In that first year of the Premier Division there had been an important change in sponsored football in that the Texaco Cup ceased to be and was replaced by an Anglo-Scottish Cup involving the teams that would have taken part had the sponsorship remained operative. This new tournament would be run by a sub-committee of both Leagues but would encounter very much the same difficulties as its predecessor. In September 1976 Newcastle United fielded a reserve side for their match against Ayr United at Somerset Park. Spectators were being cozened and Tom Lauchlan, representing the Scottish League, described the side turned out by Newcastle United as "a disgrace". He asked that Newcastle United should be at once disqualified and fined heavily and that there should be an urgent meeting between the Scottish League and Football League to prevent any repetition of the fiasco.

Try as they might, football legislators find themselves more often acting to close loopholes than to make genuine innovations. In April 1977 there was widespread applause when both bodies, S.F.A. and Scottish League, decided that suspensions of players should be for matches rather than a term of days, when clubs might have no fixture or weather impose a cancellation. This was good thinking by the legislators but they had to move to close a further bolthole as clubs suddenly resurrected long-defunct county competitions in order to get spurious matches played which could work off suspensions. No club wanted to be without a key player who was perfectly fit when pools money now stood at £359, £331 and £331 a point in the three divisions.

Celtic won the Premier Division on its second running, a success all the more noteworthy in that it would be the last major achievement of Jock Stein with the club before severing his connection with it.

It was a period of considerable crowd misbehaviour, so frequent and troublesome that it would soon require specific legislation and there was one major bout of disagreement between Association and League. In a match between Motherwell and Rangers at Fir Park, Rangers supporters had invaded the ground early in the proceedings when Motherwell were leading 2–0. Play was suspended and when it resumed Rangers went on to win 5–3. Certain Motherwell players claimed that they had been affected by the pitch invasion and the S.F.A. had ordained that the match should be replayed. Rangers dissented strongly from this decision and they were backed by the League, the result of the match eventually standing. The League issued the following Press release:

> "The Management Committee at its meeting today unanimously decided not to accept the recommendations of the

S.F.A. Disciplinary and Refereeing Committee. The matter is therefore referred back to the S.F.A. The Scottish Football League, like the S.F.A. is anxious to rid football of hooliganism. The Management Committee will be placing before the clubs for their approval rules which would be in operation early next season whereby any attempt to influence the result of a game will result in the club concerned being severely dealt with. It is the avowed intent of The Scottish Football League that they will in no way tolerate an invasion of the pitch in any match under their jurisdiction. We consider it to be the responsibility of all persons, Chairmen, Directors, Officials, Players and Supporters to ensure that clubs do not suffer for the indiscretions of hooligans. We will co-operate with the S.F.A. and the civil authorities to stamp out hooliganism."

This was a fine clear statement of intent, even if in the short run it was of singularly little consolation to the luckless Motherwell. In the end wire fencing would be the answer to pitch invasion though at the cost of creating even more dreadful situations.

The topic of the national stadium continued to exercise minds. The fine old stadium, Hampden, was exactly that, a fine old stadium and the very features which had made it pre-eminent—sheer size and wide-open terracings—had ensured that it would be overtaken by time. It could be argued that the Scottish League had no great need for Hampden, they only required it for the League Cup final now that Inter-League matches had had their day, but the League committee men were lovers of Scottish football and there was an almost-involuntary attachment to the place.

A thorough reconstruction would cost £5.5 million and in July 1978 the Government announced that it was prepared to find half of this money subject to certain conditions, among which were that the clubs themselves had to be seen to be active in the matter of donations and fund-raising. It was suggested that clubs should donate £70 a point from their pools money which would have raised £101,640 but there was no eagerness to respond. The League itself was not prepared to make any capital contribution but might perhaps assist in the upkeep of Hampden. In response to a questionnaire sent out to clubs there was overwhelming support for a world-wide appeal for donations rather than direct League action. Clubs approved this course by 35 votes to 2 although why Venezuelans, Danes, Australians and Malays should have been expected to discharge a purely Scottish responsibility does not seem very clear.

Meanwhile, in 1979, the League made a change in the Secretaryship in less than happy surroundings. Misgivings had been expressed for some time about the calibre of the day to day administration in the League office. League Secretary Tommy Maule had a long history of service to the League, having joined as a clerk in 1949 and, after a period as Assistant Secretary, succeeded to the top job on the death of Fred Denovan in 1970. He had been asked to resign in January 1979 but did not do so and was dismissed personally by the then League President, Tom Lauchlan in May of that year. For the last few months he had been working without an assistant following the departure of Campbell Ogilvie to become Assistant Secretary of Rangers. There had been 150 applications for the post of Assistant Secretary of the League but for some reason the post remained unfilled. Tommy Maule was only the third full-time Secretary in the history of the League, the others being Willie MacAndrew and Fred Denovan.

That the parting was less than harmonious can be seen from the statement issued at the time by Tom Lauchlan:

> "The Scottish Football League have reluctantly decided to terminate Mr. Maule's appointment as Secretary of the Scottish Football League as of today. He has been made a very good offer to accept the decision but has decided to take it to an Industrial Tribunal."

The League intimated that it would defend its decision at the Tribunal but a few days later Mr. Lauchlan had happier news for the waiting reporters.

> "The management of the Scottish Football League are happy to announce that the dispute between them and Mr. Maule, arising out of the latter's dismissal from the secretaryship, has been resolved amicably. They are pleased now to have the opportunity to express their gratitude to Mr. Maule for 29 years of service to the Scottish Football League. They are confident that his wide knowledge of football will secure a post for him within the football context and assure him that he will always be a welcome figure throughout the League."

In 1980 Tommy Maule was to be asked to become the Secretary of the Canadian National League. His hard work there did not bear fruition since the project fell through because most of the leading Canadian clubs were already in the North American Soccer League and in the end a competition that could only bring Toronto, Montreal, Hamilton, Calgary and Halifax to the starting line was simply not viable.

Tommy Maule's replacement was Jim Farry who came from the

S.F.A. at the age of 25 and who combined an extraordinary talent for day-to-day administration with a far-seeing eye where the commercial and marketing side of the game was concerned. He was emphatic that the game was underselling itself and neglecting potentially lucrative areas of exploitation. He suggested early on that this was something which the League might think worthy of prolonged consideration.

The late 1970s was a period of severe inflation and rapidly escalating costs and it was a difficult job to keep revenue ahead of expenditure. In July 1979 an exclusive three year contract was agreed with B.B.C. Radio with payments of £150, £175 and £210 over that period (the figure changing each year) for normal live broadcasts and £300, £350 and £420 for the League Cup final. Over the same period on television recording highlights would go from £2000 in 1979 to £2800 in 1982 while the price of League Cup final coverage rose dramatically from £4560 to £6000.

This was gratifying, but in that very same month of July 1979 notification was received that police charges were to be increased and there would for the first time be a charge made by the police where a match was postponed on the day of the game, presumably on the grounds that duty rosters would by that time have already been made out. The very high police charges meant that Sunday football was hardly a feasibility and even New Year's Day matches were now being looked at seriously, with a view to their discontinuance. Indeed, for a couple of years, the League, temporarily unsure of its product, would move away from New Year's Day but fortunately soon realised that this was a mistake and that there was certainly a public for matches on that day.

Sponsorship was secured for the League Cup, Bell's of Perth, the whisky firm, being the company which picked up the tag. At that time the competition stretched through until December and priority had to be given to League Cup ties over League fixtures to allow the competition to finish in time. Elsewhere, sponsorship was not proving so successful. Aberdeen had nipped in to take the League title in 1979–80 under their dynamic young manager Alex. Ferguson and they would win in successive years in 1984 and 1985, something that only Hibernian and Dumbarton had accomplished outside the Old Firm in the League's long history. The Dons had also won the Drybrough Cup in 1980 in front of a disappointing crowd at Hampden because of what the League described as "the time of the final and disappointing press coverage."

The League were perhaps rather hard on the Press here for it was not that body's remit to be uncritically appreciative of every new tournament that came upon the market. There were, equally,

WILLIE MILLER (*Aberdeen*)

Without doubt the greatest servant the Pittodrie club has ever had. No Scottish defender has read a game better and all major honours, including a European Cupwinners' Medal, have come his way. The senior partner in the defensive pairing with Alex McLeish he has competed with notable success at the pinnacle of achievement, the World Cup finals.

reservations expressed about the Anglo-Scottish tournament because there was not a single First Division club from England taking part but the Scots case was not helped by the defeat of Rangers by Chesterfield in that particular season and the Football League pointed out rather icily that they had no powers of compulsion to compel their clubs to enter. They could well have cited the initial reluctance of the major English clubs to become involved with their own League Cup which led to a stream of unlikely finalists in that competition's earliest years. That defeat of Rangers, was mercifully veiled in the future but even so a first-round draw which read: Blackpool v Kilmarnock, Rangers v Chesterfield, Notts County v Morton and Airdrieonians v Bury was not calculated to set the pulses racing. It was felt, and justifiably so, that this constituted a slight to Scottish football and the Secretary was instructed to notify the Football League that Scots clubs would not take part the following season if better-class opposition could not be guaranteed. It could not, and so the Anglo-Scottish competition died in comparative infancy.

Keeping the spectator informed was becoming ever more important. Clubs were now to exchange team lines at least 30 minutes before the match in the referee's room with this in mind. It did not eliminate entirely the very late announcement of teams or on occasion their non-announcement but it deprived clubs of an excuse for not informing the crowd of the identity of those players they were about to see. In 1979 too the decision was taken to bring out a Scottish League Review in association with the Clydesdale Bank and over the years the League Review has become a collectors' item, renowned for its blend of statistical accuracy and vigorous, informative writing.

The whole question of sponsorship could be very complex as indicated by the deal concluded on footballs. The League had reached an agreement with Mitre that the latter would provide 1000 footballs free for the clubs in League membership together with a 5 per cent royalty on every ball sold, but this cut across a contract which Aberdeen had already concluded on their own behalf with Adidas. Naturally enough, Mitre wanted total League coverage and the League instructed Aberdeen to make the switch. The result was that Adidas took legal action against the club and it was some time before an amicable settlement was arrived at which allowed the change to be made.

Always the main problem which the League had to address was "How do we preserve a high standard of professional football in a relatively small consumer market?" Sponsors tended to go almost as fast as they came. Drybrough's, severely disillusioned, with-

THE PREMIER DIVISION — THE 1970s 205

BILLY McNEILL (*Celtic*)

His nickname, "Caesar", identifies him as one of nature's leaders. He was an inspirational Captain in the great Stein days and an under-used International centre-half. His command in the air was legendary. He has subsequently had two fine spells as manager of his playing Club, divided by forays to England which were less successful.

drew in November 1980 and were followed five months later by Bell's. Figures released by the Scottish League showed that 70 per cent of Scottish professional footballers were part-time and certainly the whole of the Second Division was playing out of a love of the game rather than for thoughts of any immediate pecuniary reward.

Several steps were taken to put matters to rights. In January 1980 the League President Tom Lauchlan stated that Inter-League matches against the two Leagues in Ireland should be carried on to give encouragement to those players remaining in Scotland. Games would therefore be played on consecutive days in March 1980 in Dublin and Belfast. Scotland had to be made attractive for Scots players and for that matter managers, since over the next few years such as Alex. Ferguson and Billy McNeill would be lured away and this after Jock Stein had had his brief flirtation with Leeds United.

There was a need for greater discipline from the clubs in membership. From the chair Tom Lauchlan pointed out that it was vital that the League should be empowered to act as a unit on behalf of all members, especially in cases of money accruing to the League. He added sternly that individual clubs should not use the Press to publicise a particular grievance, real or alleged. At the same meeting there was a move to allow home clubs to retain the entire gate and although it was defeated it had come to pass within a year.

It began to look as if the number of Scottish League clubs would be permanently frozen at 38. Inverness Caledonian, Keith and Hawick Royal Albert all applied for admission to the League in 1980 and all were rejected. That did not mean that the composition of the three Divisions was immutable as Motherwell argued in a submission on that hardiest of annuals, League re-organisation:

> "The Premier Division is hard, tight, entertaining and uncompromising in every way. Spectators love it, managers hate it and directors get ulcers from it. It has revived the fortunes of many dying clubs and simultaneously it has thrown several well-known full-time teams into disarray."

The submission went on to argue that on the whole, however, the penalties for failure were too severe:

> "The cost of failure and of consequent relegation is horrifying. For this reason, and for this reason only, we suggest an increase in the number of Premier Division clubs to 12 from 10."

There was a fair amount of sympathy and support for Motherwell's views on reconstruction but as yet not enough. The topic which demanded the total attention of clubs in 1980 was the violent behaviour of spectators which eventually required the direct intervention of the lawmakers, that is to say, the judiciary.

The emerging pattern of crowd violence had been clearly discernible since the late 1960's when the fashion of pitch invasions began. In the early stages these were the speciality of small boys and not over-intelligent youths, intent on the congratulation of scorers and irritating rather than sinister. There were those who from the outset proclaimed that infringement of playing space by spectators must lead to eventual serious trouble and others who saw such events as mere manifestations of the exuberance of a modern youth which was for ever being exhorted to "do its own thing."

As the number of pitch invasions increased and as they took on a more sinister turn (we have mentioned the Motherwell v Rangers match and there had been a serious invasion by Celtic supporters during a Scottish Cup semi-final at Ibrox against St. Mirren as far back as 1960) it became clear that the adherents of the first party had been proved correct and that crowds had no status whatsoever on the pitch, no matter the circumstances, except possibly in the event of fire in the ground or overcrowding.

Matters came to a head with the infamous Scottish Cup Final of 1980 in which supporters of Celtic and Rangers fought a pitched battle on the playing field which was only terminated by the vigorous though extremely belated action of mounted police. The price to be paid for that outburst of savagery was the Criminal Justice (Scotland) Act 1980. The Act is overlong to quote in full but its main provisions can be summarised thus:

1. The transport of intoxicating liquor on buses or special trains was forbidden.

2. The licensee of a vehicle and his employees and agents were liable for any infraction of the above injunction.

3. There were to be no controlled containers in a football ground, i.e. there was not to be any portable container open or sealed, which is or was in its original manufactured state capable of containing liquid. (It is worth noting that this effectively banned flasks which carried nothing more harmful than tea, coffee or soup.)

4. Possession of alcohol within the confines of a football stadium was an offence.

5. It became an offence to be drunk within a ground or while attempting to enter one.

6. Powers of search of persons or vehicles were given to the police.

It has to be said that although the provisions were severe, the effect of the Criminal Justice (Scotland) Act 1980 has been wholly beneficial and in a very large measure has preserved the Scottish game from the worst of the excesses which have manifested themselves in England. It could be argued that it is because of this Act that Scottish clubs are still taking part in European competitions in this season of 1990–91. It would also lead eventually to a slowing of the appalling rapidity with which police surveillance charges were rising, although there were heavy initial costs for the installation of the electronic equipment which would enable that surveillance to be exercised.

If the Premier Division was doing nothing else it was making clubs think long and deep about the future of the game in Scotland. Aberdeen were the next to express strong reservations about the new set-up in a letter signed by their chairman, Dick Donald. What the northern club had to say was of especial interest in that it was widely recognised that their three-man Board was amongst the most progressive in Scotland and that since Aberdeen had done well since the establishment of the Premier Division, they were absolved from the charge of arguing from short-term self-interest. The letter signed by the Aberdeen chairman read as follows:

"The official statistical information available shows that the reconstructed Scottish League has achieved some of the original aims, particularly increased attendances. Nevertheless, the consensus of clubs in the Premier Division is that the time is now opportune for further changes to be made in the organisation of competitions in the Scottish League.

The reasons for further changes to be made urgently can be summarised as follows:

(*a*) The intensity of competition in the 10 Club Premier Division with 20 per cent of its clubs relegated each year has stultified the standard of play and has created fear and negativeness in the play of most teams.

(*b*) The high relegation or failure rate each season is a major disincentive for clubs to make financial and other plans for the improvement and development of their stadia and facilities.

(*c*) The need for greater stability in the Premier Division so that (1) programmes for the development of young players can be implemented and (2) the fulfilment of contracts for young players can be assured.

(*d*) The serious effect on and consequences to Scottish football arising from the "Freedom of Movement" contracts available to players as from season 1980–81.

(*e*) The need for increased revenue to meet the additional high cost especially from (*d*) which will accrue to Clubs as from next season, in order to offer contracts to players that are attractive enough to keep them in Scottish football.
(*f*) The danger that the present great uncertainty in the Premier Division, linked with the inadequate revenue available for clubs, will have a catalystic and deleterious effect on Scottish football whereby, *inter alia*, very few clubs will have the financial resources to maintain full-time contracted players.
(*g*) The need to help clubs to market their games to the best possible advantage by a re-arrangement of the playing season to eliminate the poorly-supported Christmas and New Year period."

The letter went on to suggest that there should be only one club promoted to the Premier Division from the First Division with only one club suffering relegation. Alternatively it argued for a 12–14–12 structure which was very similar to that which was to be tried in the middle 1980s.

The Aberdeen letter was well researched and thought out but it is indicative of the deep division within Scottish football on the subject of league formation that about the same time East Fife received almost as much support for their plan to return to two divisions of 18 and 20 clubs respectively.

As has been mentioned before the Criminal Justice (Scotland) Act 1980 would necessitate the provision of equipment for the new safety measures demanded in the wake of such tragedies as the Ibrox Disaster of 1971. Immediately, safety measures had been put in hand in 1971 but these would now have to be reviewed and upgraded. A Football Grounds Improvement Trust had been set up with the emphasis on safety measures but it was felt that it was almost exclusively English-oriented and Scotland, lacking a Trustee on the board, was perceived to be at a severe disadvantage. Eventually Mr. Tom Wharton, the distinguished referee and supervisor, would become the national representative on the board.

The footballing authorities were quick to resent the imputation that they had not taken hooliganism either seriously enough or had acted sufficiently promptly. In October 1980 the Town Clerk of Glasgow got short shift when he wrote to the League on football hooliganism. The Secretary was requested to detail the many steps taken by clubs to deal with this problem and to suggest that perhaps the answer lay in the imposition of stronger deterrents by the courts.

Chapter Ten

THE SCOTTISH FOOTBALL LEAGUE IN THE 1980s

The radicals among football men in Scotland were convinced that the three division set-up was the best way forward but they needed heart and nerve because the new system was not seen to be immediately successful. League and League Cup attendances had spiralled downwards from 6,338,000 in 1956–57 to 4,433,000 in 1969–70 to 2,870,000 in 1980–81. Even allowing for the spectacular decline in the League championship fortunes of Rangers over the last few years, this was very worrying.

An informal meeting of club chairmen at S.F.A headquarters in Glasgow in the autumn of 1980 tried to work out what was wrong with each of the three divisions and came up with the following criticisms:

The Premier Division was felt to be too tight and therefore it encouraged purely defensive play. It stifled attacking flair, was well described as a pressure cooker and made managers unwilling to experiment with young players.

The First Division drew the strange remark that promotion was heavily contested, which might well have been thought to be a good thing. The yo-yo symptom was mentioned whereby clubs could secure promotion to the Premier Division but found themselves unable to survive there. They thereupon returned to the First Division for a new promotion campaign which, when successful, was equally short-lived. The system of clubs playing each other three times was fiercely attacked and the common complaint was, why do we have to play once at home and twice away against X?

The Second Division pointed, with almost total justification, to their neglect by the media. They never appeared on television, got a passing mention on radio and the column space they were allotted in newspapers had dwindled to vanishing point. They argued that if no one could read or hear of their existence there was no chance of turning round the decline in attendances. They likewise felt that 39 games was a bad idea and raised the issue of one home and two away matches against X. An additional burden for them, being entirely part-time, was the heavy cost of travel to away mid-week matches with players having to be compensated for time taken off work.

These were sufficiently accurate diagnoses, but finding the cure would prove to be more difficult. On the matter of field discipline, or rather field indiscipline, which was thought to deter spectators from attending although some felt that spectators enjoyed on-field confrontations, there was the suggestion that the Scottish League should take over the policing of its own competitions, the League and League Cup. In the event the S.F.A. was not prepared to waive its powers of regulation but it is fair to say that this has been a periodic source of friction between the two bodies. The last major incident occurred in season 1988–89 when the League refused to remove referees Louis Thow and Kenny Hope from the ballot after they had been disciplined by the S.F.A.

On a happier note the League had detected a significant improvement in crowd behaviour within a year of the application of the Criminal Justice (Scotland) Act 1980. Hampden Park, which had been the scene of the last outbreak of mob violence continued to cause concern. The League agreed in August 1981 that any further commitment it might make should be preceded by the ascertaining of the Stadium's long-term viability. On the assurance that the terracing would be concreted, given by Peter Buchanan, President of Queen's Park, it was agreed to continue support for Hampden as the national stadium.

A major revolutionary measure had slipped through comparatively unnoticed when on February 19 1981 clubs were given permission to keep their home gates. This removed the necessity for the League to recommend minimum admission prices for championship matches and allowed clubs to vary the cost of entrance with regard to the calibre and attraction of the opposition.

The Scottish League could certainly not be accused at this time of failing to consider the views of its members. As yet another informal meeting of club chairmen in October 1981 the subject for discussion was radio broadcasting and the feeling that emereged from the meeting was that Independent Radio would have to be watched. Desmond White of Celtic felt, as ever, that the marvellously comprehensive coverage given to the game by Radio Clyde in particular deterred people from actually going to football matches and in this belief he was supported by James Ferguson of Airdrieonians. There was a willingness to concede that Independent Radio was doing very good work in promoting and criticising the game in general but the overwhelming impression was that it was abusing certain privileges, especially that with regard to delayed live commentary and that this was detrimental to the League's existing contract with the B.B.C. The Management Committee took the feeling of the meeting and recommended a ban on live and delayed commentaries by Independent Radio, having regard to the exclusive B.B.C. contract.

This particular problem was resolved a year later when in January 1982 Radio Clyde were allowed to cover six matches with four score flashes, two in each half of 30 seconds each although complaints came in almost immediately from the clubs that the score flashes were in fact brief reports. The criticism lost some of its pith when it became apparent that against all British and European trends, attendances were beginning to recover, but the duration of the score flashes was reduced to 15 seconds.

Acceptance of sponsorship undoubtedly meant some loss of total liberty of action. Any notion of altering the season by a mid-December to mid-January close-down foundered on the difficulties that going on to May or even June would cause with World Cups and European club competitions. The moving of the season would, as previously mentioned cause insuperable difficulties with the Pools Promoters Association who were tied contractually to taking Australian fixtures during the British summer. It was impossible to ensure that any shifting of the season would have the desired beneficial effect, given that unpredictability of the British weather. Very often February was the most severe month of the year and although the League made strenuous efforts, it was unable to find an insurance company which would touch a compensation policy for fixtures lost.

The administration of the game needed to be stream-lined, not least the Registration System which was needlessly involved and almost Dickensian. Five separate forms were in use by the Association, the Full Professional Form, the Form A Professional (used by Seniors and Juniors) and Form B Amateur (Juniors and Seniors). Form Y (minor grades) and Form S (Schoolboys). In addition The Scottish Football League used a Full Profesional Contract, an Apprentice Professional Contract, a Professional Registration Form, an Amateur Registration Form and each organisation had its own Transfer Form. It was a tangled skein, made all the more complicated by the fact that the Scottish Amateur Football Association did not use the amateur form! Jack Steedman of Clydebank led the move for this particular re-organisation.

The cumbrous administrative process reflected the overwhelming number of part-time players in Scotland. This now created its own difficulties when part-time players were refused unemployment benefit in certain areas of Scotland because their contracts stated that "they can be called upon at any time to play football." If that were the case then clearly they would be unavailable for other work which might be offered to them. As this kind of decision seemed to be arrived at by offices on an area rather than a national basis the League decided not to take any action since this might focus even wider attention on the problem.

Scottish football could live with the fact that such clubs as East Stirling, Stirling Albion and Alloa might be experiencing hard times. That was more or less a permanent condition for them and the clubs had become extremely adept in overcoming adversity. It was another matter when one of the country's leading clubs, Heart of Midlothian was in such straitened cirumstances that in May 1982 its debts were so extensive that it was the subject of a registration enbargo until it had substantially reduced sums owed for players to Dundee United and Celtic.

The trouble had been caused by relegation from the Premier Division and even more by an antiquated company structure. In 1980 one of Scotland's leading clubs, Hearts, was attempting to compete at top level with a share capital of just over £5000, the price of a basic motor car. As voting rights were severely restricted (to a maximum of 20 shares) there was no incentive for anyone to put a large sum of money at the club's disposal. The solution lay in a radical restructuring of the Articles of Association and the floating of a share issue (£350,000) to the general public. This, in conjunction with much hard work from the new Board of Directors, eventually chaired by Wallace Mercer and the shrewd appointment of a joint managerial side of the ex-Rangers players Alex. MacDonald and Sandy Jardine, would turn the Tynecastle side round in a comparatively short time and make them once more a force in Scottish football.

Dundee United were to show in 1983 what could be done by prudent stewardship and continuity of skilful management. To their League Cup successes of 1979–80 and 1980–81 they now added the League championship. Those who thought that the frequent changing of managers indicated nothing more than the inability of Boards of Directors to select properly were delighted. Dundee United had had just two managers since 1958, Jerry Kerr and Jim McLean and that statement remains true in 1990. Jerry Kerr put the club on a sound financial footing by his introduction of the highly-successful Taypools in the mid 1960s and he was, with Hal Stewart of Morton, a pioneer in the bringing of Scandinavian

THE SCOTTISH FOOTBALL LEAGUE IN THE 1980s

CELEBRATIONS
Dundee United's players go wild with delight as the final whistle announces their first-ever championship after their victory over Dundee at Dens Park in the last match of the 1982–83 season.

footballers to Scotland. He picked up several fine players such as Finn Dossing and Lennart Wing for bargain-basement prices. His successor Jim McLean brought to the job the most keenly analytical brain in Scottish football. Not the least pleasing feature of Dundee United's championship win was that it had to be clinched with a game at Dens Park against Dundee on the last day of the season. The match was inevitably keenly-contested but with scrupulous fairness and the behaviour of the crowd was a credit to both clubs. Beyond question the Premier Division had been good for the Tannadice club and since in the next two years the flag would rest with Aberdeen the New Firm could claim at least temporary supremacy.

The splendid spirit in which the Dundee–Dundee United match was played is all the more noteworthy because the extremely competitive Premier Division had bred serious field indiscipline. The number of players ordered off rose from 73 in 1965 to 182 in 1981, while over the same period bookings rocketed from 503 to 2948, reflecting more than anything else the increasing unwillingness of players to accept the decision of a referee.

On the subject of indiscipline, clubs who were frequently exposed on television—and it was almost inevitable that the Old

Firm would be over-exposed—felt that they were harshly done by in that the indiscretions of their players were disclosed on the screen, giving the disciplinary bodies a further chance to take action. Celtic decided at this time to ban all live radio commentaries, not entirely to the liking of the League who, conceding that the club had the right to do so, expressed themselves as unhappy that they should choose to exercise it.

By the spring of 1983 dissatisfaction among the biggest clubs with the running of the Scottish League had come to a head. There was a real threat of a breakaway by nine of the Premier Division clubs. These felt that the League was inevitably over-influenced, because of its management structure, by clubs which had no real claim to be considered full-time professional organisations. It was deemed essential that any proposed changes be made within a constitutional framework. On April 21 1983 Mr. Peter Gardiner of Stirling Albion proposed at a Management Committee meeting that the spokesmen for the Premier Division clubs should be approached with a view to announcing to the Press that no intention of breakaway was being considered and consultation was sought to progress constitutional changes. Thereafter, the office-bearer, no longer under threat of duress, should meet with the Premier Division clubs.

Such a statement was made and the meeting duly took place on April 29 with Desmond White of Celtic stating the case for the bigger clubs. In putting forward the requests of the Premier Division he requested that the Management Committee acknowledge that a new state of affairs existed in Scottish football and that the differential in club situations should be recognised. Leadership from the Management Committee was vital. That body responded by agreeing that where sponsorship money was earned by the efforts of a certain section of League clubs, then the bulk of any such monies received should be remitted to that section. This went some way towards defusing the discontent felt by the major organisations.

Two months previously, on March 22 1983 at a meeting of First and Second Division clubs, David Will of Brechin City had proposed divisions of 12–12–14 with one up and down between First Division and Premier Division. Pointage money would be equally divided but T.V. monies would go entirely to those teams actually appearing. Ian Paterson of Clyde spoke for everyone at the meeting when he said that an essential of any agreement for a new structure was that clubs must have the chance to play for a season to earn their place in it.

Outside advice was not lacking. The League met with the National Federation of Supporters Clubs. That body applauded the introduction of the Criminal Justice (Scotland) Act 1980 and stated that it had significantly improved behaviour. This information, coming from regular and committed supporters, was both valuable and welcome. There followed however a weird contradictory statement in which the Federation mentioned "destructive comments by journalists and T.V. reporters which are influencing and in most cases deterring supporters from attending matches."

Current attendance figures did not bear out this statement which read all the more oddly when the next question asked by the Federation was "Are certain clubs producing dull defensive football?" The answer was that they were and that it might reasonably have been taken to be the duty of Pressmen and media reporters to mention this adversely wherever they found evidence of it.

The game was becoming very dependent indeed on pools money. Of the Revenue Account of £1,464,462 in the year ending March 31 1983 pools money accounted for £1,080,147 of it. The Football Grounds Improvement Trust was willing to provide money in the first place for designated grounds i.e. grounds with a capacity of 10,000 or more. Moreover, it went on to say that where Local Authorities made unreasonable safety demands on clubs, then the latter should appeal, if the Trust's advisers and local trustees concurred, and the Trust would be responsible for the costs of any action.

In May 1983 the Management Committee took the decision to award £1000 to each club eliminated in the first round of the League Cup. This went far towards ensuring that no League club lost out in a competition which they were compelled by rule to enter. The Management Committee was less successful in persuading the First and Second Division clubs to support the suggestion that henceforth there should be only one club movement between First and Premier Divisions. The non-Premier Division clubs voted unanimously at the Annual General Meeting to retain the two-thirds majority needed for any important constitutional change and they were also firm over the need to have three representatives from each division on the Management Committee.

There were some second thoughts on the admission to the League of Meadowbank Thistle. Football did tend to sit uneasily in what was primarily a stadium for international athletics and Meadowbank Thistle were warned in May 1984 about the inadequacy of changing facilities at their ground. As tenants they were not invariably guaranteed first call on the Stadium's facilities and in August of that year they requested that they should be given three consecutive away fixtures. They were helped out by Clyde, who reversed one of their own fixtures even although it meant that the Shawfield side would be playing four away matches in a row.

If the Football Grounds Improvement Trust was to come to the aid of Hampden Park it would require some long-term assurances on that ground's future. It therefore asked for, and got, a letter of intent from the Scottish Football Association and The Scottish Football League that Hampden Park would be used for all major football matches except in special circumstances.

A most important development in the middle 1980s was the sponsorship of the League competition itself. League officials and committee men had managed to persuade the commercial world that there were more opportunities in sponsoring an existing prestigious competition than in funding a separate competition which would enjoy reluctant participation until after a few years it became a footnote in football history. The Scottish League Championship was sponsored for the first time officially in 1985–86 when the League competition became known as the Fine Fare League. The indirect spin-off to the sponsors was considerable as their brand name was mentioned, to give but one example, with every reading of the Scottish results on radio or television. Fine Fare were to sponsor League football in Scotland until 1988 when B. and Q. took up the sponsorship and what was especially gratifying was that there was no lack of potential future sponsors who wished to be identified with what had become a remarkably successful product.

This may be the moment to point out some of the problems on which the Management Committee were now being asked to adjudicate. Shirt advertising is now so commonplace that it comes as rather a shock to remember that it was as late as 1977 that Hibernian became the first Scottish side to conclude a deal for shirt sponsorship, the sportswear firm Bukta being their patrons. This at once raised the question of televised games since B.B.C. were implacably opposed to product advertising and I.T.V. would infinitely have preferred that Bukta should have advertised with them in the form of commercials. Hibernian were therefore debarred from appearing in televised League matches with their sponsored shirts and there were those who, thinking back to the battling Tom Hart's confrontations with television, could not entirely suppress a wry smile.

Shirt sponsorship would of itself cause one or two problems and not only with the television companies, although the endorsement on the shirts would require to comply with the permitted dimensions. The League office staff would now have to keep, in addition to their other duties, a register of sponsorship to aid potential sponsors and to avoid possible embarrassing conflicts of interest. It was also decided that while League sides were not permitted to carry any direct industrial affiliation in their names this did not apply to reserve teams and therefore Motherwell were given permission to dub their reserve team Stelrad Motherwell.

The game was more and more becoming a subject of interest for the legal profession with a distinction increasingly being drawn between the sort of risk a player might be assumed to undertake in playing a contact sport and injuries which if inflicted elsewhere might have been the subject of criminal assault charges. One such case arose in June 1983 when the Scottish League with their insurers and legal adviser attended a meeting to discuss the case of *James Brown v John Pelosi and St. Johnstone Football Club*. The insurance brokers advised the League that where a deliberate assault resulted in serious injury, the League would be covered for the club's liability but not for that of the offending player.

In all this welter of legislation, internal and external, it was easy to forget that the primary purpose of the League was to encourage the playing of football. It was therefore particularly gratifying when in August 1983 it was announced that Scotland had topped the points chart for points gained in European competitions in 1983, a position which owed much to the outstanding feat of Aberdeen in winning the European Cup Winners' Cup in Gothenburg against Real Madrid. Scottish performance in Europe had been consistently strong for some time and over the previous four years only five countries had a better record. The reward for this gratifyingly uniform standard of excellence was a fifth place in European competitions, since three places were now allocated to Scottish clubs in the U.E.F.A. Cup, a tremendous achievement for a country of just over five million inhabitants.

Clubs needed all the money that European competition could bring for their running expenses and those of the League were climbing inexorably. Insurance alone was costing the League £42,000 per annum, a sum which included £4000 for permanent total disability cover. The clubs suffered from a rating system so punitive that Celtic and Rangers were paying several times in rates what was demanded of English clubs such as Arsenal and Manchester United. A well-researched and tenacious campaign was fought against this glaring inequality, a campaign which owed much to the vision and acumen of Desmond White of Celtic. Playing records might be of more immediate interest to the fans but unless something could be done about rating, there might well be considerably fewer clubs playing in Scotland. The clubs were seeking redress in two principal directions.

1. They wished immediate de-rating for grounds, that is, the aim was to acquire industrial de-rating status. This would not mean any alteration of the assessment itself but there would be an alleviation of rate poundage.
2. There should be a relaxation of the appeals procedure to allow comparisons, so that a Scottish club's ground could be compared directly with an English one, something that was not permissible under the present system.

Like an ever-encroaching tide, the Premier Division cry of "1 up, 1 down" would not be denied. Meetings took place of the Premier Division clubs and, at another time, the First and Second Division clubs but agreement seemed as far away as ever. Those outside the top ten were bitterly hostile to any notion that Premier Division votes might be weighted to give the highest division an outright majority. The First and Second Division clubs brought the following points from their meeting of December 15 1983:

A There should be no change to the requirement that a two-third majority was needed to implement change at an Annual or Special General Meeting.
B The Management Committee should continue to be composed of three members from the three divisions, plus office-bearers.
C Area meetings should be re-introduced.
D The clubs were very much against a system of 1 up and 1 down from the Premier Division.
E The system of paying out the Pools Money, i.e. the ladder system, should be changed.

The beleaguered Management Committee had to have an official opinion on each of these points. On the first three they favoured the *status quo*, but they expressed themselves very much in support of one up one down from the Premier Division. With regard to the distribution of Pools Money the Management Committee made the very reasonable point that the ladder scheme was in its infancy and should be persevered with for some time longer. It was, for once, no exaggeration to say that Scottish football stood at a crossroads, with every chance of a dozen or so clubs going off in a different direction from the majority.

Desmond White and Ian Livingstone of Motherwell at a meeting in January 1985 emphasised the problems faced by a full-time club relegated from Premier Division. Those not in "uppah succles" as the Victorians had invariably called the top division of any league, naturally saw things otherwise and asked why mediocrity should be protected. Alex Jackson of Dumbarton and Hugh Currie of Morton put the effective counter-argument that it was difficult for a side going for and missing the one promotion place available to remain full-time.

Perhaps the most cogent point was that made by Peter Gardiner of Stirling Albion who argued that one club down from 10 might be fair but one club up from 14 was most certainly not. Past President Tom Lauchlan of Kilmarnock pointed out that the Premier Division had initially been accepted on a basis of two up, two down. For every argument, there was a telling riposte, and inevitably, charity began at home. Thus, Rae Simpson of Rangers made the point that under the Premier Division Scots clubs had done well in Europe and this had resulted in their attracting larger domestic crowds. Willie Harkness of Queen of the South cited the loss of spectators in the provincial grounds because the big clubs no longer went there.

Change would come and come soon, day to day matters would not wait. What to do about Meadowbank Thistle was a recurring problem. On the playing side, the club had performed most creditably and had long since ceased to be a walking source of pools money for opponents. Meadowbank Stadium itself however was something of a makeshift as a ground. The League had to balance fairness to opponents with the desire not to harm a go-ahead club whose limitations were scarcely of their own making. Yet changing facilities were inadequate and Thistle were given a specified time in which to improve them. In summer the ground was used for American football, enjoying a momentary boom in popularity in Britain and there were complaints that Scottish League matches had been played there with illegal coloured lines on the pitch. Ayr United, who owned their ground, could be told to stop holding such games but Meadowbank were beholden to the District Council for their ground. It was always going to be a difficult situation for them.

Those in search of a little light relief at this time could have found it in a match between Queen's Park and Alloa where, in a complete reversal of the normal order of things, the junior linesman, the category 3B man, was reported for having sworn at players on several occasions. It was decided that he be not offered any further Scottish League engagements.

Early in 1985 the rates levied on the offices of The Scottish Football League shot up from £4788 to £16,200 so the news that the League would now get 2.25 per cent instead of 2 per cent of the total stakes after the Pools Betting Tax had been paid was doubly welcome. This apparently microscopic percentage rise would mean that in a full season The Scottish Football League would benefit by an additional £300,000.

For the first time ever, the League Championship had a sponsor. Henceforth, from the beginning of season 1985-86 The Scottish Football League would be known as the Fine Fare League after the Scottish food store chain which had assumed sponsorship. By the terms of the deal every Premier Division club would receive £10,000 with £3000 for First Division Clubs and £2000 for those in the lowest grade. Turnstile drawings were thus accounting for an ever-smaller percentage of a club's income.

Before that season had even started football was reeling from the twin catastrophes of the violence at the European Cup Final at the Heysel Stadium Brussels, during the match between Liverpool and Juventus and the horrific fire at Valley Parade, Bradford, on the day on which the home side, Bradford City were celebrating their Third Division promoter with a subsequent match against Lincoln City. Neither of these events had any direct connection with Scotland but it was naive to think that the repercussions would not equally affect the northern country. The implications for the safety of grounds arising from the Bradford fire were enormous, for there would be an immediate survey of all grounds, whether they had previously required a safety certificate or not, and inevitably there would be a reduction in ground capacities.

Scottish clubs were encouraged by the League to resist designation for clubs in the First Division and the Second Division where capacity was less than 10,000 but every assistance was to be given to local firemasters to inspect the grounds immediately. The Government was also to be informed that clubs would welcome the categorisation as a criminal offence of the unlawful presence of spectators on the pitch itself.

It was a melancholy time for British football in general but Scottish football sustained an additional blow in the sudden death in August 1985 of Desmond White. His services to Scottish football as player, administrator and legislator had spanned more than half a century. Beginning as a player with the ill-starred Edinburgh City, he had gone on to keep goal for the formidable Queen's Park side of the mid 1930's before becoming Celtic secretary and chairman. He had led the fight against a truly penal system of rating of sports clubs in Scotland and it was fitting that his efforts and those of others would eventually be crowned with success almost in the very centenary year of the League, in 1989 when the Government admitted the justice of the claim.

Hard on the heels of that death came another, a figure much better-known to the Scottish footballing public. Jock Stein, whose unbroken run of success in the 60s and 70s had made all the current reconstruction talks necessary, died literally in the moment of

JOCK STEIN (*Dunfermline Athletic, Hibernian, Celtic, Scotland*)

An ordinary club player, never considered for a full cap, Stein became the greatest manager in Scottish football history. He saved Dunfermline from relegation, won the cup with them, made them a real force in Europe, then after a brief successful spell with Hibernian came to Celtic. There he totally dominated Scottish football for ten years and later he was a successful if cautious manager at national level. His death at Cardiff in 1985 was a numbing blow to Scottish football supporters everywhere.

salvaging Scotland's World Cup hopes in Cardiff. By no means the least of his contributions was the self-belief he had given Dunfermline Athletic for a decade and the lift he had given to Hibernian in his brief spell of less than a year with them. Scottish provincial sides such as Dunfermline could achieve, at least in the short term, if only the manager was charismatic enough and the Board sufficiently dynamic, That was his legacy.

He left a game that was scarcely any longer in control of its own destiny. In the wake of Bradford, venues would be decided by the police every bit as much as by the ballot box. Wherever there was any consideration of safety, e.g. Forfar Athletic v Rangers the police would have a considerable say in where the match would take place. Almost all the money available from the Football Grounds Improvement Trust would go on the provision of safety equipment rather than in improving grounds for the benefit of spectators.

The next topic concerning grounds to cause a stir in Scottish football was that of artificial pitches. Stirling Albion had negotiated a deal with Stirling District Council whereby the latter would take over the club's ground, Annfield, and then lease it back to them. It was a condition of the sale and re-lease that the ground should be available for a considerable part of the week for community activities, something that would clearly be impracticable on the traditional grass pitch.

The club therefore decided to invest in an artificial surface but, by the time they had done so, artificial surfaces which were already in operation at several English grounds, notably those of Luton Town and Queen's Park Rangers, were beginning to receive a bad press. So widespread was the opposition to them in England that visiting clubs were refusing to play cup-ties on those composition pitches which had been seen, only a few years before, as the answer to all the problems of ground maintenance caused by the British climate.

There was, therefore, no possibility that Stirling Albion's decision to invest in an artificial pitch would go uncontested. On being canvassed for their opinions on the development, there was an equal number of clubs in favour and in opposition. The League suggested a compromise whereby clubs due to play at Annfield would be given acclimatisation facilities in the week before the match, while a week was set apart in the close season for any clubs who might wish to familiarise themselves with the new Annfield surface.

This was perfectly acceptable to the club itself, Stirling Albion. What was not was Point Nine on the League's shopping list which said that in the event of the scheme going ahead, Stirling Albion would be debarred from promotion of any kind for the first three years of the new pitch's existence. On appeal by the club this was overturned, but they remained barred from the Premier Division—they were then in the Second Division—and clubs could not be compelled to play a League Cup tie at Annfield, a rather illogical distinction since both competitions, League Cup and League, were under the control of the Scottish League and a visiting club had no choice of venue where League matches were concerned.

A decision, however contentious, would be taken on artificial pitches. Early in 1986 it was also necessary to decide the shape of the Divisions and also the amount of television to be permitted. In January 1986 a split in the League seemed extremely probable with only Clydebank of the Premier Division clubs loyal to the *status quo* and their own tenure in the Premier Division was extremely shaky. At a meeting of First and Second Division clubs all 28 were asked to affirm their loyalty to the Scottish League. They heard the League President, Ian Gellatly, himself in a difficult position since his own club, Dundee, was one of the nine potential breakaways, state that the present publicity was most damaging for The Scottish Football League particularly in the discouragement of potential sponsors.

There was no doubt that the Premier Division clubs wanted change to a one up one down system immediately but they were stymied by the rule which required a two-thirds majority for any major constitutional change. They could have secured this under their own proposed new voting system which would have given each Premier Division club 4 votes. This, with the help of significant support from the First and Second Division clubs, would have been sufficient to pilot through any desired change.

It was precisely for this reason that the other 28 clubs would have none of this proposal. In vain did Jack McGinn and John Paton, of Celtic and Rangers respectively, say that the changes proposed were not intended to be detrimental to any Scottish League club and that they would be adopted within the present Scottish League structure. John McBeth of Clyde pointed out, unanswerably, that the proposed 4-2-1 voting structure within the three divisions gave absolute power to the Premier Division clubs and this was totally unacceptable to the others. There was also a considerable amount of ill-feeling arising from the notion that the whole package was largely being put together to save Motherwell from relegation when the Lanarkshire club had similarly been beneficiaries from the re-organisation and extension of 1955.

LAST DAY 1

Albert Kidd of Dundee, extreme left, turns away after scoring his own and Dundee's second goal against Hearts on the final afternoon of season 1985–86, the goal that effectively destroyed the Edinburgh side's chances of taking the League title.

LAST DAY 2

Meanwhile at Love Street where Celtic were four goals up against St. Mirren, Danny McGrain on the left and Neil Mochan lean out of the dug-out to pass on to their players the news from Dundee.

LAST DAY 3
The final whistle has gone at Dens Park, Hearts have lost the flag to Celtic and for at least one young supporter it has all been too much.

Compromise prevailed in the end, as it usually does. The allocation of Trading Accounts monies (which had replaced the Pools shareout) would henceforth be on a 75 per cent flat rate, the remaining 25 per cent reflected positions on the ladder. The 4-2-1 voting structure was adopted. No one would be relegated at the end of season 1985–86 though two clubs would be promoted to give a Premier Division of 12 clubs, a First Division of 12 and an unchanged Second Division. In season 1986–87 there would be two up two down as usual, but the following season, that of 1987–88, three clubs would be relegated from the Premier Division and only one promoted. Thereafter, i.e. from the beginning of 1988–89, the Premier clubs would have the one up one down for which they had fought so long and hard.

The arrangement meant that the top Scottish clubs were committed to playing 44 League matches and a successful run in European and domestic competitions could easily take this total to nearly 60 games to be played in the season. Fortune was on the side of the League in the shape of two of the mildest winters in living or indeed written memory and the programmes went through almost completely uninterruptedly. The major item salvaged from the wreckage by the First and Second Division clubs was that their Premier Division brethren had undertaken not to block the relegation from that body of any full-time club. There was no doubt that the big clubs had not been bluffing. When it seemed as if there might indeed be a breakaway league, but that its composition might be unacceptable to the Scottish Football Association, Wallace Mercer of Hearts let it be known that in that case the new league would apply to the Glasgow Football Association or the Highland League for temporary affiliation.

As it happened the 1985-86 season provided an astonishing climax with Hearts faltering in the last ditch against Dundee at Dens Park while a relaxed Celtic rattled in five goals against St. Mirren at Love Street.

Those who had favoured amalgamation of clubs or at least a sharing of grounds were interested in the news, made public in April 1986 that Clyde would henceforth be sharing Firhill with Partick Thistle. Immediately parallels were drawn with the European situation, parallels drawn none the less enthusiastically for being totally erroneous. In Europe the municipality owns the ground and two clubs from that city share it on equal terms. In the case of Clyde, they were about to become semi-permanent lodgers at Firhill, a vastly different thing. The club was genuinely grateful to Partick Thistle for their hospitality but the Clyde supporters did not take to the move then or afterwards and absented themselves from home matches in perceptible numbers. The episode underlined once more how the non-Old Firm clubs of Glasgow had gone into a seemingly irreversible decline. Although the directors of Clyde F.C. came under heavy fire for their decision it was difficult to see where any realistic alternatives lay. If the nation could scarcely finance the re-structuring or building of a national stadium, it was highly improbable that one individual club could find the necessary resources for a similar exercise.

Unlikely, but not impossible, for one club was about to do just that. St. Johnstone were fortunate in that their ground, Muirton Park, lay ten minutes from the centre of Perth on highly-desirable ground for development. They successfully negotiated with a food store, so that a completely new all-seated ground on the outskirts of the city was in readiness for them before they had to leave their original home. In a foreshadowing of things to come the capacity of the new ground, McDiarmid Park, at 10,000 was just half that of the ground they were in the process of vacating. They were in their new quarters for the beginning of season 1989–90.

There was a growing feeling of confidence in the game as attendances continued to rise dramatically, up 16.4 per cent in the first half of 1985–86 against every European trend. That was in League games only, the rise in Skol Cup attendances was even more gratifying. Seemingly intractable problems were being resolved. In television the clubs had opposed the showing of even one live match per year, feeling that the T.V. companies would speedily want an increase in the number of matches shown live and would not be over-enthusiastic to continue with the showing of recorded highlights. For their part the companies were becoming increasingly irritated by the powers which individual clubs had to refuse access to the cameras, often at extremely short notice.

Scottish Television, which had shown considerable forbearance, now took the bit between its teeth in December 1986. It stated that if a new contract were signed and a club subsequently refused access to them, they would pay only 50 per cent of the money due till then for recorded highlights and the contract would be terminated forthwith. This gave the major clubs pause and the upshot was a proposal for a new rule which came to pass as Rule 83 (2). It stated:

"A club involved in any fixture which may be the subject of such a contract shall be bound, as far as it is within its power, to secure compliance by the League with such obligations as have been undertaken by the League in terms of such contract, and in particular, and without prejudice to the foregoing generality, to make available appropriate facilities for the radio or television coverage of any such fixture."

It was a happy resolution to a long-standing area of contention even although the picture would soon be clouded by the arrival on the scene of satellite television. The medium had the capacity to be of great help to the game, and arguably it had been of great help. Programmes had caused discussion and created interest. Television had introduced people to the game in some cases. The problems it posed for football were real ones, however and legislators such as Robert Kelly and Desmond White had not expressed strong misgivings out of sheer bloodymindedness. Players need a live audience if they are to perform to maximum potential. Supporters who have taken the trouble to queue up for tickets for big

SPOT THE PLAYER/MANAGER
Graeme Souness has an uneasy view of his club's first triumph at Pittodrie under his managership. He had previously been sent off and so had an anxious spell on the sidelines while his teammates clinched the flag.

matches are entitled to feel betrayed if they subsequently find that they could have seen the match as it happened from the warmth and comfort of their homes. Relations between television and football although based on a genuine inter-dependence, are always likely to be uneasy.

By the beginning of the 1987–88 season broadcasting monies were going almost entirely to the clubs appearing on television and in essence this meant the half-dozen leading clubs in the Premier Division. Membership of that elite band did not automatically

LEAGUE CHAMPIONS YET AGAIN
A sight that was to become increasingly familiar in Scottish football in the 1980s. Graeme Souness and Walter Smith of Rangers hold the League Championship trophy aloft in 1987.

mean that the cameras would visit the ground. In the previous season no matches had been televised by B.B.C. Scotland from Clydebank or Hamilton or by S.T.V. from Dens Park, Dundee or Motherwell. A welcome development in 1988–89 was a Goals Highlights programme which gave camera exposure to First and Second Division clubs but contractual difficulties delayed its re-appearance the following season.

Traditional honours were still held dear. Dunfermline Athletic, having been given 15 medals for the League championship success in the Second Division of 1985–86 and having been allowed three further medals, were rebuffed when they requested another nine which would have taken the total to 27 championship medals. The Scottish Football League were in no doubt that to make awards on such a scale would be to detract seriously from their intrinsic worth and Dunfermline were informed that an additional three medals, taking the total to 21 in all, were as much as the League was prepared to sanction.

It had long been a source of grievance that Scotland had been unrepresented on the Football Grounds Improvement Trust and there had therefore been considerable satisfaction when Tom Wharton, the former referee, had been appointed to that body. He was able to announce that the maximum grant available for work on a designated ground which came under the category of safety rather than of cosmetic improvement, had been raised to 75 per cent of £700,000, i.e. £525,000.

Between the World Wars Scottish League football had at times appeared a rather somnolent affair, set in its ways and resistant to change. In contrast, the game had been a whirlpool of activity since the mid 1950s and was about to receive yet another powerful impetus from the arrival in Scotland of a young player-manager Graeme Souness of Rangers who would set new marks and invite his competitors to aim at them. Scottish football had already taken a larger share of Continental notice than before because its teams could still compete in Europe where English sides could not. It would now achieve an even greater prominence with the wholesale importation of Football League and foreign players of the very highest calibre. Rangers would lead and, if only for their own preservation, the other major Scottish clubs would follow.

Chapter Eleven

THE LEAGUE CUP —A TOURNAMENT REDISCOVERED

The history of the League Cup competition is one of the strangest chapters in the story of Scottish football. For a quarter of a century since its inception it was an outstanding success and then for the next decade 1967–77 it increasingly lost its way, to such an extent that the tournament at one stage seemed scarcely viable. A rescue operation at the eleventh hour gave temporary breathing space and the chance to adopt a formula which over the last eight years has been brilliantly successful so that it is now a model for other similar competitions.

The idea of a League Cup came about almost as an accidental by-product of the Second World War although James Bowie of Rangers had floated an astonishingly similar idea in an article in the *Sunday Mail* of May 1939. In season 1940–41 there were only 16 clubs still playing league football in Scotland and these 16 constituted the entire membership of the Southern League. By this time the Government wanted as much football played as could possibly be played without undue interference with the war effort. As the S.F.A. had suspended the Scottish Cup for the duration of the war and the Southern League programme offered only 30 matches as against the 38 of the pre-war First Division, there was a considerable gap in the football calendar.

In the spring of 1941 it was decided to institute a League Cup with four sections of four teams which would play each other home and away on a league basis. One team from each section would qualify to produce two semi-finals which would be decided on a traditional knock-out basis. The sections were unseeded so that such pairings as Celtic, Hearts, Motherwell and Clyde and Rangers, Hibernian, Partick Thistle and Falkirk were quite possible.

Of the war-time competitions, which of course were the responsibility of the Southern League rather than The Scottish Football League, Rangers virtually monopolised the honours.

LOWER LEAGUE WINS
In 1947 East Fife became the only Second Division side to win the League Cup when they defeated Falkirk in a replayed final. Here players Laird, Philip, McGarrity, Brown, Aitken, Davidson and Black admire the trophy.

From six competitions they won four, lost a fifth by a corner to Hibernian, (corners in those days fulfilled the function of shots from the penalty mark today) and that after losing their goalkeeper Jerry Dawson with a broken leg early in the match. Their only other reverse was in the last Southern League Cup Final in 1945-46 when Aberdeen won 3-2, interestingly the competition was officially called the Southern League Cup final despite the illogicality of including Aberdeen in any such tournament.

Even then, Rangers exacted a double revenge. The trophy which had eluded them that day was taken back and presented by the S.F.A. for competition as the Victory Cup, a competition which Rangers won in 1946. The League Cup had been such a success that when peace-time football was resumed there was no thought of jettisoning it. The competition was moved to early September and a new cup put up for the new tournament, now officially the Scottish League Cup. Rangers put their name on it first, extracting full payment from Aberdeen in the form of a 4-0 drubbing. The new trophy was the gift of Mr. John McMahon, then President of The Scottish Football League.

The League Cup got off to a great start because it had been instituted at a time when the post-war football boom was coming to its height. Moreover, no club monopolised it in the 15 years or so after the war. In that time, East Fife would win it three times— once as a Second Division club to add to their astonishing feat of having won the Scottish Cup while in the same division—Hearts were likewise successful on three occasions, Dundee twice, Celtic twice with wins for Motherwell and Aberdeen. In this period Rangers, who by 1990 had far outstripped the other clubs in this competition, managed only three successes, far below their accustomed striking rate.

Some idea of the competition's pulling power can be gauged from the attendances at three finals which at first sight do not appear to be of pre-eminent attraction. In 1947–48 East Fife and Falkirk brought 52,781 to Hampden and over 30,000 for an afternoon mid-week replay. Two years later 38,897 paid to see East Fife take on Second Division Dunfermline Athletic and in 1952–53 51,830 saw Dundee register their second consecutive success in defeating Kilmarnock 2–0.

The League Cup would function perfectly well as a competition for either 16 or 32 clubs. Matters became slightly more awkward after 1955 when the number of League clubs went up from 32 to 37 with the admission of the five small clubs from Division C. This means that a ninth section of five clubs had to be created, playing each other once only and then playing a decider against one of the other Second Division sections. The public liked the idea of the First Division clubs being drawn together but once the First Division clubs increased to 18 in 1955 there had to be at least one mixed section—that is of both First and Second Division clubs—in the draw.

The League Cup, nevertheless, remained firmly entrenched in the good graces of the supporters right through the 1960's. There would be no surprise in learning that the Celtic v Rangers League Cup Final of 1965–66 attracted the highest crowd ever of 107,609 but it is much more astonishing to reflect that Rangers and Morton had played to 105,907 in 1963–64 and that at a time when Morton were a Second Division side.

The League Cup attracted because it abounded in high-scoring matches and strange statistics. That Old Firm Cup final just alluded to was the first of Celtic's five consecutive League Cup successes, but although they were to appear in the next nine finals as well, they would only be victorious on one further occasion, making their haul six from fourteen consecutive final appearances in total. In the course of that run they would twice score six goals against Hibernian in a League Cup final. The second match would indeed produce two hat-tricks and one of those, from Joe Harper,

RANK WILL OUT!
Morton in 1963 had the chance to repeat East Fife's feat of winning the League Cup as a Second Division side. On the day Rangers were much too good and Jim Forrest had a field day. Here he is scoring his own third and Rangers fourth in a 5–0 victory.

would be achieved by a player on the losing side. In a match in an earlier year of the competition in 1968–69, two Celtic players each scored five goals, Lennox and Chalmers going nap against the luckless Hamilton Academical.

The last six-figure crowd to attend a League Cup final was that of 1970–71 when 106,263 saw Derek Johnstone make an immediate impact on Scottish football by scoring the only goal of the game for Rangers. There would never again be a crowd which approached to within 30,000 of this total and the reasons for this were complex. The following year Partick Thistle recorded one of the greatest upsets ever in Scottish football in drubbing Celtic 4–1.

To some extent crowd comparisons would be misleading after the Ibrox Disaster of January 1971 following the match between Rangers and Celtic. Crowd capacities would be cut drastically and never again would huge throngs seethe and sway uncontrollably on ricketty and antiquated terracings. That said, it is impossible to resist the conclusion that by the early 1970's the League Cup was a competition that had gone badly wrong.

The attraction of it for the fans, the chance to see such as Rangers, Hearts, Motherwell and Morton in the same section, was

A RARE ENJOYABLE TRIUMPH
Alex. Rae who skippered Partick Thistle to a totally unexpected win against Celtic in the League Cup Final of 1971, shows off the trophy to jubilant fans outside Hampden.

not likely to recommend it to the big clubs themselves. They wished the glamour of a cup competition without its essential ingredient, prominent casualties at an early stage, and they set themselves to eliminate, as far as possible, the chances of unhappy accident. Some of this elimination was praiseworthy, especially on the financial side. Since one of the semi-finals was then traditionally played at Hampden and the other elsewhere, there was a lot to be said for the decision of May 1962 to pool the League Cup semi-final drawings.

The big clubs had found out that a genuine all-in draw could create problems. By 1971 the Old Firm had been drawn in the same section four times in the last five years, a fact pointed out by the Glasgow senior magistrate, Baillie James Anderson. He expressed himself disappointed that they had not been kept in separate sections as over this period there had been quite a history of crowd trouble. The League in reply stated that they had considered all aspects of this money-spinning competition in previous years and were against the idea of segregation in the early stages.

Unfortunately they were not long to persevere with this courageous viewpoint. Powerful forces were working for a new form of competition. In that same interview in which he delivered his opinion of the Drybrough Cup in August 1971 Desmond White of Celtic had this to say of the League Cup.

> "Speaking on a purely personal basis I believe we could, with advantage, reorganise the League Cup competition. It's significant that the sectional draw under the tournament rules as they now stand throws up First Division side against First Division side and Second Division side against Second Division side. This must lead to the elimination early on of some of our top clubs.
>
> "By arranging the sections so that they consist of say, two First and two Second Division clubs we would, among other things, bring top class football to some of our soccer outposts. Imagine what a fillip the game in the Brechin area would get from visits from either Celtic or Rangers or perhaps Hearts or Hibs."

As Professor C. E. M. Joad was wont to say "it depends what you mean." A section of 1972–73 which threw up Aberdeen and Hibernian with Queen's Park and Queen of the South as cannon-fodder would administer several things to the Scottish game but a fillip was not one of them. Only 4,000 went to Palmerston to see Queen of the South play Hibernian, with a beggarly 1508 at Hampden the same evening as football-starved spectators flocked to the national ground for the visit of Aberdeen. Nor were they taken by a competition which meandered its weary way across half a season, so that the opening game on the second Saturday in August led to a final in early December. The other egregious error was to allow two sides from each section to proceed to the next stage, thereby rendering some of the sectional matches completely meaningless.

THE LEAGUE CUP — A TOURNAMENT REDISCOVERED

It rarely pays to under-estimate the intelligence of supporters and they deserted the already gaping terracings in large numbers.

The following year, 1973–74 was no better for with two clubs qualifying from Section 1 which contained Celtic, Rangers, Arbroath and Falkirk, good judges of form were not over-taxed in predicting the two successful sides. As often happens, an inherently bad competition was not helped by a severe stroke of ill-fortune. Because of a miners' and power-workers strike, there was a ban on artificial lighting when the League Cup final fell due to be played on its midwinter date of December 20 and worse, the day was pitiless, covering an ice-bound pitch with a layer of surface water. Only 27,974 thought it worthwhile to go along to see Dundee defeat Celtic 1–0, a match which ex-Celt Tommy Gemmell, by that time with Dundee, must have been almost alone in relishing.

The competition was struggling yet it was inherently very important, guaranteeing as it did entry to European competition to its winners. There was no sign of matters improving and veteran sports correspondent Hugh Taylor had this to say in 1976 after even an Old Firm pairing failed to attract 60,000 spectators to Hampden:

> "It is hardly surprising that the League Cup final failed to thrill for the League Cup is not one of the best of Scotland's tournaments. Not only are the early sectional games a distraction before the real cup-tie business begins and the quarter-finals usually a yawn but the final comes at a bad time. The days of the huge League Cup final gates are over and, it must be repeated, this tournament could do with a different dressing."

Matters appeared to have mended when, coinciding with the arrival of Jim Farry as Secretary, sponsorship was secured for the first time for the League Cup competition. The reluctance of sponsors to become involved hitherto could itself be seen as a criticism of the state of the competition. Now the Perth whisky firm of Bell's offered sponsorship for three years, although they would in the event pull out after two. The Bell's League Cup is memorable for two things. Only one club, Dundee United, can claim to have won the Bell's League Cup and they are the only side never to have won it at Hampden Park. In the first year of sponsorship they defeated Aberdeen in a replay at Dens Park and on the same ground a year later they had the better of exchanges with their city neighbours. The League showed a refreshing commonsense in switching venues to accommodate the vast bulk of supporters and although Bell's withdrew from sponsorship prematurely, it could be argued that these were the two matches which turned the League Cup round.

A CLINICAL FINISH
Colin Jackson outjumps the Aberdeen defence to register the winning goal for Rangers in the contentious League Cup final of 1979.

There remained some little way to go. Bell's withdrawal meant considerable financial loss as the amount of sponsorship would have gone from £80,000 in 1979 to £100,000 in 1981. No other sponsor could immediately be found, hardly surprising when Section 1 of the 1982–83 competition read Celtic, Arbroath, Alloa, Dunfermline Athletic. It was pointless for the League to complain of hostile press and media coverage. Better to admit that for once things had gone spectacularly wrong and the obvious reason for failure was that over two-legged matches the weaker side had as near no chance of success as mattered. Effort and luck could cause an upset in the course of ninety minutes but in the longer term superior skill and fitness would assuredly assert themselves. The fans simply would not watch Clyde against Rangers, Hibernian against Montrose or Aberdeen against Meadowbank over two games and they were right not to do so. League and League Cup attendances which had stood at 6,338,000 in 1956–57 had nose-dived to 2,870,000 by 1980–81. Allowing for the fact that Rangers at this time were making little or no impact on the championship the fall was profoundly worrying.

There was tinkering where major surgery was required. Few would have quarelled with the decision to seed the four European entrants each season but this caused problems when soon after-

DAVE NAREY (*Dundee United*)
Nearly always unflurried, thinking ahead, Dave Narey has been the lynch-pin of a Dundee United side which rose from obscurity to a leading role in Scottish Football. A thinking player in a thinking team, he led his side on several outstanding European campaigns while at home only a Scottish Cup winners' medal has eluded him.

wards Scotland's quota for European competition was increased to five. Salvation came at length with the involvement of the Alloa Brewery Company Ltd. in what came to be known as the Skol Cup. Almost overnight the tournament was transformed. Clubs were phased in in ascending order to a competition which was decided on the night over one game and immediately David had his successes against Goliath. There were additional rewards for Second Division sides beating First or Premier sides and for First Division sides toppling any of the top ten. Henceforth the League Cup, now the Skol Cup, would no longer be lost in the thickets of the Scottish football calendar as it plodded wearily across the year. In its place would be a compact tournament, easy to understand and with the obvious device of moving the final to a Sunday so that it need not compete with the rest of the League calendar.

From a quiet beginning, 44,698 to see Rangers beat Dundee United 1–0 in 1984 and 40,065 at Aberdeen's convincing 3–0 win over Hibernian the following year, the Skol Cup soon built up a considerable head of steam. The 1986 match between Rangers and Celtic ended in considerable disorder with the dismissal of Maurice Johnston of Celtic against the club for whom he would one day play after Rangers had gone ahead 2–1. Yet although the behaviour of both sets of players and officials led to a commissioned report from the Secretary, there had been much splendid play before then and the sponsors pronounced themselves well-pleased.

They were to be abundantly rewarded for their confidence for the next three years, 1987, 1988 and 1989 were to produce three superlative matches, defying the odds all the more in that the same two teams, Rangers and Aberdeen, would be involved on each occasion. The 1987 match which Rangers eventually won on a penalty shoot-out after the sides remained at 3–3 after extra time, has strong claim to rate as the finest domestic final ever seen at Hampden and indeed perhaps has only been excelled in all matches at that ground by the classic European Cup final of 1960 between Real Madrid and Eintracht Frankfurt. So exceptional was the performance in this Skol Cup final that a special award was made to Aberdeen as losers.

The teams tried again the following year and astonished onlookers by achieving the same standard of excellence, Rangers just getting through 3–2. In the last pre-centenary League Cup final the wheel turned for Aberdeen and they took the Skol Cup north by dint of a 2–1 win. The most eloquent testimony of a sponsor's satisfaction is a willingness to renew and Skol's association with the League Cup is now set to continue until at least 1992.

And so, a competition which started extremely successfully and then dwindled in popularity until it became a near-embarrassment has triumphantly re-established itself. Its rehabilitation has been perhaps almost the most important factor in the strong revival of Scottish football and it is all the more meritorious in that eventually the game's legislators were prepared to take account of the wishes of the fans as represented by the media.

Chapter Twelve

THE LEAGUE ON THE FIELD—INTER-LEAGUE MATCHES

Almost from the inception of The Scottish Football League there was the wish amongst its officials to measure swords with the senior body, the Football League, and to see how the playing standards of the two Leagues compared. Given that over the century since 1890 many of the leading Scottish players have been enticed to England and have therefore been ineligible to take part in this fixture, it would be reasonable to assume that Scotland would do less well in inter-league matches than in full internationals and indeed it has so proved. The Inter-League fixture declined from the point where it was the second most important game in the football calendar (certainly when the match was played in Scotland) to the position where the match increasingly became an embarrassment, cancelled if the fixture list became too heavy or played with ever less representative sides.

The first meeting of the two Leagues took place in April 1892 at Pike's Lane, Bolton, when the teams fought out a 2–2 draw. It is not intended to give a game by game account of this fixture throughout its 90 years duration but the teams for this very first match are specifically worthy of record:—

FOOTBALL LEAGUE: Reader (West Bromwich Albion); Holmes (Preston North End); Gow (Sunderland); Reynolds (West Bromwich Albion); Gardiner (Bolton Wanderers); Groves, Bassett (both West Bromwich Albion); McInnes (Notts County); Goodall (Derby County); Chadwick (Everton); Daft (Notts County).

SCOTTISH LEAGUE: McLeod (Dumbarton); Hannah (Renton); Doyle, Maley (both Celtic); Boyle (Dumbarton); McBride (Renton); Taylor (Dumbarton); McCall (Renton); McCallum, McMahon (both Celtic); Bell (Dumbarton).

The Football League included four Scots, Gow, Reynolds, Groves and McInnes but this was not a practice that would last and

A VERY EARLY CAP
Cap awarded to an unknown player for Scottish League v Scottish Alliance in 1892 . The following year the Scottish Alliance became the Second Division of The Scottish Football League.

---

after the initial matches Scots would not be selected again for the Football League until the 1960's when the fixture had almost run its course. On the Scots side there were no Edinburgh players nor were Rangers represented, while of the Celtic players Willie Maley would earn greater distinction in managing the club over the next fifty years and incidentally becoming President of the Scottish Football League. The attendance of 9,500 was paltry when put alongside the 31,000 who watched the first-ever match between the two Leagues in Scotland, which event took place in April 1893 at Parkhead. Before that date the Scots had played their opening match against the Irish League in Belfast.

The discrepancy in attendances when the match was played in Scotland and England was to be a permanent characteristic of the series although certain venues in England were better than others. Thus, even when the fixture was approaching terminal decline, Newcastle could usually be depended upon to turn out spectators in large numbers.

If The Scottish League did not attract magnetically in England, the same was true of the Irish League in Scotland. This fixture had to be massaged carefully and located with discretion, the home side bearing a considerable correlation to venue. Thus a poor crowd of 5,000 for this match at Parkhead in 1896 was doubled when the match moved to the romantically named Carolina Port in Dundee two years later. This gratifying increase owed much to the fact that the city of Dundee had a considerable immigrant Irish population and the politic inclusion of a Dundee player. When the match was staged at Easter Road in 1900 there were no fewer than seven local players in the side and each of the four senior Edinburgh sides was represented.

The match against the Football League in 1900 was played at Crystal Palace, an odd choice of venue on the face of it as the Football League was almost exclusively recruited from North and Midland clubs and the lands south of the River Trent were in the grip of a separate organisation, the Southern League. There may have been something of the trail-blazing instinct in the decision to go to Crystal Palace, much as Rugby League clubs would later take their Challenge Cup final to Wembley, but the financial returns were indifferent, the crowd, as at Bolton, being in the region of nine thousand.

David was much more keen to see Goliath laid low and in 1901 there were 37,000 at Ibrox to see the Scottish League score its most emphatic victory ever. In the 6–2 score R. C. Hamilton of Rangers became one of only four Scots ever to score a hat-trick against the Football League. In the same year the Irish League match in Belfast had produced two historical curios. In the course of the match the Irish brought on A. L. Bamford of Glentoran as substitute for A. Kearns of Distillery (presumably with the agreement of the Scots) and G. C. McWattie of Queen's Park was in goal for the visitors, the first Hampden player to be honoured by selection for the League.

When the match was played in Scotland it regularly attracted crowds of 40,000 and in 1903 when Celtic Park was chosen to host the game the selectors were sufficiently confident in the fixture's drawing power not to pick any Celtic players, although since the Football League won 3–0 the selectors might have been well advised to think again. The year before, when bad weather at Newcastle had kept the crowd down to 11,000, John Campbell of Celtic had the misfortune to score three and still be on the losing side, England doing twice as well.

The increasing importance of organised football, in the south of England was recognised when in October 1910 the Southern League was met for the first time at Millwall. The game was lost but the sting was eased by the reflection that the Football League had also lowered their colours that year to the same opposition. When the Southern League again won at Millwall in 1912 piquancy

MANY CAPS

The impressive array of caps amassed by the great Bobby Walker of Heart of Midlothian in the early years of the century.

was given to the 1–0 scoreline by the fact that the Southern League goal was unfortunately scored by a Scots defender, Alec McNair, who in years to come would form a redoubtable partnership with the opposing goalkeeper of that day, Charlie Shaw, when the latter moved to Celtic.

In the years immediately before World War 1 the Scottish League was doing rather well against its English neighbour. It had won twice in England within four years, something that was very necessary if the fixture was to retain credibility. The war did not put an immediate stop to representative games, the Southern League was met in London in October 1914 and the Football League at Parkhead in March 1915. There was also a journey to Belfast to take on the Irish League but thereafter the temper of the time was against such representative matches. The strenuous efforts made to play the Irish fixture were rather surprising, given the strain on public transport at that time.

The end of the war brought about a great upsurge of enthusiasm for football, as would happen again 25 years later. There were 70,000 at Ibrox for the Victory Inter-League match of 1919 which Scotland won 3–2 and an astonishing 83,000 at Parkhead a year later who were less well rewarded for their enthusiasm in a match which the Football League won 4–0.

The balance was tilting inexorably towards the Football League. As recession began to bite Europe after the initial though short-lived peacetime boom, Scotland with its heavy industries was particularly affected. With the exception of Rangers and Celtic and, for a remarkably long time, Motherwell, Scottish clubs were unable or unwilling to resist the English cheque-book. The Scottish League had to recruit where it could and was fortunate enough to have two non-Scottish players of genuine international ability available to them. Only technically were they non-Scots because they had been educated in Scotland and played all their football there. As however they had been born when their parents were, however briefly, domiciled in England, neither Robert Ferrier of Motherwell nor J. B. McAlpine of Queen's Park could ever represent their country in a genuine international, something which seemed hard then and much more so now, Scotland having been represented in recent years by players who did not have a tenth of their ancestral claim.

J. B. McAlpine or "Mutt" as he was known, because of his contrast in stature with his original wing partner Alan Morton of Queen's Park, was not quite the typical Scottish inside-forward, being rather larger than most but he had the individual skills and ability to pass the ball which distinguished the breed. Ferrier had a powerful shot and was a prolific scorer from the wing during all his years at Motherwell but even had he been fully eligible to play for Scotland he would have faced daunting competition from Alan Morton who by the early 20's had moved on to Rangers. Curiously, Ferrier was withdrawn from the first Scottish League side from which he was selected, on the grounds of having been born in England, but fortunately he was quickly restored, the League in which the player was involved rather than the country of his birth being what influenced eligibility for selection.

Individual scoring feats brightened the 1920's. Hughie Gallacher in 1925, when still with Airdrie rattled in five goals against the Irish League in Belfast (curiously, 22 years later another Airdrieonian, Bobby Flavell, would be equally successful in the same match in the same city) and the superbly-named Barney Battles also scored five against the unlucky Ulstermen in 1928 at Firhill. These were minor triumphs however when set beside the crushing defeats by the Football League who won 6–2 at Ibrox in 1928, Dixie Dean scoring twice, and in 1930 even more humiliatingly won 7–3 at Tottenham, not even the great John Thomson of Celtic in the Scots goal being able to do more than keep the margin down.

The adverse balance in results was not simply a matter of unequal resources. There was a feeling that the Scottish League was not clear on its methods of selection. Too often, a player seemed to be given a League cap against the Irishmen because his club wished him to be put in the shop window, or, applying more to the Football League fixture, because of long or loyal service or because he was a well-liked fellow.

Increasingly, the Football League was making concerned noises about the match, particularly because the playing of it on a Saturday interfered greatly with League fixtures at a time when in that pre-floodlit era, all postponements had to be played on mid-week afternoons with the certainty of considerable financial loss. Yet, paradoxically, the Football League did well out of its biennial visits to Scotland and did not wish to be too hasty in arguing for change. The inherent problem was that the more powerful Football League found it difficult to motivate its spectators or players for the Scottish match. They should be able to account for the Scottish League and it was no major achievement if they did. Only a run of consecutive victories by the Scots would make the English take matters seriously.

The exotic element in the make-up of sides was on the increase. Celtic's Canadian replacement for goalkeeper John Thomson, Joe Kennoway, was chosen against the Irish League in 1932 and he was to gain the unusual honour of representing three different countries, Scotland, Canada and the United States, at full international level.

Meanwhile the Irish League had returned the compliment by selecting Jackie Donnelly, an inside forward who had been with Queen's Park before going over to play for Linfield. Donnelly would be followed into Irish League sides by Isaac McDowell of Cowdenbeath, Eric Trevorrow of Parkhead Juniors and Johnny Deakin of St. Mirren who played for The Scottish League against the Irish League and vice versa.

In the run-up to the Second World War, another English-born player, Willie Lyon of Celtic was chosen at centre-half in the last pre-Hitler joust with the Football League. Unusually, in a representative game, Lyon was flanked by his two Celtic colleagues, Chic Geatons and George Paterson. Early in 1939 the Scots took on new opposition in the form of the League of Ireland, the clubs in the Irish Free State having formed their own League at the time of the political division of 1922. Football in the south of Ireland was not highly regarded, mistakenly so since the League of Ireland won this first-ever meeting 2–1. The Scots could not use a weak selection as excuse because they had sent a very strong side, its composition reading:

Dawson (Rangers); Hogg (Celtic); Carabine, Blair (both Third Lanark); Dykes, Brown (both Heart of Midlothian); Delaney (Celtic); Walker (Heart of Midlothian); Crum (Celtic); Venters (Rangers); McNee (Hamilton Academical).

There was nothing wrong with the selection, only with attitudes. At that time there was a terrorist I.R.A. campaign in the offing and on his next home game at Cathkin Park Jimmy Carabine was regaled with the question "Hey, Carrie, did you see any bombs?" He and his team-mates would see enough of them in all conscience over the next seven years but before that he had been back to Ireland just four days before the outbreak of war in a winning side in Belfast which included the Welshman Ben Ellis of Motherwell.

With one exception Inter-League matches ceased after the outbreak of the Second World War but that exception has its own interest. At Blackpool in October 1941 a Southern League side went down 3–2 to a Football League side but such was the disparity in strength of the sides that they are worth setting out in full.

FOOTBALL LEAGUE: Fairbrother (Preston North End); Bacuzzi (Fulham); Cook (Everton); Willingham (Huddersfield Town); Pryde (Blackburn Rovers); Mercer (Everton); Matthews (Stoke City); Mannion (Middlesbrough); Rowley (Manchester United); Doherty (Manchester City); Pearson (Newcastle United).

SCOTTISH LEAGUE: Dawson (Rangers); McGurk (Hamilton Academical); Curran (Partick Thistle); Busby (Hibernian); Baxter (Heart of Midlothian); McDonald (Celtic); McSpadyen (Partick Thistle); Bremner (Motherwell); Smith (Rangers); Wallace (Clyde); Caskie (Hibernian).

The Football League made use of four non-English players. Three of them Willie Cook, Bob Pryde and Tommy Pearson were Scots and the fourth was the gifted Irishman Peter Doherty. The noteworthy feature on the Scots side was the inclusion of Matt Busby who was then guesting with Hibernian and would not otherwise have figured in a Scottish League side since he did not at any stage play senior football in Scotland.

Post-war crowds were phenomenal. In the first regular peace-time match 84,000 turned up at Hampden on a snowy March day in 1947 to see a Scottish side overwhelmed by a magnificent display of football from Stanley Matthews and Wilf Mannion. Matthews indeed so perplexed and tormented his immediate opponent, John Kelly of Third Lanark, that the latter's promising career was to all intents and purposes snuffed out. Only the heroics of Celtic's Willie Miller in goal, playing the seond-half with a towel around his blood-stained head, kept the score down to 3–1. Some talk was caused by the choice of Ronnie Burgess, a Welshman, in the Football League side but there was no reason why he should not have taken part, playing as he was in an England-based League.

When the game was taken to Ibrox two years later, there was an even bigger crowd, 90,000, for this was the very height of post-war enthusiasm. Even the gallant no-hopers of the Irish League could attract 62,000 in losing at the same venue six months later, further proof if further proof were required of the Glasgow public's insatiable if undiscriminating appetite for football.

Not infrequently, the selector failed to judge the calibre of the opposition and the importance of the occasion correctly. A match was played against the Welsh League at Cardiff in September

DOUGLAS H. WALLACE
(Clyde F.C.)

1952, the home side using the term Welsh League for convenience, although more accurately it consisted of players attached to Welsh clubs in the Football League. The Scottish League side was an odd mixture of players of genuine international class, such as Sammy Cox, and Lawrie Reilly, and serviceable club players such as Alec Boden of Celtic, Wilson Humphries of Motherwell and Willie Sharp of Partick Thistle who found it difficult to make the step up in level. The Welshmen won 3–0, two of their goals being scored by that undoubtedly international-class inside-forward, Ivor Allchurch of Swansea Town.

The same selectors were frequently criticised for an excessive partiality towards Old Firm players and yet when they left them out, the League side did not always prosper, indeed seldom did. There were no Rangers players in the side which lost 4–0 at Stamford Bridge in 1954. There were three Celts, among them the most famous Celtic name of all, Jock Stein, who received his only major representative honour at centre-half. He did not have the happiest of matches, his immediate opponent in those days of man to man marking scoring twice, so that one would have to say that Bedford Jezzard of Fulham had had the best of things.

Johnnie Hubbard became the second South African to play for a Scottish League side in 1955 (at much the same time another such, John Hewie, was establishing himself in the full Scottish international team) and in the same year the Scottish League took on a foreign adversary for the first time, recording a good 4–0 win against the Danish Combination at Copenhagen, Hubbard repaying selection by scoring one of the goals.

The terms of trade, however were turning against the League although there were still some good performances left in the Scots. To lose 1–0 at Highbury in 1960 to a Football League side bolstered by Dave Mackay of Spurs and Welshman Jack Kelsey and Cliff Jones was a highly respectable result. Even more impressive was perhaps the best result the Scottish League ever achieved, a 1–1 draw against the full might of the Italian League which thrilled 67,000 spectators on a November night in 1961 at Hampden. The Italian side was indeed formidable but were matched in every aspect of the game by the Scots.

SCOTTISH LEAGUE:
Connachan (Dunfermline Athletic);
Hamilton (Dundee); Caldow (Rangers); Crerand (Celtic);
Ure (Dundee); Baxter, Scott (both Rangers);
Quinn (Motherwell); Black (Kilmarnock);
Brand, Wilson (both Rangers).

ITALIAN LEAGUE:
Albertosi (Fiorentina); David (A.C. Milan); Pavinago (Bologna); Zaglio (Inter Milan); Charles (Juventus); Colombo (Atalanta); Hamrin (Fiorentina); Maschio (Atalanta); Hitchens (Inter Milan); Law (Torino); Petris (Fiorentina).

The result looked even better when a week later the Italian League side, with only three changes, easily defeated the Football League 2–0 at Old Trafford. To play a return in Italy a year later with only three of the same Scottish players might have seemed foolhardy but the Scots had two superlative inside-forwards in Willie Hamilton of Hearts, a little-known genius of the Scottish game, and Charlie Cooke, then with Aberdeen. The Scots went under 4–3 but had made a vivid impression on the crowd in the Olympic Stadium, Rome. This was exactly the kind of fixture needed to revive flagging interest in Inter-League matches but it had come on the scene rather too late in the day. The growing congestion of the domestic and European calendars at club level made it almost impossible to arrange dates on which worthy teams could be fielded and so was lost an excellent chance to measure our best home-based players against the top European footballers. Italian opposition had suited the Scots. As late as 1978 there was a highly creditable 1–1 draw in Verona against a very powerful home side who were preparing for a World Cup campaign in Argentina.

Ironically, over the last fifteen years of Inter-League football there was a much more professional approach to Scottish League matches. They were seen as part of the build-up to World Cup and European Nations fixtures and several excellent matches were played between the Scottish League and Scotland XI's, from one of which John White of Falkirk burst ready-made upon the international scene. League sides were put in charge of the international manager of the day and at various times John Prentice, Ian McColl, Bobby Brown and Jock Stein were all placed in control.

There were still some sparks in the dying embers. Davie Wilson scored three in a 4–3 win at Birmingham in 1962, (R. C. Hamilton would have approved) and Joe McBride with two goals inflicted the most damage when Newcastle in 1966 saw a 3–1 win. Yet it was plain that the days of Inter-League fixtures were gone. Such matches had become expendable, players were pulled out of them in droves by their clubs if there was a European or championship involvement and such mismatches as the 11–0 win against the League of Ireland in 1962 had become a serious embarrassment. By the late 1960's the Irish League failed to attract 5,000 people to Ibrox, a situation perhaps compounded by the fact that only one

JOHN GREIG (*Rangers***)**
Coming into a highly successful Rangers side in 1962, John Greig showed that urgency and total commitment that would see him virtually single-handed carry the Ibrox Club through the dark days of the mid 1970s. In his playing career he captained his country, won innumerable honours and was in the side which took the European Cup Winners' Cup in Barcelona in 1972. He has subsequently managed Rangers and in 1990 became their Public Relations Officer.

Rangers player, John Greig, gained selection. The Irish League matches drifted out to being played once every two years. It scarcely mattered. From time to time the League of Ireland would win in Dublin. No one cared.

The end came, to all intents and purposes in 1974 when a pitifully-weak Scottish League side was destroyed by a powerful Football League one at Maine Road. Injury, Scottish Cup and European involvement had hit the Scots but no one could seriously maintain that the side fielded had any hope of doing the job:

FOOTBALL LEAGUE: Clemence (Liverpool); Storey (Arsenal); Nish (Derby County); Dobson (Burnley); McFarland, Todd (both Derby County); Bowles (Queen's Park Rangers); Bell (Manchester City); Brooking (West Ham United); Tueart (Manchester City).

SCOTTISH LEAGUE: Stewart (Kilmarnock); Hermiston (Aberdeen); Wallace (Dunfermline Athletic); Copland (Dundee United); Fleming (Ayr United); Millar (Motherwell); Brown (Heart of Midlothian); Parlane (Rangers); Ford (Heart of Midlothian); Robb (Aberdeen); Prentice (Heart of Midlothian).

Clearly, only one League had treated this match with a degree of gravity and that was the Football League. Be one never so well-disposed, there were not three members of that Scottish League side which lost 5–0 who had the remotest hope of establishing themselves as full Scottish internationals, and in the oldest of Inter-League games that should always have been the yardstick. When, two years later, there could not be found ten thousand Scots who thought it worthwhile to see a minor-key 1–0 defeat at Hampden, the end had come. Events had overtaken this prestigious and venerable fixture. It would join Queen's Park v Corinthians, Amateurs v Professionals and Glasgow v Sheffield on the list of historical curios. No longer would a League jersey represent the first step on the way to a full cap nor, as it all too often had, a consolation prize for those who would clutch in vain for the topmost rung of the ladder.

The ultimate irony is that, in the League's centenary year, 1990, if the strongest possible representative side were to be chosen, it would contain at least three Englishmen and a Dutchman and a very good case could be made for a Yugoslav, a Finn and a Pole. In an indirect way no finer indication could be given of the highly-respected position which Scottish League football occupies today in the wider circles of the game.

Chapter Thirteen

THE RUNNING OF THE LEAGUE

THE SECRETARY'S VIEWPOINT

The Secretary of The Scottish Football League does not make policy, that is not his function. Policy-making is the preserve of the League Management Committee, care having been taken to canvass the opinion of the member clubs. By the nature of his office however, the Secretary is invested with considerable day to day authority. Most of the tenants of the office have been reasonably long-lived in their occupancy of it. Jim Farry, whose filling of the post almost exactly spanned the 1980's was only the fourth man to hold the office since it became a full-time occupation and taken out of the hands of the club officials.

When he took up his appointment in May 1979 at the very youthful age of 25 he was already a seasoned administrator, having served his apprenticeship with the S.F.A., the body to which he would return in the first month of 1990. He immediately identified his two overriding priorities. These would be to restore the administrative credibility of the League and to persuade the clubs to allow the League to be marketed aggresively in the commercial sector. An instance of the administrative disarray into which the League had fallen is that Jim Farry had to spend his evenings in May 1979 putting together the fixtures list for the coming season which was almost on top of him.

At a time when gate revenue was declining, alternative sources of revenue had to be found since the game had become dangerously dependent on pools money. There would be a change in the nature of the sponsorship being sought. Henceforward the drive would not so much be for sponsors who would originate their own competitions so far as brand names were concerned, e.g. the Drybrough and Texaco Cups. What the League was now after was the sponsorship of its two traditional major competitions, the Championship itself and the League Cup.

It was with a certain amount of reluctance that Jim Farry saw the Anglo-Scottish Cup go. It had been the first example of Inter-League co-operation in the devising of such a competition. The Drybrough Cup had always suffered from the apathy shown towards it by the old Firm who felt that it took place at the wrong time of the season and deprived them of a lucrative pre-season friendly against major English sides.

In addition to this kind of sponsorship there were other deals waiting to be made, such as that for footballs by which in 1990 the Mitre company provides 1000 balls for the use of Scottish clubs, no mean contribution when one considers that the price of a top-line match ball in 1990 is £80 or more. Before this kind of negotiation could be successfully concluded, sponsors would require an assurance that the League could deliver all clubs in any deal which might be struck. This in turn meant that the larger clubs might have on occasion to forego advantageous individual sponsorship for the common good. Such an instance was that of Aberdeen's prior agreement with Adidas for the supply of match balls.

This equally affected television of course. The T.V. companies were no longer prepared to allow individual clubs the right of exclusion and would rather do without any contract whatever than permit this state of affairs to continue. The League would more and more have to act as a Co-operative and to do this the Executive would have to earn the trust and confidence of the member clubs.

It might seem odd that such a small country as Scotland should possess two separate organisations to run its football, but this is largely due to historical development. Although there have been coolnesses and causes of quarrels between Association and League, relations over the century have been remarkably good given the number of egos to be bruised. Because of its immediate connection with international matches and the major European club competitions the Association has tended to take the higher profile, the more so as the more dramatic elements of player and club punishment tend to be dispensed from Park Gardens. The League has tended to go about its business quietly, rather too much so for some of its partisans, and has not been greatly concerned if the S.F.A. administers discipline so long as its input to the disciplinary process has been considerable. Thus when the four caution system was originally mooted whereby players would become subject to disciplinary procedure after cautions totalling eight penalty points, it was the League, mindful of the fact that traditionally the fourth caution had always been the one appealed against, which recommended five cautions but with no automatic right of appeal. The League of course can and does exercise disciplinary functions of its own. A club can have points deducted for breach of rule or may be fined heavily for failing to fulfil a fixture on the appointed day without good cause shown.

In the course of the 1980's pools money, remaining very important, became less pre-eminent than it was in the days when Fred Denovan and Tom Maule performed the Secretary's duties. In 1979 pools money had accounted for almost all non-gate revenue but it has now been overtaken by sponsorship and T.V. Of the revenue money which accrues, 75 per cent is distributed equally among all clubs and the remaining 25 per cent goes to finance the ladder whereby clubs are rewarded for their position in what is effectively a 38 club league.

When Jim Farry assumed office the Premier Division had been in existence for four seasons. The leading clubs had been very strong in their agitation for a new structure. Even Celtic, nine times in succession winners of the First Division, accepted the need to meet more credible opposition than the 18 club top division was able to provide. The original proposal had been for one up and one down but the Management Committee persuaded the big clubs that the proposal stood no chance of constitutional acceptance unless the principle of two up and two down was conceded. Contrary to popular perception today the Premier Division was not an immediate success in increasing gates and it was around 1980 before gates picked up consistently.

In the last 10 years or so the League has steadily become less insular. Oddly this has happened when the day of the regular Inter-League match would appear to have gone, although there will clearly be revivals for special occasions such as the Scottish League Centenary.

Inter-League matches, even those with the Football League, were choked out of the football calendar by the proliferation of European fixtures both at club and national level. There is now no season without its three or four full internationals, be they in the World Cup qualifying matches or the European Nations Cup. In the last, sad years of a distinguished history Inter-League matches had been pushed into such unsuitable months as February with inevitable results.

The Scottish League has long since passed the time when developments abroad were interesting but peripheral. The World Cup is of tremendous importance to our premier domestic competition, the League. Qualification for the final stages has a very beneficial effect on attendances, particularly if it is achieved early in the preliminary matches since spectators relish the thought of being able to see players every Saturday who will be present at the latter stages of the competition. The recent influx of prominent English and top class Continental players to The Scottish League has likewise had its effect. It has had very positive results on the perception of Scottish football abroad. The most obvious spin-off had been a marked increase in the sale of videos of Scottish League matches in European countries.

With regard to the influence of the media on the game in Scotland Jim Farry would say that he has detected a tendency towards being hyper-critical. He would concede that criticism is a function of Press, radio and television and that it is sometimes quite justified as in the case of the League Cup which had become a most unsatisfactory competition by the late 1970's and stood in need of drastic and immediate revision. The League Newsletter was largely designed to ensure that the League's own point of view on important matters was communicated to clubs and public and did not simply go by default.

A Secretary will only be successful in so far as he is perceived to have a thorough knowledge of the rules and to be working whole-heartedly for the general good of The Scottish Football League, i.e. the member clubs. There should also be a willingness to apply these rules in a spirit of commonsense and a preparedness to give the clubs themselves the first opportunity to resolve disputes before the League need intervene as mediator. This is not always possible since in reality the Scottish League often has to resolve matters by 3 p.m. on the following Saturday. Because of this, much day-to-day power vests in the Secretary who together with President, Vice-President and Treasurer forms the League Executive. Luck is important too as in the fortunate co-incidence of two of the mildest Scottish winters in history with the two seasons of the 12 club Premier and First Divisions. Astonishingly, a potentially disastrous 44 match schedule was carried through in two successive years with scarcely a postponement.

The League Secretary has found it often very advisable to work wherever possible through club secretaries whose professional training can enable them to take the longer view of things. Nor are they handicapped by the need which club chairman and club managers sometimes feel of adopting a high and aggressive profile. At the end of the day the League Secretary will largely exist on the strength of his personal relationships with other in the game, always assuming, of course, that professional competence which the clubs are entitled to expect.

In the opinion of Jim Farry, now moved to the post of Secretary of the Scottish Football Association, the ideal formula for Scottish League football remains elusive. Perhaps it will always remain so since football is never static and indeed never dare be static. The present set-up is basically right, perhaps all that is needed is some fine-tuning. Yet the clamour for constant change can badly affect credibility and there is some evidence that it can seriously deter potential sponsors.

Structure was not the main problem for him. Rather it could be posed thus: Now that the Scottish game is internationally well-respected and well-regarded, how do we improve the entertainment content? That may prove to have ramifications well beyond League level and may demand a new outlook from schools upwards. In his new post Jim Farry will be able to bring some very heavy guns to bear to achieve his wish.

Chapter Fourteen

THE LEAGUE REACHES ITS CENTURY— TRIUMPHS AND CHALLENGES

A centenary is an occasion both for celebrating and for looking to the future. The Scottish League will have much to congratulate itself on in August 1990 and will do so with some style. There will be a formal banquet to which will be invited the good and the great of world football, and certainly the chance taken to measure Scottish League football against fitting opposition.

No doubt the speeches made at the banquet will take account of the undeniably solid achievement of the century in general and the last few years in particular. The Scottish Football League has produced in the Skol Cup the ideal blueprint for a knock-out competition in modern times, with spectators guaranteed a definite result on the day. This has proved to be one of the most successful instances of sponsorship in the entire history of sport in Britain with firms queueing up in their willingness to act as replacements when the present sponsors decide that their time has run.

The major competition, The Scottish League Championship, has been revitalised by the introduction of three divisions. In a 15 year existence the Premier Division has already been won by four clubs, Aberdeen, Celtic, Dundee United and Rangers, and was within seven minutes of being won by a fifth, Heart of Midlothian. The contrast between this period and that of the twenty years between the two wars, when one Motherwell win relieved otherwise total Old Firm domination, could scarcely be starker. In 1990, having been told for years that competitive team sports were seriously losing appeal, The Scottish League will have 38 clubs in membership. This is precisely the same number that it had in 1939 and indeed 33 of the clubs claimed membership then and now.

It could be further argued that the smaller clubs have never been freer from real financial worry, something that does not meet with the unfeigned approval of those who would like to see them disappear and the game streamlined. There will certainly always be struggle associated with the running of a club such as Cowdenbeath or East Stirling or Montrose. Yet, relatively, the £8000 that Stenhousemuir receive from the B and Q sponsorship of The Scottish League Championship is more important than the £20,000 given to Rangers, Aberdeen or Celtic. Add to that the incentive payments available through the Skol Cup and monies available from the Pools Promoters Association, television and radio and it will be understood that gate money plays an almost negligible part in the financing of the smaller clubs, not that this is by any means a totally healthy state of affairs.

The Scottish Football League is highly regarded in Europe. This is partly because the creation of the Premier Division has had as its chief result the emergence of two new clubs as European powers, Aberdeen and Dundee United. It is not over-stating the case to say that these two clubs in the 1980s gave Scottish football European credibility as the traditional standard-bearers, Celtic and Rangers, faltered badly before the continental challenge. The European connection has been greatly strengthened by the recent trend toward importing top-class players from Europe so that there are few leading Scottish clubs today which lack a strong cross-Channel influence.

If to that is added the enormous English input, largely the result of the visionary work of Graeme Souness at Ibrox, which has at various times seen such stars as Trevor Francis, Graham Roberts, Ray Wilkins, Terry Butcher and Chris Woods wear the light blue jersey, it can be seen that Scottish League football has moved far from its rather insular position of the 1960s when there was the very definite imputation that a player who spent his entire career in Scotland did so in the last analysis because of a lack of either ambition or ability at the highest level.

Some idea of the strength of the foreign contingent in Scottish football in the year 1990 can be garnered from the fact that it would be perfectly possible to pick two extremely strong elevens of non-Scots to play a match, every player being currently engaged in the Scottish Football League. Such sides might read as follows:
TEAM A: Snelders (Aberdeen); Stevens (Rangers); Wdowczyk (Celtic); Spackman (Rangers); Elliott (Celtic); Butcher (Rangers); Steven (Rangers); Dziekanowski (Celtic); Van der Ark (Aberdeen); Gillhaus (Aberdeen); Walters (Rangers).
TEAM B: Woods (Rangers); Morris (Celtic); Rogan (Celtic); Krivokapic (Dundee United); Saunders (Dundee); O'Neill (Motherwell); Paatelainen (Dundee United); Foster (Hearts); Torfarson

(St. Mirren); Houchen (Hibernian); Kozma (Dunfermline).

Missing from these teams would be yet another international goalkeeper, Pat Bonner of Celtic and the Republic of Ireland, Paul Mason, Aberdeen's Englishman, and Michael O'Neill of Dundee United and Northern Ireland.

Just as important, however, was the fact that Scotland started the last qualifying match in the World Cup against Norway at Hampden Park on November 15 1989 with ten Home Scots in the side. It is vital to the health of the game in Scotland that spectators should be able to see World Cup players appearing on a weekly basis and in the ranks of teams other than the Old Firm. This heavy home concentration was in marked distinction to that of their opponents, Norway, a country whose players have almost totally to make a living from football in other lands and in its own way was an indication of the comparatively healthy state of the Scottish game.

So far then, a tale of almost unalloyed success and worthy of much laudatory comment when the Centenary Banquet is held in the Albany Hotel, Glasgow on August 18 1990. Are there then no clouds on the horizon, no threats to be faced down? Of course there are, problems are the norm in human existence, it is only the nature of those problems that changes.

The first reservation expressed on the current state of League football in Scotland is that it has produced a Premier Division which is ultra-competitive but infra-talented. The complaint is that the fierceness of onfield rivalry has choked the traditional, skilful Scottish ballplayer out of the game. We are, argue the critics, back to Jock Stein's hundred-yard sprint for grandmothers which he described tersely as "highly competitive but just not very good." It would be ostrich-like to claim that these criticisms are totally lacking in validity but there is a strong possibility that the damage is caused long before these players reach Premier Division level, or indeed any grade of League football. Many good judges, Jim McLean of Dundee United and the national coach Andy Roxburgh among them, are on record as saying that Scots play far too much competitive football from far too early an age. Inevitably, they learn to win before they have learned how to play, and when they move into the wider sphere of foreign opposition, their deficiencies in the arts and crafts of the game are ruthlessly exposed. A change in basic thinking is required, rather than any essentially cosmetic re-organisation of the divisions.

The critics are possibly on surer ground when they maintain that reconstruction has helped top and bottom clubs in The Scottish League set-up but has been harmful to those middle-range clubs of whom Morton, Partick Thistle and Falkirk might well serve as examples. Certainly it has been extremely difficult for a First Division club having secured promotion to the Premier Division to stay there, and only Dundee United in the last thirty years have made the transition from lower to higher grade with any permanence and considerable degree of success. It could also be argued that Dundee United were in any case atypical, based as they were in one of the major cities of Scotland. The Falkirks of the world have increasingly begun to wonder about their long-term future in Scottish football, with promotion to the top division becoming much more unlikely now that it has been restricted to one club per season. Is it remotely worth keeping a club on a full-time basis when the odds are 13–1 against its attaining Premier Division status at the end of any particular season? Is there not a case in equity for having a play-off between the team which finishes 9th in the Premier Division and that which comes second in the First Division?

Yet the game has prospered astonishingly as will be seen at once from these League and League Cup statistics of 1987 (shown below). The underlying questions, say the pessimists are: How securely based is this apparent prosperity, is it not really a mirage? What will the Scottish scene look like the season after English clubs are re-admitted to Europe? Will the attraction of Scotland for English players persist in those circumstances? And, with the

SCOTTISH FOOTBALL LEAGUE ATTENDANCE FIGURES
SEASON 1987–88

Premier Division	Skol Cup	Fine Fare League Championship	TOTAL
Aberdeen	41,205	296,123	337,328
Celtic	13,711	730,388	744,099
Dundee	19,867	189,096	208,963
Dundee United	6,075	230,168	236,243
Dunfermline Ath.	17,705	203,384	221,089
Falkirk	—	146,503	146,503
Heart of Mid.	20,899	365,929	386,828
Hibernian	10,383	254,977	265,360
Morton	1,899	108,533	110,432
Motherwell	15,304	146,511	161,815
Rangers	40,920	848,493	889,413
St. Mirren	3,507	162,499	166,006
	191,475	3,682,604	3,874,079

	Skol Cup	Fine Fare League Championship	TOTAL
First Division			
Airdrieonians	—	31,116	31,116
Clyde	—	23,120	23,120
Clydebank	—	23,397	23,397
Dumbarton	9,429	18,402	27,831
East Fife	—	21,570	21,570
Forfar Athletic	—	16,268	16,268
Hamilton Accies.	—	44,957	44,957
Kilmarnock	—	40,610	40,610
Meadowbank Th.	3,255	16,143	19,398
Partick Thistle	—	43,393	43,393
Q.O.S.	2,003	28,200	30,203
Raith Rovers	7,902	46,402	54,304
	22,589	353,578	376,167
Second Division			
Albion Rovers	536	6,806	7,342
Alloa	—	11,393	11,393
Arbroath	735	11,153	11,888
Ayr United	2,378	53,125	55,503
Berwick Rangers	467	8,962	9,429
Brechin City	—	9,487	9,487
Cowdenbeath	315	5,351	5,666
East Stirlingshire	2,240	6,718	8,958
Montrose	—	7,988	7,988
Queen's Park	1,410	12,203	13,613
St. Johnstone	1,313	38,916	40,229
Stenhousemuir	394	6,809	7,203
Stirling Albion	11,737	15,208	26,945
Stranraer	390	9,362	9,752
	21,915	203,481	225,396

TOTAL 4,475,642

SKOL CUP SEMI-FINAL TIES 67,873

SKOL CUP FINAL TIE 71,961

GRAND TOTAL 4,615,476

increasing liberalisation of Eastern Europe, will there be the same incentives for, say, Polish and Hungarian players to come to Britain?

The year 1992 will in any event see practically untramelled movement within Europe with players possibly able to come and go in complete freedom on the expiration of contracts. This might mean that some very good European players will end up in Scotland. The gloomy probability is that the traffic in the reverse direction will be much heavier. There is a real danger of Scottish players embarking on "sandwich careers" by which they will make their name in Scotland, play their peak five to eight seasons abroad and then come back to spend their declining footballing years in their native Scotland. It is not an appealing prospect but one with which the major Scottish bodies, Association and League, will have to grapple.

There will be increased frequency of movement and this in itself could cause spectator resentment. There is a great need for supporters to identify with the long-term club servant, and to experience the communal emotion of the testimonial match for such great players as John Greig of Rangers, Billy McNeill of Celtic, Willie Miller of Aberdeen, Paul Hegarty of Dundee United and from an earlier generation Charlie Aitken of Motherwell, Jimmy Mason of Third Lanark and Sammy Stewart of East Fife. It is going to be very difficult to generate the same affection for players if they become short-term contract birds of passage.

There is another problem to which all sports will have to address themselves and that is that the results of the dramatically-reduced birthrate of the 1980's will become apparent in the new decade. The reality in Scotland will be that there will be three children where ten years before there were four, and football will face very strong competition for the reduced number of youngsters who will be available as potential recruits. This will happen at precisely the time when the traditional pyramidical structure through the schools will for all practical purposes have collapsed.

Clubs will have to become much more actively involved in the actual introduction of boys to the game. No longer will they be able to sit back in the happy knowledge that the natural conveyor-belt of the game i.e. the schools, will produce the latest batch of hopefuls ready for testing. It is entirely possible that ten years into the twenty-first century, almost the most important man on a club staff will be its Community Relations Officer and for there to be any worthwhile inter-action with the community, that will involve the provision of an all-weather playing pitch, at least at training level.

As life becomes materially easier, it will almost certainly be the case that association football is no longer seen as the only career escape for a working-class boy from grim and depressing surroundings. Traditionally, Scottish football flourished in mining areas and those where heavy industry was strong. It remains to be seen how football will fare in an essentially post-industrial society. Boxing offers an ominous analogy, for with the disappearance of the "hungry fighter" of the 1930s and 1940s, the sport has almost totally gone under as a mass-audience attraction and ekes out a precarious existence in a handful of Sporting Clubs.

To understand what a successful footballing career could mean to a boy from a working-class background the writer would wish to quote from two interviews which he conducted with Jerry Dawson, the great Rangers goalkeeper of the 1930's and Jimmy Delaney, the flying Celtic winger of the same period. The interviews were recorded in the course of the 1971–72 season, Dawson first:

"I signed for Rangers in season 1929–30. In my first season at Ibrox I was a part-timer as I was completing my apprenticeship, so I trained as a part-timer, training on Tuesday and Thursday nights. We were given to understand that there would be a very long apprenticeship to serve for our first team places, about three to four years.

"My parents were not at all keen on my playing professional football. They were less keen than ever when in my first match against Celtic the Celtic goalkeeper, John Thomson, sustained fatal injuries.

"We were subject to very strict physical and social disciplines. Don't swim in fresh water, don't play badminton, be immaculate on the field, always run out of the tunnel at half-time even if three goals down. To lose one's place in the side and receive a free transfer was almost certainly to return to the Labour Exchange.

"We played in the palmy days of football. In the circumstances of the time we were millionaires. We paid Income Tax at the end of the year and we made about £15 per week. We had much better tours abroad than now. We went by boat, we had time to see the country, we lived like lords and the opposition were pushovers. Now it is a very hasty flight and a really tough match."

Other professional clubs also issued guidelines to their players as witness this circular issued to members of the playing staff by Aberdeen Football Club on October 12 1938. It was somewhat quaintly called The Pittodrie Code of Honour. Issued by the then manager, David Halliday, it laid down the following requirements:

1. The players will see that they report each morning at 10 a.m. for training.
2. There must be no dancing after Tuesday.
3. There must be no smoking within three hours of any match.
4. There must be no smoking during the train trip south to any match.
5. Any tendency to "blind eye" the instructions of captain or trainer will be a breach of contract to be considered in session by the Aberdeen Club.

It is fair to say that most footballers found these rules anything but oppressive. Jimmy Delaney of Celtic, while relatively less prosperous, could also serve as a model of a very successful professional footballer in those immediate pre-World War Two days.

J. DELANEY

"I signed for Celtic from Stoneyburn Juniors in 1934. As a provisional signing I was paid £2 per week. When I became a fully-signed player I got £4 per week, after which my wages went up by about 10/- per week each season. The most I ever got from Celtic was £7-10-0d. During the war of course we were restricted to a maximum of £2 per match.

"When I moved to Manchester United in 1946 I stayed with them until 1950. The most I ever received at Old Trafford was £14–£15 per week. I then moved on to Aberdeen, to Falkirk, to Derry City, to Cork Celtic and finally to Elgin City. I finished playing senior football in 1957.

"I had left school at fourteen and worked a short time in the pits but I had been idle a good while when Celtic signed me. I lasted so long because I was a great trainer and usually in bed by 10 p.m. I have arthritis now, caused by football but I would to the same again. I would have liked to scout, not to manage. I would have loved to play in present-day football. When I was young I never thought the day would come when I would have to give up playing."

Supporters are also less hungry and more discerning. There is evidence that they prefer winter football but winter football in greatly improved facilities. In the 1940s it could be argued that the standard of housing in industrial Scotland was so bad that there was comparatively little difference between living in a damp and draughty single-end tenement flat and standing on a gale-swept, rain-lashed terracing but people's expectations have risen in tandem with their standards of living.

Covered accommodation, and seated accommodation at that, will be imperative in the next few years for even if the spectators did not want it, U.E.F.A. and those bodies responsible for public safety would insist upon it. This in turn has consequences for the ownership of clubs. The old friendly society, family business, atmosphere will simply be proved incapable of generating the necessary money for large-scale ground improvements. The large clubs have effectively two choices. They can be bought out by a large consortium or they can go public and invite their supporters to acquire a substantial shareholding in the club.

Either way presents difficulties. Widen the share structure and the chance of an eventual take-over is inevitably increased. The danger in corporate ownership is that supporters may become distanced and alienated since they may feel that in a very real sense it is no longer their club as it was in the days when they could make suggestions to, and vent their spleen on, local directors. There may also be speedy and serious repercussions for the club if the parent company should run into financial problems and most do, in the short or long term. It is another illustration of the paradox that football must be run on business-like lines but running it as a business pure and simple will certainly not guarantee its survival.

And what is the Scottish League's function in all of this? At its most basic, it is to act as a facilitator, to see that nineteen League matches are played off each Saturday of the season and that there are 57 officials present to take charge of those matches. Its real long-term concern has of course to be the health and good standing of those clubs which make up its membership. This is a more restricted remit than that of the S.F.A. which has to concern itself additionally with international football and the welfare of the minor grades at home but nevertheless there is ample opportunity for the League Management Committee to display the skills of statesmanship rather than those of politics.

The League must, wherever possible, take the long view. It must not be panicked into taking hasty decisions on such matters as a winter shut-down. Year after year this issue is raised and year after year it founders on the unpredictability of the Scottish weather. To eliminate any serious interference from that agency, there would have to be a shut-down from mid-December to mid-March. Would the customers still be there on resumption? Since many matches are cancelled because of frost in the ground, although there is some evidence that the climate is becoming milder, would not the provision of undersoil heating largely eradicate the problem? And since the great bulk of spectators attending League matches could normally be accommodated quite comfortably under cover, need matches not be postponed only when travelling conditions or the weather on the day were downright dangerous?

These are complex question as is the problem of what to do with the smaller clubs. For those who argue that there is no place in senior Scottish football for a club such as Forfar Athletic which attracts on average around 1000 spectators to its home matches, there is the valid counter-argument that this modest total represents one in ten of the town's inhabitants, a strike-rate which many larger clubs come nowhere near achieving. There is, too, the fact that League football does stimulate interest in the game in the outposts. The two regions where there is no Scottish League football in Scotland, the Highlands and the Borders, have not been noted as producers of top-class players in any number. If a club which is the lone outpost of League football closes down, the chances are heavily that the youngsters of that neighbourhood will opt for other pastimes and sports.

That is not to say that there have been no opportunities missed, most notably in the New Towns where the footballing authorities should have attempted to ensure that a League side grew up with the towns of East Kilbride, Glenrothes, Cumbernauld and Livingston, or in at least three of them as it could be argued that Fife was already adequately served for League football. That chance would appear to have gone irretrievably now, for it would be very difficult to impose a football club at this stage of development of the New Towns.

Something perhaps requires to be done to make sure that a populous area such as Inverness, with a history of good-class football, is given a chance to participate in the League structure. The obvious way to ensure this would seem to be the kind of pyramidical structure recently adopted in England whereby the bottom club in the Fourth Division of the Football League automatically drops out, to be replaced by the leading club in the GM Vauxhall Conference. This would be harder to work in Scotland where the great probability would be a gradual erosion of the small Lowland and Central Scottish clubs with their replacement by Highland League clubs in increasing numbers. To keep those clubs

ALAN MORTON

For twelve years this small but strong and elusive player was an automatic choice for the outside-left position in the Scotland side. Starting out with Queen's Park he moved to Rangers just after World War One and won every possible domestic honour with the Ibrox Club. He was especially renowed for his dribbling and crosses-cum-shots which were known as Alan Morton lobs. His nick-name, the Wee Blue Devil, testified to the fear he inspired in opposition defences.

which temporarily lost League status in existence, they would have to be guaranteed places either in the Reserve League or better still, for a couple of seasons in the Premier Reserve League. This would give them a chance to regain their lost League status. Consideration might also be given to the trying-out of a club in Galashiels where the powerful rugby club has no official second team and plays away from home on alternate Saturdays. There is the risk that a powerful non-league side could in effect force admission by gaining control of a weak Second Division side already in the League and then running it into the ground but normal vigilance should be enough to prevent this coming to pass.

This book, and it is important to re-iterate the fact, is not a history of individual clubs, it concerns itself with clubs only in so far as they have at one time or another acquired membership of The Scottish Football League. Yet it cannot be denied, that however fascinating the workings of that League, and however gratifying its successful development, the League to the man in the stand and the man on the terracings means the players. For them, the history of The Scottish League is the history of giants of far and recent past, such as Jimmy Quinn, Nick Smith, Bobby Templeton and Bobby Walker in the years before 1914, Tommy Walker, Dougie Gray, Bobby Hogg, Alan Morton and Willie Lyon in the inter-war years, together with Stevenson and Ferrier of Motherwell, who have some claim to be the greatest wing ever to play in Scottish League football, and more recently, Billy McNeill, John Greig, Willie Miller and Paul Hegarty, every single one of whom established himself in the affection and admiration of the Scottish sporting public.

Inevitably the League history is also in some part, the story of individual clubs, the tremendous triumphant surge of the Old Firm, almost uninterrupted across the century, the brief flowering of the Edinburgh sides in the 1950's, the welcome emergence of a convincing and sustained challenge from the New Firm of Aberdeen and Dundee United in the 1970's and 1980's. The shore is studded too with gallant and picturesque wrecks such as Solway Star, Mid-Annandale, Dumbarton Harp and Royal Albert, which were never more than a gleam in the collective eye of their committees and there is the more sinister disappearance of the founding Third Lanark, dead of a long and deliberate course of neglect.

Today, almost fifty years after their clubs last kicked a ball, there are old men in Scotland who would describe themselves as supporters of King's Park, Leith Athletic or St. Bernards. It is difficult to over-emphasise the hold that the game has for Scots, or the depth of perception which ordinary men can bring to their thinking on the subject. Perhaps this letter, written by a Scot in the evening of his days to a friend in Glasgow will serve as illustration. When the letter was written in 1974, the Scot, a former Scottish League footballer, had lived in the United States for many years but in the sense that mattered he had never left home.

January 15 1974 　　　　　　　　　　227 Grove Street
　　　　　　　　　　　　　　　　　　　　　　Bridgeport
　　　　　　　　　　　　　　　　　　　　Conn. 06605
　　　　　　　　　　　　　　　　　　　　　　　U.S.A.

Hello Jock,

Before going any further let me thank you for your beautiful calendar which I received and which is now hanging above my desk. As I have said before, I am afraid that I am not a very good American and the thought of my native country is always with me.

The fact that you have followed the Clyde for so long has, I'm sure, fully earned for you a reserved seat with the angels. It's a lot easier to follow the big boys but I'm sure not any more satisfactory. The Clyde have also had their day and I remember when their stand burned down and they had a little hut built in the corner to serve as a dressing room. I remember in my very very young days being helped over the turnstile by the spectators going into the ground. That was in the days of Gilligan, "Shoogly" Walker, McAndrew, etc. Years later I was to run on to the same field with Third Lanark. Our forward line was Reid, Devlin, McInally, Walker and Hillhouse and of course in the Clyde team were Singleton, Cowan, Farrell, Rae, Forrest and Marshall. Remember those players Jock? I think the result was, if I remember, 2–2. Mattha Gemmell was the trainer at that time.

I remember when I was ordered off against Aston Villa on their ground. I was suspended for a month and forbidden by the English Association of course even to enter the Birmingham Stadium. I came home and trained at Shawfield and it was the most entertaining time of my football career. Glasgow has had its quota of comedians... Tommy Lorne, Power and Bendon, Sammy Thomson... but the Clyde had Auld Mattha. I remember us taking penalty kicks, a tanner a pop. I belted three past him but he refused to pay up because he said I was a spy from another country—England! He was never stuck for a reply.

All those characters have gone, Jock, that is the reason we have to die off.

Now the old game is ruined and it will soon become a music hall profession more quickly than you think. Loyalty to a club will be at a premium with players being able to move from club to club at the end of each season. The small clubs won't be able to compete and will go to the wall. Only the clubs in heavily populated areas will survive. It is going to be like baseball and American football. There are only about 24 baseball clubs in a country this size. It (baseball) went through all the growing pains of our football and that is the way it finished up. Scotland, England and Wales could stand three leagues of sixteen teams and they would be the best. There is no such thing as big journeys anymore. Rangers could pop down to London in a couple of hours, Cardiff City to Edinburgh in three. It's too bad we won't be around to see it, Jock, but that's what is going to happen. Look at the returns from such clubs as Queen of the South, Albion Rovers, Airdrie, Clyde, nearly all of them. It's pitiful. And now with world football as it is we have just GOT to compete and the national team boss at the moment MUST get the players he wants or let us get to hell out of league football.

Bobby Calder, you remember him, he was quite a referee in his day and was the man who found all the good players for Aberdeen, wrote me a letter about his sister Mary Greenshields passing away. Although it was something which we had expected nevertheless it carried a clout. However she had a peaceful end and just fell asleep. You know, Jock, she was really an amazing woman. Mary kept up a running correspondence with me for 27 years. She lost her husband many years ago. He was a guard on the railway and was on the Preston, Birmingham and London route. The two of them, with two other neighbours played nearly every night at rummy. One night as they were sitting enjoying a cup of tea, a great big "blether", (full-size football) wet and muddy, with as many patches on it as my pants, came flying through the window right on to the middle of the table. I believe Mary fainted.

It had been raining for about three days and the back yard at 639 Dalmarnock Road was a quagmire. They came flying out into the yard in an effort to catch us but fast as they travelled they were too slow. We lost the ball but kept on denying it was us. But, as the years passed, I told them they were lucky we didn't charge them admission fee to see us. That puts me in mind of the lady who lived on the ground floor in the single close red building in Summerfield Street. I smacked a tanner ba' right through her window and we galloped as usual. However she was a stickler and a couple of hours later Big Paddy the "polisman" was up to see Maw Devlin. You would have thought I had broken into Barclay's

Bank. Maw Devlin (the writer's mother) paid for the window and I was on the receiving end of one of her right hooks. As the lady was leaving the Devlin household she said to me "and YOU, if you could play it wouldn't be so bad."

A few years later she was walking along Dalmarnock Road on her way home when a slim, young, well-dressed man behind her tapped her on the shoulders and, when she turned round, handed her a couple of stand tickets for the Third Lanark and Airdrie game at Cathkin Park on the Saturday. It was the great Airdrie side of Howieson, Gallacher, Bob Bennie, etc. "My God," she gasped... "You!"

"Yes, it's me," I said. "Remember you said it wouldn't be so bad if I could play? Well, you bring your husband on Saturday and I'll show you," and I walked on, laughing. That was another happy little East End moment. The tenements were grim and grimy but they had a warmth and friendliness which will never be surpassed. You always had a neighbour and a friend, even if you had no money.

Well, Jock, I may see you in the summer but a lot of things have got to happen. Best wishes to you both for continued good health. In case it's later than we think it was nice to have known you.

And that's the way it is, Jock,
Yours as aye
Tommy Devlin.

The letter is not only a remarkable testimony to the excellence of Scottish education at that time—Tommy Devlin left school at fourteen years of age—but it illustrates how an old man, almost blind as he mentions in another part of the letter, could foresee some of the changes which were going to have to be made in the running of the Scottish game.

So, the summer of 1990 will be one of celebration as The Scottish Football League awaits its second century. Those in charge of its destiny will reflect that although Scots occasionally exaggerate their own importance in the football world, the record of national achievement has been solid enough in all conscience. Great things have come from that initial meeting in Holton's Hotel in 1890 and certainly men such as J. H. McLaughlin and William Wilton would have welcomed whatever challenges may prove to lie ahead. It is pleasant to suppose that, from wherever he is located in eternity, the waspish editor of those early days of *Scottish Sport* might summon sufficient grace to admit that for once he had got things wrong and that The Scottish Football League has been a powerful influence for the good of the game in his native land.

HISTORICAL DATA and RESULTS

SCOTTISH LEAGUE CHAMPIONS

Division One

Year		Pts.
1890/91	Dumbarton/ Rangers *(Joint Champions)*	29
1891/92	Dumbarton	37
1892/93	Celtic	29
1893/94	Celtic	29
1894/95	Hearts	31
1895/96	Celtic	30
1896/97	Hearts	28
1897/98	Celtic	33
1898/99	Rangers	36
1899/1900	Rangers	32
1900/01	Rangers	35
1901/02	Rangers	28
1902/03	Hibernian	37
1903/04	Third Lanark	43
1904/05	Celtic *(after play-off)*	41
1905/06	Celtic	49
1906/07	Celtic	55
1907/08	Celtic	55
1908/09	Celtic	51
1909/10	Celtic	54
1910/11	Rangers	52
1911/12	Rangers	51
1912/13	Rangers	53
1913/14	Celtic	65
1914/15	Celtic	65
1915/16	Celtic	67
1916/17	Celtic	64
1917/18	Rangers	56
1918/19	Celtic	58
1919/20	Rangers	71

Division Two

		Pts.
	—	
	—	
	—	
Hibernian		29
Hibernian		30
Abercorn		27
Partick Thistle		31
Kilmarnock		29
Kilmarnock		32
Partick Thistle		29
St. Bernards		25
Port Glasgow		32
Airdrieonians		35
Hamilton Accies.		37
Clyde		32
Leith Athletic		34
St. Bernards		32
Raith Rovers		30
Abercorn		31
Leith Athletic		33
Dumbarton		31
Ayr United		35
Ayr United		34
Cowdenbeath		31
Cowdenbeath		37
— *(No Competition)*		
— *(No Competition)*		
— *(No Competition)*		
— *(No Competition)*		
— *(No Competition)*		

Division One			Division Two	
Year		Pts.		Pts.
1920/21	Rangers	76	— (*No Competition*)	
1921/22	Celtic	67	Alloa Athletic	60
1922/23	Rangers	55	Queen's Park	57
1923/24	Rangers	59	St. Johnstone	56
1924/25	Rangers	60	Dundee United	50
1925/26	Celtic	58	Dunfermline	59
1926/27	Rangers	56	Bo'ness	56
1927/28	Rangers	60	Ayr United	54
1928/29	Rangers	67	Dundee United	51
1929/30	Rangers	60	Leith Athletic (*on goal average*)	57
1930/31	Rangers	60	Third Lanark	61
1931/32	Motherwell	66	East Stirlingshire (*on goal average*)	55
1932/33	Rangers	62	Hibernian	54
1933/34	Rangers	66	Albion Rovers	45
1934/35	Rangers	55	Third Lanark	52
1935/36	Celtic	66	Falkirk	59
1936/37	Rangers	61	Ayr United	54
1937/38	Celtic	61	Raith Rovers	59
1938/39	Rangers	59	Cowdenbeath	60
1939/40	— (*No Competition*)		— (*No Competition*)	
1940/41	— (*No Competition*)		— (*No Competition*)	
1941/42	— (*No Competition*)		— (*No Competition*)	
1942/43	— (*No Competition*)		— (*No Competition*)	
1943/44	— (*No Competition*)		— (*No Competition*)	
1944/45	— (*No Competition*)		— (*No Competition*)	
1945/46	— (*No Competition*)		— (*No Competition*)	
1946/47	Rangers	46	Dundee	45
1947/48	Hibernian	48	East Fife	53
1948/49	Rangers	46	Raith Rovers (*on goal average*)	42
1949/50	Rangers	50	Morton	47
1950/51	Hibernian	48	Queen of the South (*on goal average*)	45
1951/52	Hibernian	45	Clyde	44
1952/53	Rangers (*on goal average*)	43	Stirling Albion	44
1953/54	Celtic	43	Motherwell	45
1954/55	Aberdeen	49	Airdrieonians	46
1955/56	Rangers	52	Queen's Park	54
1956/57	Rangers	55	Clyde	64

HISTORICAL DATA AND RESULTS

Division One			Division Two	
Year		Pts.		Pts.
1957/58	Hearts	62	Stirling Albion	55
1958/59	Rangers	50	Ayr United	60
1959/60	Hearts	54	St. Johnstone	53
1960/61	Rangers	51	Stirling Albion	55
1961/62	Dundee	54	Clyde	54
1962/63	Rangers	57	St. Johnstone	55
1963/64	Rangers	55	Morton	67
1964/65	Kilmarnock	50	Stirling Albion	59
	(on goal average)			
1965/66	Celtic	57	Ayr United	53
1966/67	Celtic	58	Morton	69
1967/68	Celtic	63	St. Mirren	62
1968/69	Celtic	54	Motherwell	64
1969/70	Celtic	57	Falkirk	56
1970/71	Celtic	56	Partick Thistle	56
1971/72	Celtic	60	Dumbarton	52
			(on goal difference)	
1972/73	Celtic	57	Clyde	56
1973/74	Celtic	53	Airdrieonians	60
1974/75	Rangers	56	Falkirk	54

Premier Division		1st Division		2nd Division	
1975/76					
Rangers	54	Partick Thistle	41	Clydebank	40
				(on goal difference)	
1976/77					
Celtic	55	St. Mirren	62	Stirling Albion	55
1977/78					
Rangers	55	Morton	58	Clyde	53
		(on goal difference)		*(on goal difference)*	
1978/79					
Celtic	48	Dundee	55	Berwick Rgrs.	54
1979/80					
Aberdeen	48	Hearts	53	Falkirk	50
1980/81					
Celtic	56	Hibernian	57	Queen's Park	50
1981/82					
Celtic	55	Motherwell	61	Clyde	59
1982/83					
Dundee Utd.	56	St. Johnstone	55	Brechin City	55

	Premier Division		1st Division		2nd Division	
1983/84	Aberdeen	57	Morton	54	Forfar Ath.	63
1984/85	Aberdeen	59	Motherwell	50	Montrose	53
1985/86	Celtic *(on goal difference)*	50	Hamilton	56	Dunfermline	57
1986/87	Rangers	69	Morton	57	Meadowbank	55
1987/88	Celtic	72	Hamilton	56	Ayr United	61
1988/89	Rangers	56	Dunfermline	54	Albion Rovers	50
1989/90	Rangers		St. Johnstone		Brechin City	

SCOTTISH LEAGUE CUP FINALS

1946/47	Rangers v Aberdeen	4–0
1947/48	East Fife v Falkirk *(after 1–1 draw)*	4–1
1948/49	Rangers v Raith Rovers	2–0
1949/50	East Fife v Dunfermline Athletic	3–0
1950/51	Motherwell v Hibernian	3–0
1951/52	Dundee v Rangers	3–2
1952/53	Dundee v Kilmarnock	2–0
1953/54	East Fife v Partick Thistle	3–2
1954/55	Hearts v Motherwell	4–2
1955/56	Aberdeen v St. Mirren	2–1
1956/57	Celtic v Partick Thistle *(after 0–0 draw)*	3–0
1957/58	Celtic v Rangers	7–1
1958/59	Hearts v Partick Thistle	5–1
1959/60	Hearts v Third Lanark	2–1
1960/61	Rangers v Kilmarnock	2–0
1961/62	Rangers v Hearts *(after 1–1 draw)*	3–1
1962/63	Hearts v Kilmarnock	1–0
1963/64	Rangers v Morton	5–0
1964/65	Rangers v Celtic	2–1
1965/66	Celtic v Rangers	2–1
1966/67	Celtic v Rangers	1–0
1967/68	Celtic v Dundee	5–3
1968/69	Celtic v Hibernian	6–2
1969/70	Celtic v St. Johnstone	1–0

1970/71	Rangers v Celtic	1–0
1971/72	Partick Thistle v Celtic	4–1
1972/73	Hibernian v Celtic	2–1
1973/74	Dundee v Celtic	1–0
1974/75	Celtic v Hibernian	6–3
1975/76	Rangers v Celtic	1–0
1976/77	Aberdeen v Celtic	2–1
1977/78	Rangers v Celtic	2–1
1978/79	Rangers v Aberdeen	2–1
1979/80*	Dundee United v Aberdeen (*after 0–0 draw*)	3–0
1980/81*	Dundee United v Dundee	3–0
1981/82	Rangers v Dundee United	2–1
1982/83	Celtic v Rangers	2–1
1983/84	Rangers v Celtic	3–2
1984/85†	Rangers v Dundee United	1–0
1985/86†	Aberdeen v Hibernian	3–0
1986/87†	Rangers v Celtic	2–1
1987/88†	Rangers v Aberdeen (*after extra time 3–3*) (*Rangers won 5–3 on kicks from the penalty mark*)	
1988/89†	Rangers v Aberdeen	3–2
1989/90†	Aberdeen v Rangers (*after extra-time*)	2–1

*Competition known as the Bell's League Cup
†Competition known as the Skol Cup

THE SCOTTISH FOOTBALL LEAGUE
v
FOOTBALL LEAGUE

Played 72;   Scotland won 18;   England won 40;   Drawn 14

		Match Scores	
Year	Venue	S.L.	F.L.
1892	Bolton	2	2
1893	Glasgow	3	4
1894	Liverpool	1	1
1895	Glasgow	1	4
1896	Liverpool	1	5
1897	Glasgow	3	0
1898	Birmingham	2	1
1899	Glasgow	1	4
1900	London	2	2
1901	Glasgow	6	2
1902	Newcastle	3	6

Year	Venue	S.L.	F.L.
1903	Glasgow	0	3
1904	Manchester	1	2
1905	Glasgow	2	3
1906	London	2	6
1907	Glasgow	0	0
1908	Birmingham	0	2
1909	Glasgow	3	1
1910	Blackburn	3	2
1911	Glasgow	1	1
1912	Middlesbrough	0	2
1913	Glasgow	4	1
1914	Burnley	3	2
1915	Glasgow	1	4
1920	Glasgow	0	4
1921	London	0	1
1922	Glasgow	0	3
1923	Newcastle	1	2
1924	Glasgow	1	1
1925	Liverpool	3	4
1926	Glasgow	0	2
1927	Leicester	2	2
1928	Glasgow	2	6
1928	Birmingham	1	2
1929	Glasgow	2	1
1930	London	3	7
1931	Glasgow	4	3
1932	Manchester	3	0
1933	Glasgow	2	2
1934	London	1	2
1935	Glasgow	2	2
1936	Liverpool	0	2
1937	Glasgow	1	0
1938	Wolverhampton	1	3
1947	Glasgow	1	3
1948	Newcastle	1	1
1949	Glasgow	0	3
1950	Middlesbrough	1	3
1951	Glasgow	1	0
1952	Sheffield	1	2
1953	Glasgow	1	0
1954	London	0	4
1955	Glasgow	3	2

HISTORICAL DATA AND RESULTS

Year	Venue	Match Scores S.L.	F.L.
1956	Sheffield	2	4
1957	Glasgow	3	2
1958	Newcastle	1	4
1959	Glasgow	1	1
1960	London	0	1
1961	Glasgow	3	2
1962	Birmingham	4	3
1964	Sunderland	2	2
1965	Glasgow	2	2
1966	Newcastle	3	1
1967	Glasgow	0	3
1968	Middlesbrough	0	2
1969	Glasgow	1	3
1970	Coventry	2	3
1971	Glasgow	0	1
1972	Middlesbrough	2	3
1973	Glasgow	2	2
1974	Manchester	0	5
1976	Glasgow	0	1

Note: Inter League Matches in abeyance 1915–19 and 1939–46.

THE SCOTTISH FOOTBALL LEAGUE
v
IRISH LEAGUE

Played 62; Scotland won 56; Ireland won 5; Drawn 1

Year	Venue	Match Scores S.L.	I.L.
1893	Belfast	2	3
1894	Glasgow	6	0
1895	Belfast	4	1
1896	Glasgow	3	2
1897	Belfast	2	0
1898	Dundee	5	0
1899	Belfast	1	3
1900	Edinburgh	6	0
1901	Belfast	2	1
1902	Dundee	3	0
1903	Belfast	0	1
1904	Paisley	3	1

		Match Scores	
Year	Venue	S.L.	I.L.
1905/07	Not played		
1908	Belfast	2	1
1909	Glasgow	2	0
1910	Belfast	3	1
1911	Glasgow	3	0
1912	Belfast	3	1
1913	Belfast	2	1
1914	Belfast	2	1
1916/18	Not played		
1919	Belfast	2	0
1921	Glasgow	3	0
1921	Glasgow	3	0
1922	Glasgow	3	0
1923	Belfast	1	0
1924	Edinburgh	3	0
1925	Belfast	7	3
1926	Edinburgh	5	2
1927	Belfast	2	1
1928	Glasgow	8	2
1929	Belfast	4	1
1930	Glasgow	5	0
1931	Belfast	2	3
1932	Glasgow	4	1
1933	Belfast	0	3
1934	Glasgow	3	2
1935	Belfast	3	2
1936	Glasgow	5	3
1937	Belfast	3	2
1938	Glasgow	6	1
1939*	Belfast	3	2
1940/45	Not played		
1946	Belfast	7	4
1947	Glasgow	3	0
1948	Belfast	1	0
1949	Glasgow	8	1
1950	Belfast	4	0
1951	Glasgow	3	0
1952	Belfast	5	1
1953	Glasgow	4	0
1954	Belfast	5	1
1955	Glasgow	3	0

*Played in season 1939/40 prior to the outbreak of war.

		Match Scores	
Year	Venue	S.L.	I.L.
1956	Belfast	7	1
1957	Glasgow	7	0
1958	Belfast	5	0
1959	Glasgow	7	1
1960	Belfast	2	1
1961	Glasgow	7	0
1963	Belfast	4	1
1965	Glasgow	6	2
1967	Belfast	2	0
1969	Glasgow	5	2
1978	Motherwell	1	1
1980	Belfast	4	2

THE SCOTTISH FOOTBALL LEAGUE
v
LEAGUE OF IRELAND

Played 22;   Scotland won 18;   Ireland won 2;   Drawn 2

		Match Scores	
Year	Venue	S.L.	L.I.
1939	Dublin	1	2
1948	Dublin	2	0
1949	Glasgow	5	1
1950	Dublin	1	0
1951	Glasgow	7	0
1952	Dublin	2	0
1953	Glasgow	5	1
1954	Dublin	3	1
1954	Glasgow	5	0
1955	Dublin	4	2
1956	Glasgow	3	1
1957	Dublin	5	1
1958	Glasgow	1	0
1959	Dublin	4	1
1960	Glasgow	5	1
1961	Dublin	1	1
1962	Glasgow	11	0
1964	Dublin	2	2
1966	Glasgow	6	0
1968	Dublin	0	0
1970	Glasgow	1	0
1980	Dublin	1	2

THE SCOTTISH FOOTBALL LEAGUE
v
DANISH FOOTBALL COMBINATION

Played 1;   Scotland won 1;   Danish Football Combination won 0

Year	Venue	Match Score S.L.	D.F.C.
1955	Copenhagen	4	0

THE SCOTTISH FOOTBALL LEAGUE
v
WELSH LEAGUE

Played 1;   Scotland won 0;   Wales won 1

Year	Venue	Match Score S.L.	W.L.
1952	Cardiff	0	3

THE SCOTTISH FOOTBALL LEAGUE
v
ITALIAN LEAGUE

Played 3;   Scotland won 0;   Italy won 1;   Drawn 2

Year	Venue	Match Scores S.L.	I.L.
1961	Glasgow	1	1
1962	Rome	3	4
1978	Verona	1	1

THE SCOTTISH FOOTBALL LEAGUE
v
SOUTHERN LEAGUE

Played 5;   Scotland won 2;   Southern League won 2;   Drawn 1

Year	Venue	Match Scores S.L.	Sth.L.
1910	Millwall	0	1
1911	Glasgow	3	2
1912	Millwall	0	1
1913	Glasgow	5	0
1914	Millwall	1	1

LEAGUE ATTENDANCES SINCE 1961/62

Season	Matches	Division I	Division II	Total
1961/62	648	3,411,129	576,659	3,987,788
1962/63	648	3,043,567	590,452	3,634,019
1963/64	648	2,962,114	498,309	3,460,423
1964/65	648	2,908,508	350,788	3,259,296
1965/66	648	2,667,380	346,432	3,013,812
1966/67	686	2,836,762	405,620	3,242,382
1967/68	648	2,869,815	345,280	3,215,095
1968/69	648	3,060,783	334,747	3,395,530
1969/70	648	3,045,994	371,919	3,417,913
1970/71	648	2,893,652	412,566	3,306,218
1971/72	648	3,132,141	484,241	3,616,382
1972/73	648	2,816,106	467,763	3,283,869
1973/74	648	2,452,562	451,107	2,903,669
1974/75	648	2,673,655	445,656	3,119,311

Season	Matches	Premier Division	First Division	Second Division	Total
1975/76	544	2,422,833	451,153	140,391	3,014,377
1976/77	726	2,131,848	636,410	208,861	2,977,119
1977/78	726	2,356,440	790,111	268,830	3,415,381
1978/79	726	2,324,799	538,735	249,791	3,113,325
1979/80	726	2,225,650	599,958	205,452	3,031,060
1980/81	726	1,759,856	601,152	166,175	2,527,183
1981/82	726	1,704,140	512,242	151,675	2,368,057
1982/83	726	1,859,856	474,879	140,709	2,475,444
1983/84	726	2,019,949	321,749	156,078	2,497,776
1984/85	726	1,949,788	366,785	188,283	2,504,856
1985/86	726	2,260,411	351,610	225,831	2,837,852
1986/87	801	3,094,224	402,236	180,733	3,677,193
1987/88	801	3,682,604	352,578	203,481	4,239,663
1988/89	726	2,827,519	670,158	137,522	3,635,199

GLOSSARY OF CLUBS FORMERLY IN MEMBERSHIP OF THE SCOTTISH FOOTBALL LEAGUE

ABERCORN (1890–1915)   One of the original members of the League, Abercorn were a Paisley side who eventually could not compete for the town's favours with St. Mirren. With the foundation of a Second Division in 1893 they were immediately assigned to it although they had one season's First Division football again in 1896–97. They were champions of the Second Division in 1909 and second in 1912 but on neither occasion were they re-elected to the First Division. They dropped out of League football in 1915 when the Second Division went into abeyance and the impossibility of gaining a suitable ground meant that they closed down permanently in season 1920–21.

ARMADALE (1921–32)   At the end of the First World War football was flourishing in the West Lothian mining district. Armadale came into the Second Division following the absorption of the Central League and in their first season, 1921–22, did well to finish third. Like other clubs from this area they found themselves unable to meet the obligations of League football. Their playing record deteriorated, they consistently finished in the bottom three clubs and in 1932–33 inability to pay the guarantee to visiting clubs led to their expulsion after 17 league matches had been played. Their record for that season was disregarded. Their ground, Volunteer Park, is still used for Junior football, a pattern which will be found to be not uncommon among departed Senior clubs.

ARTHURLIE (1901–15, 1923–29)   In the early years of the twentieth century Renfrewshire had six Scottish League clubs and one of them, Arthurlie, played at Dunterlie Park, Barrhead. Fourteen years of modest achievement in the Second Division were recorded before that Division closed down in 1915, but Arthurlie did not immediately resume operations with the end of hostilities. They waited until 1923 to apply for membership of the newly-created

Third Division and were its first champions. Four reasonably successful seasons followed but financial pressures were too great and with six matches of the 1928–29 season to go they resigned from membership. A Junior club of the same name has played at Dunterlie Park from the early 1930s.

AYR F.C. (1897–1910) Members of the Second Division between 1879–1910, Ayr held respectable positions most years without ever seriously challenging for First Division status. In 1910 they amalgamated with the other Ayr side, Parkhouse, changing their name to Ayr United without formally resigning from the League. This is the only occasion of a merger between two League clubs from the same town in the history of Scottish football.

AYR PARKHOUSE (1903–1904, 1906–10) Parkhouse were the more recent creation of the Ayr clubs, joining the Second Division in 1904, finishing bottom but not seeking re-election. They came back in 1906 and were like their fellow-citizens a middle of the league club. The amalgamation brought about the hoped-for First Division status almost immediately. The new club, Ayr United played on the ground of the former Ayr F.C., Somerset Park, but Parkhouse's ground Beresford Park, remained in use for some years and interestingly was used by Ayr United for a time during the First World War.

BATHGATE (1921–28) Another of the West Lothian clubs which joined the Scottish League from the Central League, Bathgate were no more fortunate than their county neighbours. Again the pattern was of a bright start in 1922 and in 1924 they missed promotion to the First Division by one place. The Coal strike of 1926 savagely affected them however and on March 2nd, 1929, they were compelled to resign from the League, their record for season 1928–29 being expunged. Some half-hearted attempts to revive the club were made but Bathgate's footballing future lay with the Juniors.

BEITH (1923–26) This small Ayrshire town club had a League history which exactly co-incided with that of the Third Divison. When that collapsed in 1926 they then played in the Scottish Alliance with Galston (q.v.) and the reserve teams of the First Division clubs. When the latter decided that only First Division clubs could play in the Reserve League the small Ayrshire clubs were unjustly expelled in 1938. With no proper league in which to play, the decision to go Junior was accelerated by the war and today Beith Juniors still play at Bellsdale Park.

BO'NESS (1921–32)   Bo'ness were by far the most successful of the West Lothian sides and indeed briefly attained First Division status. Coming in from the Central League at the beginning of season 1921–22 they startled Scottish football when after five modest seasons they won the Second Division championship in 1926–27. They narrowly failed to retain their First Division place but the slide afterwards was protracted and irreversible. They faltered, as did others, on the question of payment to visiting clubs of the guarantee and ceased to be members of The Scottish Football League in November 3 1932. They remained senior until the outbreak of war in 1939, playing in various minor leagues but on the resumption of peace-time football in 1945 opted to become one of the most powerful Junior clubs in Scotland, although still playing on their traditional Newton Park.

BROXBURN UNITED (1921–26)   Coming from a very small town, it is astonishing that this club was formed from two other Broxburn Senior clubs, Broxburn F.C. and Broxburn Athletic. They were unlucky to be voted out in 1925–26 since although they had finished bottom of the Second Division that year they had been in seventh place the season before. They played as seniors for another year in a minor league, (the Scottish Alliance), before ceasing to exist as a serious force.

CAMBUSLANG (1890–92)   Original members of the Scottish Football League, this little village club found the pace far too hot. They did very well to finish fourth in the League's first season but were bottom of eleven clubs the following year and after 1892 appear to have made no effort to seek re-election even when the League became a two-division structure.

CLACKMANNAN (1921–22, 1923–26)   This club, from the little Midlands town of the same name, were the surprise admission when the Second Division was formed in 1921. They finished bottom and withdrew for a year, only to try again when the Third Division was created in 1923. They played for all of its three seasons without distinction and the collapse of the Third Division was also the end of Clackmannan's senior career.

CLYDEBANK I (1914–15, 1917–31)   The figure has been used to indicate that this club bore no relation to the one which currently plays under the same name in The Scottish Football League. They were admitted to the Second Division for the last season before World War One and when that Division was discontinued in 1915 spend the next two years in the Western League. In 1917 they had a great stroke of good forture when war conditions meant that

Aberdeen, Dundee and Raith Rovers had to withdraw from League football. Clydebank were invited to take one of their places. They spent the next five years in the top flight and although relegated in 1922 and 1924, got back immediately on each occasion. They were, however especially vulnerable to the industrial downturn of the late 1920s and after threatening to resign in 1929, eventually did so in May 1931.

COWLAIRS (1890–91, 1893–95)   Original members of The Scottish Football League, Cowlairs, hailing from Springburn in the North of Glasgow finished bottom of the Scottish League in the body's inaugural season. They were suspended the following season for breaches of the rules affecting professionalism, following inspection of their books by a League sub-committee. They could fairly be adjudged to have been extremely unlucky as there were certainly instances of other clubs who were equally culpable. In 1893 they came back for two seasons but the heart had gone from the club, Second Division football was not an attractive proposition and several experienced administrators had been lost. The result was that by 1895 Cowlairs had severed their connection with League football and the club folded completely soon afterwards.

DUMBARTON HARP (1923–24)   Harp belonged to the category of 'one-season wonders', in their case the first of the three seasons of Third Division football, i.e. 1924–25. They attempted another season but had to resign in January 1925 and a club of the same name later featured for a few years in Junior football.

DUNDEE WANDERERS (1894–95)   Their career in League football was even shorter than that of Dumbarton Harp. They had a season in the Second Division in 1894–95 but the all-amateur side finished with only 9 points and two of those were awarded because Renton (q.v.) failed to fulfil a fixture. Their ground Clepington Park became the present Tannadice Park, home to Dundee United.

DYKEHEAD (1923–26)   This club, from the Shotts district of Lanarkshire, was yet another product of the era of Third Division over-expansion. The industrial climate of the 1920s made it impossible for a small mining town to sustain a League club over a long period of time and so when the Third Division was disbanded in 1926, Dykehead, who had finished a creditable fourth had no realistic field of competition at senior level and disappeared after struggling on for about two years.

EDINBURGH CITY (1931–39, 1946–49)   This amateur club was the least-successful of all those who were members of the Scottish

League for more than five years. In eleven seasons it won fewer than one game in six. The stark record is dealt with elsewhere, but being bottom of the Second Division six times in the eight season between 1931–39 tells its own story. The club closed down during the Second World War and was not invited to rejoin the Second Division in 1946. It struggled on for three seasons in C Division before joining the Junior ranks but even this lower grade had proved over-demanding by 1955.

GALSTON (1923–25)   The history of this small Ayrshire club is broadly similar to that of Beith although they only managed the first two seasons of Third Division football, those of 1923–24 and 1924–25. Galston were the first side to pull out of the Third Division in February 1926 and were blamed for accelerating that Division's collapse. For a while they played as an amateur side then joined the Scottish Alliance which was basically a league run for the reserve sides of First Division clubs. They were expelled in 1938 with Beith because the Qualifying Cup commitments of the two small clubs caused problems. There seems to have been no serious attempt to turn Junior and the outbreak of war in 1939 effectively meant the demise of Galston Football Club.

HELENSBURGH (1923–26)   The Dunbartonshire seaside town had a club of this name in membership throughout the three years of the Third Division. In its last incomplete season Helensburgh did very well, finishing third, and with a ground of considerable potential, Ardencaple Park, it is surprising that no serious attempt was made to acquire Second Division status which had certainly been accorded to less promising material.

JOHNSTONE (1912–15, 1921–26)   Elected to the Second Division in 1912 Johnstone were establishing themselves nicely when The Scottish Football League reverted in 1915 to one Division only. Johnstone transferred to the Western League and kept going thoughout the First World War but although re-admitted immediately on the re-establishment of the Second Division in 1921 some of the original impetus had gone. They were relegated to Division Three in 1925 and when that Division ceased operations in 1926 they were forced to play in a minor senior league. Shortly afterwards, around 1929, their ground was taken over by a Junior side.

KING'S PARK (1921–39)   The Stirling club's League career neatly spans the inter-war period. War-time football had suited King's Park and they came in from the Central League in 1921. For the next 18 seasons they were a typical middle-of-the-table Second Division side only once, in 1927–28, coming within a place of promotion. They seemed one of the least-vulnerable clubs even when the Second World War closed them down in 1940 but a bomb from a stray aeroplane destroyed their ground, Forthbank, in 1941 and when football resumed after the war, Stirling businessmen took the decision to proceed with a new club, Stirling Albion, and a new ground, Annfield.

LEITH ATHLETIC (1897–1915, 1924–26, 1927–39, 1946–53)
The broken record of League membership is an indication that Leith Athletic were in some respects the unluckiest of the clubs now gone. Denied promotion when they won the Second Division in 1906 and finished first equal in 1910, they also suffered by winning the Third Division in 1926 when its collapse that year meant that there was no promotion from it. There is little doubt that their advancement in the early days was blocked by the two senior Edinburgh sides. They managed a brief First Division existence from 1930–32 but withdrew from football during the war after one unsuccessful season in the North-Eastern League (q.v.) in 1941–42. They had moved from Logie Green to Portobello to Old Meadowbank in an attempt to attract a following but following five years of scraping an existence in C Division they refused to continue there in 1953 and were expelled from the League. Ironically, had they held on for two more years they would have found themselves part of the reconstituted and expanded Second Division and might well have profited from the maintenance of a separate Leith identity as the old port revived.

LINTHOUSE (1895–1900) Theirs is a curious though brief history. They came in with the second wave of League clubs and were probably admitted because the South side of the city (Glasgow) had fewer clubs and therefore the League was willing to overlook the previous grim example of Thistle and Cowlairs across the river. Rangers were too firmly established to brook a rival in the Govan district however and after five undistinguished years in the Second Division, Linthouse fell out of League football.

LOCHGELLY UNITED (1914–15, 1921–26) Their chance of a successful League career was marred by the outbreak of World War One at the end of their first full season in 1914–15. Oddly enough, they then played in the Eastern rather than the stronger Central League but after three seasons in the Second Division they perished in the wreck of the Third Division in 1925–26 and after a year or so in the Scottish Alliance disappeared from the map.

MID-ANNANDALE (1923–26) This poetically-named side from the town of Lockerbie in Dumfrieshire had a brief League history which exactly co-incided with that of the Third Division. In the last season of that body's existence they finished a respectable fifth but with its collapse they had to find shelter in the Scottish Combination. An interesting survival was that throughout the 1930s Hamilton Academical adopted Mid-Annandale's name for an annual charity match against Queen of the South.

NITHSDALE WANDERERS (1923–27)   In their second season as Third Division members Nithsdale Wanderers were champions and won promotion to the Second Division. They did well enough in their first season there, 1925–26, finishing a healthy twelfth, but were bottom the following season and did not seek re-election. They played in various minor Senior competitions after that but the Dumfriesshire town of Sanquhar, whence they hailed, was too small to support senior football in any shape and the side turned Junior after the Second World War, still using the original ground, Crawick Holm. Even Junior football proved beyond Wanderers and the club was gone by the mid 1960s.

NORTHERN (1893–94)   Northern were a Glasgow club, located near Springburn which was then famous as being the 'railway workshop of the world'. Their career was of the briefest, one season in the Second Division which saw them gain nine points, ninth place and fail to secure re-election. There is reason to believe that they may have suffered indirectly for the shortcomings of Cowlairs (q.v.).

PEEBLES ROVERS (1923–26)   Another club whose sole experience of Scottish League football has been in the Third Division. Lack of a strong economic base has at various times caused the club to play both Junior and Amateur football but each time it has come back to take part in minor Senior leagues.

PORT GLASGOW ATHLETIC (1893–1911)   Moderately successful by Scottish standards, Port Glasgow Athletic had eight continuous seasons in First Division football between 1902–1910 although only in the first of them were they free entirely from relegation trouble. They were unusual in that stringent financial circumstances compelled them to operate for much of the time as an amateur concern. In 1911 they finished in the respectability of eighth position in the Second Division but surprisingly were not re-elected and that marked the end of this club, the present Junior side having no direct connection with the old Athletic.

RENTON (1891–1898)   Renton are perhaps the most celebrated example of a club which found the rigours of League football too demanding. Their early expulsion for playing against Edinburgh Saints in the first few weeks of League football in Scotland totally destroyed what little chance the Dunbartonshire village side had of adjusting to the new regime. They were re-admitted but were clearly out of their depth, gathering only four points from a possible 36 in season 1893–94. Their attitude towards League obligations tended to be somewhat cavalier and they were expelled again in what proved to be their last season, 1897–98, Hamilton Academical taking over their programme after four games had been played and lost by Renton. By 1898, a club which ten short years before had proudly styled itself 'champions of the world' had disappeared from top-level existence.

ROYAL ALBERT (1923–26)   The club's name gives no clue to its geographical origin but in fact they came from the little Lanarkshire town of Larkhall. They did not challenge seriously for promotion in their three years of Third Division membership and by the very early 1930s, certainly by 1931, the club had turned Junior, continuing to play at Raploch Park though rather the minor partner to the other Junior side in the town, Larkhall Thistle.

ST. BERNARDS (1893–1915, 1921–39)   This famous old Edinburgh side started in the First Division and after seven consecutive seasons there were only relegated after a Test match with St. Mirren. They immediately won the Second Division but were not elected to the First, a fate which also befell them in 1907 and indeed they were never again to play in the top flight. In the middle 1930s they were a force to be reckoned with in the Second Division, finishing third twice and fourth once while in 1938 they took the eventual winners of the Scottish Cup, East Fife, to three games in the semi-finals. Their position seemed financially sound, even after a bad season in the Scottish Regional League (East) in 1939–40. Even when the club closed down after one season in the North-Eastern League, 1941–42, there seemed no possibility of not re-starting at the end of the war. In 1943, however, their ground, Royal Gymnaisum Park was sold abruptly and efforts to continue even a partial existence as a united club with Leith Athletic met with no success. Scottish football lost one of its oldest and most respected members.

SOLWAY STAR (1923–26)   South of Scotland clubs tended to be noted for attractive names rather than football skill but this little side from Annan in Dumfrieshire were perhaps an exception. They missed promotion from the Third Division by only one place in 1925 but the collapse of the Third Division the following year left them no realistic prospects of promotion. They appeared in various Scottish Cup ties but the outbreak of war in 1939 killed off any lingering League aspirations in Annan.

THISTLE (1893–94)   Not to be confused with Partick Thistle, one season was enough to convice the Scottish League that the national emblem had no future as a member club. In their one season in the Second Division they finished comfortably last and recieved no support in a bid for re-election. They were located in the West of Glasgow.

VALE OF LEVEN (1890–1892, 1905–15, 1921–26)   By the time the Scottish Football League was formed Vale of Leven's great days were behind them. In the second season of League football they failed to win a single First Division game and did not seek re-election. They came back to the Second Division in 1905 and from then until the outbreak of war in 1914 lived out an undistinguished Second Division existence. They were bottom of the Division three times in the five years just before World War One. Relegated from the Second Division in 1924 they went down with the Third Division ship two years later. Their ground lay vacant from some years until, with macabre timing, Millburn Park became the home of Vale of Leven Juniors in July 1939.

THIRD LANARK (1890–1939, 1946–67)   The death of the Third Lanark club in 1967, fully described in the text, is perhaps the most painful of all the losses sustained by Scottish League football. It meant the departure of a founder member, a Scottish Cup winner and a Scottish League champion. Moreover, unlike the other demises, the club had been doing well at the gate and had finished third in the First Division as recently as 1960–61, scoring 100 goals in the process. Its full name, Third Lanark Rifle Volunteers, showed the close connection that had once existed between association football and the Territorial movement. The closure of the club alerted football in general to the dangers of unscrupulous chairmen, and the attraction of football grounds to commerce as town and city sites ripe for development. All attempts to relocate Third Lanark either within the City of Glasgow or in one of the new towns failed, and with their going went one of the last links with the earliest origins of Scottish League football.

INDEX

A

ABBOT, James (Galston) 103
ABERCORN F.C. 6, 7, 8, 20, 33, 37, 40, 62, 66, 135
ABERDEEN F.C. 46, 49, 62, 67, 101, 110, 113, 116, 118, 120, 123, 124, 126, 127, 129, 147, 152, 177, 197, 198, 202, 204, 208, 215, 219, 234, 235, 238, 240, 242, 258, 263, 264, 274
ADAMSON, Sandy 119
ADVENTURERS F.C. 17, 19
AIRDRIEONIANS F.C. 29, 39, 43, 50, 71, 112, 113, 114, 147, 183, 184, 197, 204, 276, 277
AITKEN, C. (Motherwell) 268
AITKEN, G. (East Fife) 141
ALBION ROVERS F.C. 46, 55, 63, 67, 114, 118, 135, 165, 183, 197, 276
ALLOA F.C. 68, 69, 70, 112, 127, 129, 133, 214, 221, 240
ANDERSON, Baillie James 238
ANGLO-SCOTTISH CUP 199, 258
ARBROATH F.C. 69, 76, 77, 82, 110, 111, 112, 126, 182, 239, 240
ARCHER, Ian 189
ARMADALE F.C. 68, 69, 77, 83, 85, 94, 95
ARMSTRONG, M. 71
ARTHURLIE F.C. 43, 45, 62, 69, 76, 77, 78, 80, 85
AVONSIDE, Lord 166
AYR F.C. 38, 47
AYR PARKHOUSE F.C. 46, 47
AYR UNITED F.C. 46, 47, 62, 64, 74, 82, 101, 104, 112, 114, 127, 129, 133, 191, 199, 221

B

B & Q League 218, 264
BATHGATE F.C. 68, 69, 78, 83, 85.
BATTLES, B. (Heart of Midlothian) 250
BAULD, W. 145, 148
BAXTER, J. 181
BEATTIE, F. 176, 180
BECCI, A. (Arbroath) 96
BEITH F.C. 77, 103, 104

BELL (Hurlford F.C.) 15
BELL'S LEAGUE CUP 239
BENNET, A. 55
BERWICK RANGERS F.C. 95, 150, 152, 156, 165, 191
BLACK, A. (Heart of Midlothian) 71, 86, 96, 115
BLACK, B. (Kilmarnock) 180
BLAIR, D. 85
BODEN, A. 253
BO'NESS F.C. 68, 69, 82, 83, 88, 95
BONNER, P. 265
BOWIE, J. 66, 233
BRAND, R. 172
BRECHIN CITY F.C. 77, 78, 86, 109, 137, 142, 165, 166, 180, 181, 191, 193
BREMNER, G. 128
BRITTLE, W. 153
BROWN, A. (East Fife) 141
BROWN, J. 219
BROWN, R. (Rangers) 125, 254
BROWNLIE, J. 51, 77
BUCHAN, W. 115, 125
BUCHANAN, P. 212
BULLOCH, W. 66
BROXBURN SHAMROCK 27
BROXBURN UNITED F.C. 68, 69, 76, 79, 81, 83
BUSBY, Sir Matt 123, 125, 252
BUTCHER, T. 264

C

CAMBUSLANG F.C. 6, 7, 8, 15, 20, 22
CALDER, R. 276
CAMERON, A. 186
CAMPBELL, "Bummer" 4
CAMPBELL, J. 247
CAMPBELL, P. 8
CAMPBELL, W. (Morton) 139
CASKIE, J. 118
CELTIC F.C. 6, 8, 9, 12, 15, 19, 20, 25, 27, 28, 29, 30, 31, 35, 36, 39, 40, 49, 50, 51, 57, 60, 62, 74, 79, 83, 86, 94, 101, 103, 104, 108, 112, 113, 117, 118, 119, 121, 125, 126, 137, 139, 140, 141, 145, 151, 161, 164, 177, 179, 182, 185, 186, 188, 189, 197, 198, 199, 207, 214, 216, 218, 219, 228, 235, 236, 239, 240, 242, 246, 263, 264

301

INDEX

CHALMERS, S. (Celtic)   236
CHISHOLM, K.   125
CLACKMANNAN F.C.   68, 69, 76, 77
CLARK, R. (Aberdeen)   183
CLARK, T. (Clyde)   183
CLYDE F.C.   7, 8, 13, 15, 21, 27, 30, 31, 35, 39, 42, 46, 50, 51, 62, 94, 97, 104, 115, 118, 175, 182, 186, 188, 217, 228, 240
CLYDEBANK F.C. (original club of that name)   56, 62, 63, 76, 83, 85, 88, 90
CLYDEBANK F.C. (second club of that name)   172, 197, 225, 231
CLYDESDALE F.C.   3
COLQUHOUN, T. (Clydebank)   90
COMBE, R. (Hibernian)   117, 125
COMPTON, D. C. S.   140
CONN, A. (Heart of Midlothian)   145
COOKE, C.   254
COUSIN, A. (Dundee)   172
COWDENBEATH F.C.   49, 111, 112, 116, 127, 129, 133, 264
COWLAIRS F.C.   6, 7, 8, 10, 15, 16, 19, 21, 26, 27, 32
COX, S. (Rangers)   147, 253
CRAIGMYLE, P.   92
CURRIE, H.   221

D

DALGLISH, K.   187
DAVIDSON, R. H.   155
DAWSON, J.   234, 269
DELANEY, J.   270
DENOVAN, J. F. (Scottish Football League Secretary)   135, 150, 170, 182, 201, 259
DOLLAN, Sir Patrick   119
DONALD, D. (Aberdeen)   208
DONNELLY, J.   251
DOSSING, F.   215
DRYBROUGH Cup   202, 204, 258
DUMBARTON F.C.   6, 7, 8, 11, 14, 15, 19, 20, 22, 30, 32, 37, 70, 75, 113, 114, 116, 123, 186, 202
DUMBARTON HARP F.C.   77, 79, 274
DUMBRECK F.C.   3
DUNDEE F.C.   26, 27, 30, 31, 32, 39, 40, 44, 49, 62, 67, 70, 76, 103, 113, 114, 116, 118, 126, 127, 132, 135, 161, 183, 184, 215, 225, 228, 231, 235, 239
DUNDEE HARP F.C.   27, 47
DUNDEE HIBERNIAN F.C.   47, 54, 62, 76, 77
DUNDEE UNITED F.C.   76, 77, 88, 112, 113, 114, 116, 120, 126, 182, 183, 197, 198, 214, 215, 241
DUNDEE WANDERERS F.C.   29, 32
DUNFERMLINE ATHLETIC F.C.   17, 19, 49, 68, 113, 114, 116, 150, 177, 183, 184, 224, 231, 235, 240
DYKEHEAD F.C.   77

E

EASTERN F.C.   3
EASTHAM, George (Newcastle United)   160
EAST FIFE F.C.   68, 69, 112, 114, 141, 142, 209, 234, 235
EAST STIRLINGSHIRE F.C.   42, 62, 68, 76, 77, 78, 82, 99, 134, 137, 142, 150, 160, 165, 193, 214, 264
ES/CLYDEBANK F.C.   170, 171
EDINBURGH CITY F.C.   90, 91, 109, 112, 134
EVANS, R. (Celtic)   140

F

FAIRLY, Peter (Renton)   6
FALKIRK F.C.   37, 42, 44, 60, 64, 95, 101, 113, 116, 123, 235, 239, 266
FARRY, J. (Secretary of the Scottish Football League)   201, 239, 257, 258, 259, 260, 261
FERGUSON, A. (Aberdeen)   202, 206
FERGUSON, J. (Airdrieonians)   212
FERGUSSON, T. (Stirling Albion)   115
FERRIER, R. (Motherwell)   75, 249, 250, 274
FINE FARE LEAGUE   218, 222
FINNIGAN. W. (Hibernian)   125
FLAVELL, R. (Airdrieonians)   250
FORFAR ATHLETIC F.C.   69, 79, 81, 109, 137, 193, 224, 272
FORREST, J. (Rangers)   236
FRANCIS. T. (Rangers)   264
FURST, E. H. (Heart of Midlothian)   83

G

GALLACHER, H.   71, 250, 277
GALLACHER, P.   54, 60, 124
GALLACHER, T. (Dundee)   124

INDEX

GALLAGHER, W. G. ("Waverley") 68, 81, 113, 115, 116, 119
GALSTON F.C. 77, 78, 79, 116, 119
GARDINER, P. 216, 221
GEATONS, C. (Celtic) 251
GELLATLY, I. 225
GEMMELL, Mattha (Clyde) 275
GEMMELL, T. (Dundee) 239
GILLICK, T. (Rangers) 128, 145
GILLIES, John (Clyde) 96
GILZEAN, A. 172
GOODFELLOW, J. (Third Lanark) 172, 173
GORDON, J. (Rangers) 54, 68
GRAHAM, Mr. (Renton) 9
GRANVILLE F.C. 3
GRAY, D. (Rangers) 274
GRAY, M. (Third Lanark) 172
GREIG, J. (Rangers) 193, 255, 256, 268, 274
GROVES, Wm. (Hibernian) 19
GUNN, Felix (Dumbarton) 63

H

HALLIDAY, D. (Aberdeen) 269
HAMILTON, R. C. (Rangers) 247, 254
HAMILTON, W. (Heart of Midlothian) 254
HAMILTON ACADEMICAL F.C. 38, 39, 50, 59, 182, 231, 236
HARKNESS W. (Queen of the South) 221
HARLEY, A. (Third Lanark) 172
HARRIS, N. (Partick Thistle) 63
HARPER, J. (Hibernian) 235
HART, T. (Hibernian) 188, 189, 198, 218
HART, T (St. Mirren) 57
HAY, James (Celtic) 51
HAYNES, Johnny (Fulham) 160
HEART OF MIDLOTHIAN F.C. 6, 8, 15, 20, 23, 25, 31, 32, 37, 40, 41, 44, 49, 57, 60, 63, 64, 71, 75, 100, 101, 110, 111, 112, 113, 118, 121, 127, 141, 145, 152, 153, 164, 177, 182, 183, 184, 188, 214, 235, 236, 263
HEGARTY, P. (Dundee United) 268, 274
HELENSBURGH F.C. 77, 78, 81
HENDERSON, G. (Cowlairs) 10, 11, 12
HENDERSON, W. (Rangers) 172
HERD, A. (Hamilton Academical) 125
HEWIE, J. (Charlton Athletic) 253
HIBERNIAN F.C. 19, 20, 26, 27, 33, 35, 37, 49, 75, 91, 110, 112, 113, 117, 121, 123, 138, 141, 145, 152, 153, 164, 177, 182, 183, 184, 188, 198, 202, 218, 234, 235, 236, 263
HIDDLESTON, W. G. (Third Lanark) 172, 175
HIGGINBOTHAM, H. (St. Mirren) 63
HILLEY, David (Third Lanark) 172
HOGG, R. (Celtic) 274
HOPE, K. 212
HOULISTON, W. (Queen of the South) 142
HOWAT, H. 118
HUBBARD, J. (Rangers) 253
HUMPHRIES, W. (Motherwell) 253
HUNTER, John (Motherwell) 51, 54
HURLFORD, F. C. 77, 78

J

JACKSON, A. 221
JACKSON, A. A. 42
JARDINE, S. (Rangers) 193, 214
JOAD, Professor C. E. M. 238
JOHNSTON, M. 242
JOHNSTONE F.C. 49, 55, 62, 79
JOHNSTONE, D. (Rangers) 236
JOHNSTONE, J. (Celtic) 75
JOHNSTONE, R. (Hibernian) 145
JORDAN, J. (Morton) 184
JULIUSSEN, A. (Dundee United) 125

K

KEITH, Hon. Henry Shanks, Q.C. 173
KELLY, A. (Hearts) 130
KELLY, James (Renton) 16, 23
KELLY, John (Third Lanark) 252
KELLY, Sir Robert (Celtic) 23, 139, 146, 151, 166, 198, 229
KENNOWAY, J. (Celtic) 250
KERR, Jerry (Dundee United) 100, 214
KIDD, A. (Dundee) 226
KILMARNOCK F.C. 28, 32, 40, 44, 71, 104, 114, 126, 129, 137, 177, 182, 204, 235
KING'S PARK F.C. 26, 68, 69, 81, 83, 95, 112, 114, 115, 126, 131, 274
KINNEAR, D. (Rangers) 107

INDEX

L

LAMB, J. (Arbroath) 128
LAUCHLAN, T. (Kilmarnock) 199, 201, 206, 221
LAW, Denis 155
LAWTON, Tommy 125
LAWRENCE, A. (Dumbarton) 8, 11, 12, 22, 23, 36, 101
LEISHMAN, A. H. 92

Mc

McINNES, J. 172, 180
MACKAY, D. 155, 253
McKENNAN, P. 131
McKENZIE, G. H. 63, 75
McLAUGHLIN, J. H. 9, 12, 13, 20, 21, 22, 23, 28, 29, 33, 36, 37, 38, 39, 41, 42, 277
McLEAN, J. 214, 216, 265
McLEISH, A. (Aberdeen) 203
McMAHON, J. (Clyde) 234
McMAHON, A. (Celtic) 26
McMENEMY, J. 54
McMILLAN, I. 172
McNAIR, A. (Celtic) 74, 249
McNAUGHT, W. (Raith Rovers) 142
McNEILL, W. (Celtic) 205, 206, 268, 274
McPHAIL, R. (Rangers) 71
McSTAY, P. (Celtic) 122
McTAVISH, J. (Queen's Park) 7, 14
McWATTIE, G. C. (Queen's Park) 247

M

MACARI, L. 189
MALEY, W. (Celtic) 25, 50, 55, 56, 79, 82, 122, 246
MARTIN, A. (Celtic) 26
MARTYN, D. (Airdrieonians) 63
MASSIE, A. (Heart of Midlothian) 71
MASON, J. (Third Lanark) 132, 136, 268
MASON, P. (Aberdeen) 265
MATTHEWS, S. 125, 188
MAULE, T. (Scottish Football League Secretary) 182, 201, 259
MEADOWBANK THISTLE F.C. 191, 192, 217, 221, 240
MEIKLEJOHN, D. (Rangers) 115
MELLISH, J. 9

MERCER, W. (Heart of Midlothian) 214, 228
MID ANNANDALE F.C. 77, 81, 274
MILLER, J. (Rangers) 172
MILLER, W. (Aberdeen) 203, 252, 268, 274
MILLS, W. (Aberdeen) 71
MOCHAN, N. (Celtic) 226
MONTGOMERY, D. R. (Third Lanark) 12, 33, 36
MONTROSE F.C. 77, 86, 101, 109, 137, 193, 240, 264
MORTENSEN, S. (Blackpool) 125
MORTON, A. (Rangers) 90, 249, 250, 273, 274
MORTON F.C. 26, 29, 36, 42, 44, 113, 118, 183, 184, 204, 235, 236, 266
MOTHERWELL F.C. 26, 36, 39, 42, 51, 54, 62, 71, 100, 112, 123, 182, 183, 184, 199, 200, 206, 207, 219, 225, 231, 235, 236, 266

N

NAREY, D. (Dundee United) 241
NELLIES, P. 67
NITHSDALE WANDERERS F.C. 77, 79, 82, 90
NIVEN, G. (RANGERS) 164
NORTHERN F.C. 26

O

O'NEILL, M. (Dundee United) 265
ORMOND, W. (Hibernian) 145
ORR, R. (Falkirk) 101

P

PARNELL, C. S. 27
PARTICK THISTLE F.C. 26, 37, 39, 42, 44, 59, 62, 123, 125, 127, 138, 152, 175, 188, 228, 236, 266
PATERSON, I. (Clyde) 216
PATERSON, G. (Celtic) 107, 132, 251
PATON, J. (Rangers) 225
PAUL, H. 25
PEEBLES ROVERS F.C. 77

INDEX

Q

PELOSI, J. (St. Johnstone) 219
PENMAN, A. (Dundee) 172
PORT GLASGOW ATHLETIC
F.C. 26, 30, 42, 44, 49, 50, 135
PRENTICE, J. 254
PRIMROSE URE, Bailie 18

Q

QUEEN'S PARK F.C. 2, 3, 4, 7, 8, 9, 13, 14, 19, 29, 31, 32, 35, 42, 44, 47, 50, 57, 64, 70, 79, 81, 89, 91, 97, 116, 119, 133, 135, 137, 175, 191, 221, 238
QUEEN OF THE SOUTH F.C. 79, 100, 114, 118, 129, 133, 137, 193, 238, 276
QUEEN OF THE SOUTH WANDERERS F.C. 76, 77
QUINN, J. (Celtic) 41, 54, 90, 274

R

RAE, A. (Partick Thistle) 237
RAISBECK, A. (Partick Thistle) 54, 55, 59
RAITH ROVERS F.C. 44, 62, 67, 114, 118, 123, 126, 183
RANGERS F.C. 6, 14, 15, 18, 20, 28, 35, 40, 42, 44, 57, 60, 62, 71, 74, 75, 79, 83, 86, 87, 100, 101, 104, 111, 112, 113, 116, 117, 118, 119, 122, 123, 124, 126, 127, 128, 132, 135, 137, 138, 141, 145, 147, 155, 161, 164, 165, 177, 179, 180, 182, 188, 189, 191, 197, 198, 204, 207, 211, 219, 232, 233, 234, 239, 240, 242, 246, 263, 264
REID, W. (Rangers) 54
REILLY, L. (Hibernian) 138, 145, 253
RENTON F.C. 6, 7, 8, 13, 15, 16, 17, 18, 19, 20, 22, 29, 31, 32, 34, 38
REYNAUD, Mr. 9
RICHARDSON, J. 30, 67
ROBERTS, G. (Rangers) 264
ROBERTSON, H. (Dundee) 172
ROBERTSON, J. R. (Dumbarton) 186
ROUGHHEAD, M. (Stenhousemuir) 196
ROYAL ALBERT F.C. 77, 274
ROXBURGH, A. 265
RUSSELL, R. (Ayr United) 101

S

SHANKLY, J. 163
SHANKLY, R. 163
SHANKLY, W. 115, 163
SHARP, W. 143, 253
SHAW, C. (Celtic) 54, 66
SHORTT, J. (Stenhousemuir) 79
SIMPSON, R, (Celtic) 221
SINCLAIR, J. S. 64
SKOL CUP 229, 242, 243
SLIMAN, J. 23
SMITH, G. (Hibernian) 117, 125, 145, 161, 162, 172, 186
SMITH, N. (Rangers) 274
SOLWAY STAR F.C. 77, 79, 81, 274
SOUNESS, G. (Rangers) 230, 232
STAROSCIK, F. (Third Lanark) 128
ST. BERNARD F.C. 6, 8, 11, 13, 17, 18, 25, 26, 29, 37, 39, 42, 76, 109, 112, 114, 119, 120, 121, 131, 135, 148, 274
STEEDMAN, C. 170, 172
STEEDMAN, J. 170, 172, 213
STEEL, W. (Dundee) 145, 146
STEIN, Jock 174, 177, 179, 185, 188, 194, 199, 206, 222, 223, 253, 256, 265
STENHOUSEMUIR F.C. 68, 69, 70, 79, 101, 112, 114, 160, 165, 166, 182, 196, 264
STEVENSON, G. (Motherwell) 274
STEVENSON UNITED 63
STEWART, H. 214
STIRLING ALBION F.C. 131, 133, 134, 135, 142, 214, 224, 225
ST. JOHNSTONE F.C. 49, 112, 113, 114, 116, 126, 127, 129, 133, 164, 170, 219, 228
ST. MIRREN F.C. 6, 8, 11, 30, 33, 47, 104, 112, 115, 118, 124, 207, 228
STRANRAER F.C. 135, 137, 165
STRAUSS, W. (Aberdeen) 71
STRUTH, W. (Rangers) 50, 86, 117
SYMON, J. S. (Rangers) 155

T

TAYLOR, H. 188, 239
TEMPLETON, R. (Kilmarnock) 46, 274
TERRIS, W. W. 156
TEXACO CUP 198
THOMSON G. (Berwick Rangers) 152
THOMSON, J. (Third Lanark) 9
THOMSON, J. S. (Morton) 155, 159
THORNTON, W. (Rangers) 107, 132, 145

INDEX

THOW, L. 212
THYNE R. (Kilmarnock) 141
THIRD LANARK F.C. 3, 6, 8, 14, 30, 35, 40, 48, 62, 75, 77, 80, 81, 118, 123, 141, 172, 175, 188, 274, 277
TOWNS, D. (St. Mirren) 11, 36
TREVORROW, E. 251
TROUP, A. (Dundee) 75
TURNBULL, E. (Hibernian) 145
TURNER, John Moncrieff 173
TURPIE, R. 171

V

VALE OF LEVEN F.C. 3, 4, 6, 7, 8, 9, 14, 19, 22, 30, 32, 55, 63, 78, 81
VENTERS, A. (Rangers) 120

W

WADDELL, W. 134, 145, 180, 185
WALKER, R. 49, 248, 274
WALKER, T. (Heart of Midlothian) 71, 108, 122, 132, 274
WALL, F. 55
WALLACE, D. (Clyde) 252
WALLACE, J. (Rangers) 193
WASHBROOK, C. 140
WHARTON, T. 209, 232
WHITE, T. 117
WHITE, D. M. (Celtic) 185, 189, 212, 216, 219, 220, 222, 229, 238
WHITE, J. (Falkirk) 254
WILKINS, R. (Rangers) 264
WILKINSON, J. (Dumbarton) 75
WILLIAMSON, A. B. 85
WILL, D. (Brechin City) 216
WILSON, D. (Rangers) 254
WILTON, W. (Rangers) 33, 36, 39, 40
WING, L. (Dundee United) 215
WOODS, C. (Rangers) 264
WRIGHT, J. 66

Y

YOUNG, G. (Rangers) 147, 175